Build
watchOS Apps

DEVELOP AND **DESIGN**

Build watchOS Apps

DEVELOP AND DESIGN

Mark Goody

Maurice Kelly

PEACHPIT PRESS
WWW.PEACHPIT.COM

Build watchOS Apps: Develop and Design

Mark Goody and Maurice Kelly

Peachpit Press

www.peachpit.com

To report errors, please send a note to errata@peachpit.com.
Peachpit Press is a division of Pearson Education.

Copyright © 2016 by Mark Goody and Maurice Kelly

Editor: Connie Jeung-Mills
Production editors: Maureen Forys and Lisa Brazieal
Development editor: Robyn G. Thomas
Compositor: Kim Scott, Bumpy Design
Technical editor: Stepan Hruda
Copyeditor: Scout Festa
Proofreader: Liz Welch
Indexer: James Minkin
Cover design: Mimi Heft
Interior Design: Mimi Heft

ISBN-13: 978-0-13-417517-1
ISBN-10: 0-13-417517-4

9 8 7 6 5 4 3 2 1

Printed and bound in the United States of America

To my darling wife, Rebecca, and our sons,
Reuben and Joel, who give us so much joy. Thank you for your love, patience,
and support as I kept disappearing to "work on the book" at what
turned out to be a particularly busy time in our family's life.
The three of you are my world.

—*Mark Goody*

I am ever grateful once more to my beautiful wife, Fiona,
who showed me so much support in getting through another
one of these books, and for giving us our sensitive angel Aoibhínn,
and our cheeky little monkey Caoimhe.

—*Maurice Kelly*

ACKNOWLEDGMENTS

We would like to thank the engineering management chain at our employers, ShopKeep Inc., particularly Joshua Vickery, Duncan Grazier, Jason Ordway, and Miriam Kerbache. They supported this endeavor by giving us the permission and space to work on it, and by giving us an enjoyable and progressive engineering environment to return to. They also gave us access to Stepan Hruda, one of the most awesome engineers we've worked with and a fearsome force when it comes to reviewing code as our tech editor. We also can't forget our fellow iOS engineers in ShopKeep: Robert and Team Charlie (Kieran, Wes, Zack, and Jordan) in Belfast, as well as James and Gabe in New York City. You all make us much better developers.

Once again, we have had the utmost pleasure in working with Robyn Thomas on this book. This time, we ganged up on Robyn and tried to force the UK/US English matter, but she along with our copyeditor, Scout Festa, held firm. We *sympathise* greatly with them.

This time around, we had a new project editor: Connie Jeung-Mills. We're very pleased to have had the opportunity to work with Connie and extremely grateful that she was able to wrangle us some more pages when we couldn't stick to our page budget. Thanks also to Clifford Colby for starting the project off (twice, actually); we miss you in our weekly conference calls, though you still owe Robyn an Apple Watch.

ABOUT THE AUTHORS

Mark Goody spends most of his time writing software, concentrating on Apple platforms—though he can be tempted to experiment with most things. He lives just outside Belfast, Northern Ireland, with his wife and two sons. They look after him by making sure he remembers to step away from his computer from time to time. Mark blogs sporadically at marramgrass.org.uk and more reliably tweets as @marramgrass.

Maurice Kelly has been engineering software since leaving university in 2001. After spending many years working on server software for mobile telecoms, he took a change of direction to work at the user-facing end by becoming an iOS developer. He has a love for synthesizers and music, and still dreams of owning a Land Rover Defender someday. He lives with his wife and children just outside Dromara, a small village in Northern Ireland.

CONTENTS

PART I Getting Started

PART II Creating Apps

PART III Making the Most of the Platform

INTRODUCTION

For some, the idea of a smartwatch is characterized by the wrist-borne communicator devices in *Dick Tracy* cartoons, but for a child of the eighties few pop-culture memories remain as vivid as seeing Michael Knight communicating with his car K.I.T.T. through his wristwatch. The idea of being able to see information that had been beamed to your wrist, to talk with an intelligent car, and to sport such a perm was to remain a symbol of the future for many children who grew up as fans of the TV show *Knight Rider*.

THE WATCH OF OUR DREAMS

The announcement that Apple had been working on a watch that could respond to voice commands and also run apps and communicate with the Internet via an iPhone set the Mac and iOS developer community alight. Not only did it signal the potential for yet another app gold rush, but it tickled the imaginations of those former children for whom the wristwatch was the perfect device on which to control your digital life.

Sure, the iPhone was revolutionary, but it was still just a phone, and we've always had phones (depending on your age, of course). The iPad has changed the face of personal computing, but it's still just a computer, albeit a lot smaller than the ones we had when we were kids.

The Apple Watch is different. We never needed the other devices in the same way that we wanted the ability to talk to our watches. We dreamed of being able to tap the watch face and have it respond to the commands. We yearned for the day that critical information would arrive directly to our wrists.

THE APPLE WATCH OF OUR REALITIES

As developers, we have been spoiled by what we can achieve using iOS. The first iPhones were not accessible to developers (at least not officially), but with the release of iPhoneOS 2.0 in 2008, Apple gave third-party developers the ability to create fully fledged apps that took advantage of the full hardware of the devices.

In many ways, watchOS has followed the same pattern; the first release of watchOS (which wasn't even called watchOS at the time) provided a somewhat restricted subset of functionality. Rather than running full apps, the watch ran iOS app extensions that were much more restricted in the level of processing they could do and the range of interactivity available to them.

watchOS 2 is the release that developers have really been waiting for. We now get access to fully native apps that run directly on the watch and have access to much more in the way of software APIs and hardware features.

ABOUT THIS BOOK

In this book, we aim to get you up to speed on how to create and design watchOS apps. We'll guide you through the process of creating apps and illustrate how to visualize and interact with user interfaces for the Apple Watch using storyboards. We delve into communications between the Apple Watch and the iPhone and how to present quick summaries of information to the user using glances.

This book is not an introduction to iOS or CocoaTouch programming and is instead aimed at existing developers who want a guide to the features available in watchOS. We'll also be presenting most of our code samples in Apple's new Swift programming language. In many cases, it will be apparent what the code is doing and how it can be re-implemented in Objective-C if necessary. If you have not yet delved into the world of Swift, you may find *Swift Translation Guide for Objective-C Developers* (also published by Peachpit) to be a helpful companion.

HOW TO USE THIS BOOK

Writing and distributing watchOS apps requires that you have a solid foundation in iOS development. We assume that you have intermediate knowledge of iOS development as well as of provisioning and configuring iOS devices in the Apple Developer Center.

ORGANIZATION
We have split this book into three main sections:

Part 1, "Getting Started"
We start with a quick example project before taking the time to examine the structure of watchOS apps in more detail, and then we provide an overview of the main user interface controls available to your apps.

Part 2, "Creating Apps"
This section begins a deeper examination of what you can do with WatchKit, and it offers guidance on how to design and optimize the interface of your app, as well as how to entice your users through glances, complications, and notifications.

Part 3, "Making the Most of the Platform"
In the third section, we go deeper into the platform and look at how to take advantage of the hardware and software features that make watchOS the most compelling developer platform that Apple has produced in many years.

CODE SAMPLES
Many of the chapters feature short example projects that you can follow along with in order to gain a better understanding of the material. We have published the source code repositories to the GitHub account that accompanies the book, at github.com/bwa-book. Each chapter that has a sample project has a companion repository, and we have endeavored to make the commits to the repositories logically follow the progress in the book.

TEXT FORMATS

Code samples that you should enter will be marked as follows:

```
@IBAction func saySomething() {
    messageLabel.setText("Hello Wrist!")
}
```

Highlighted code identifies changes to a snippet of code or is meant to draw your attention to specific sections of code:

```
@IBAction func buttonTapped() {
    spinnerImage.startAnimating()
}
```

You'll also find notes containing additional information about the topics:

> **NOTE:** The Utility face (and others) actually features a fourth complication when you enter its customization mode. It corresponds to the date display in Figure 7.3, and we won't consider it here because it can show only the date (in a number of styles) or be turned off. It is not yet open to third-party developers.

SOFTWARE VERSIONS

All the code samples have been tested with watchOS 2.0 and iOS 9.0. To follow along with the examples in the book, you should ensure that you are using at least Xcode 7.0. Where there are incompatibilities with future versions of watchOS, we will endeavor to post corrections to our website, http://watchosapps.build.

WELCOME TO WATCHOS

Apple's watchOS could be its most exciting new operating system since the introduction of iOS in 2007. It introduces new ways for users to interact with your applications and provides you with new and improved methods of getting up-to-date information in front of your users.

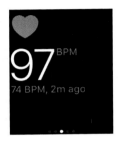

GLANCES

Present critical information to your users at a glance. A summary of everything they need to know is just a swipe away.

COMPLICATIONS

Display small pieces of information directly on the main watch face. Complications also provide a compelling way to quickly launch your application.

NOTIFICATIONS

With a push notification service, you can send the latest data directly to your users. With a flick of their wrist they can see, and even act upon, the information as they receive it.

HARDWARE INTEGRATION

New APIs allow for interaction with watch hardware features, such as the accelerometer, the heart rate sensor, and the Taptic feedback engine.

PART I

Getting Started

CHAPTER 1

Creating a WatchKit Project

Apple frequently refers to Watch apps as standalone entities: miniature equivalents of iOS apps that can exist independently of your iPhone, iPad, or iPod touch. Although Watch apps are becoming more independent, creating a watchOS app means creating a new iOS project and giving it a few extras.

LIFELONG COMPANIONS

The first generation of third-party WatchKit apps required that you have an extension to an iOS app running on an iOS device. The extension acted as the brains of the app while the user interface ran on the watch. In watchOS 2 the split nature still exists, but the extension and the interface now both run on the watch. Therefore, to create your Watch app you'll need to create a new iOS project in Xcode and add a companion watchOS target to it.

NOTE: The next chapter explains the split nature of watchOS apps more fully so you can understand the implications of using it. For now, we focus on getting a watchOS app up and running as soon as possible, and we skip over some of the finer details here and there.

1. Open Xcode, and create a new iOS project by selecting File > New > Project from the main menu.

2. In the project template chooser (**Figure 1.1**), navigate to the watchOS Application category, select the iOS App with WatchKit App template, and click Next.

FIGURE 1.1 The WatchKit App target template

3. Give your project a name (we use **HelloWrist**), choose Swift from the Language menu, and choose Universal as the Devices type (**Figure 1.2**).

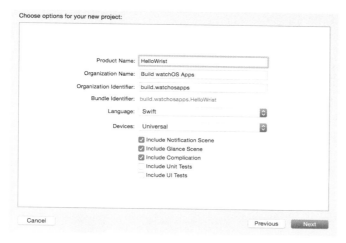

FIGURE 1.2 The WatchKit
App target options

4. Ensure that the Include Notification Scene, Include Glance Scene, and Include Complication options are selected, and click Next.

5. Choose a location to save your project, and click Create to finish creating the project.

When the project has been created, you'll have what looks like a standard iOS project but with a number of extra items in the File Navigator, the list of targets, and the list of schemes in your project. Chapter 2 explains the significance of these new items in detail.

ADDING CODE TO YOUR WATCHKIT APP

You now have a working app that you could easily try running at this point; jump ahead to the section "Trying Out HelloWrist!" if you feel so inclined. However, you may be a bit underwhelmed if you do because there isn't much to the default templates. Instead let's add some extra code to some of the template files created by Xcode to demonstrate a little more of the watch functionality.

UPDATING THE WATCH INTERFACE

The main interface to the WatchKit app is defined as a scene in a storyboard file. WatchKit has its own selection of UI components designed to work on the restricted interface, so let's see what we can do with them.

1. In the Xcode File Navigator, expand the HelloWrist WatchKit App folder, and click the Interface.storyboard file to load the WatchKit App user interface in the Storyboard editor of Interface Builder.

When the storyboard file loads, it displays four scenes (**Figure 1.3**).

FIGURE 1.3 The Watch-
Kit App Interface.
storyboard file

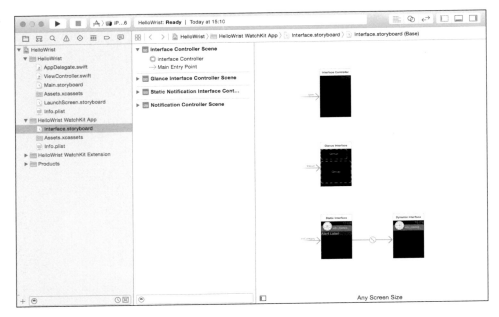

FIGURE 1.3 The Watch-Kit App Interface.storyboard file

2. Select the Interface Controller Scene option.

3. In the Object Library, search for the user interface element named Label (or
   WKInterfaceLabel) (**Figure 1.4**).

   This is the equivalent of a UILabel in a full iOS app, but as you'll see later, it comes with
   some limitations compared to its more fully featured counterpart.

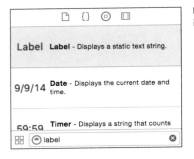

FIGURE 1.4 The WatchKit Label element
in the Object Library

NOTE: The Label element uses the underlying WKInterfaceLabel class. If you
need more information about any element, you can click it in the Object Library
to show a popover with more information, including the class name.

4. Drag the Label element from the Object Library onto the interface controller scene
   (**Figure 1.5**).

5. Use the Attribute inspector to style the element as you please.

Figure 1.6 shows the full range of customization options available to you for a WatchKit Label element. We have chosen to center the label horizontally (**Figure 1.7**).

> **NOTE:** Unlike in a regular iOS storyboard, you cannot place the label anywhere you choose. WatchKit uses a flow-layout system in which elements are placed in the order they should appear. Chapter 5 covers this in more detail.

FIGURE 1.5 A freshly placed Label element

FIGURE 1.6 Customization options for a Label element

FIGURE 1.7 A customized Label element

WRITING CODE FOR THE WATCH APP

What you have created so far is pretty much a vanilla "Hello World!" introduction. Again, if you want to run it right now, you can skip ahead to the "Trying Out HelloWrist!" section, but let's add some more interactivity before running it.

As with UIKit apps, WatchKit relies on a button user interface element to provide a lot of its interactive capabilities.

1. In the Object Library, search for a Button (or WKInterfaceButton) element (**Figure 1.8**), and drag it onto the interface controller scene.

Figure 1.9 highlights that, due to the flow-layout system, the Button element cannot be absolutely positioned on the interface, but can be placed relative only to the existing Label element. The button can be styled using the Attribute inspector; we'll set the Button title to **Say Hello**.

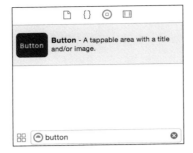

FIGURE 1.8 The WatchKit Button, or WKInterfaceButton, element

FIGURE 1.9 Dropping the Button element after the label

To make the button do something useful, you need to hook it up to an action method; this process is identical to that which would be carried out with a regular iOS storyboard. The easiest way to create the action is to enable the assistant editor, which should cause the InterfaceController.swift file from the HelloWrist WatchKit Extension folder to be displayed.

2. Control-click your new button, and drag it into the assistant editor. When Xcode displays an insertion line and the text "Insert Outlet or Action" (**Figure 1.10**), release the drag operation.

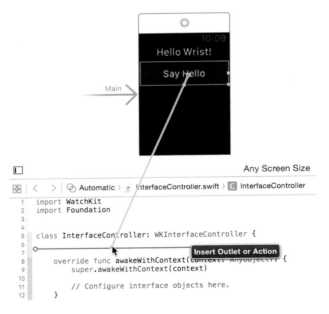

FIGURE 1.10 Inserting the saySomething action

3. In the popover that appears, select Action as the Connection type, and name it **saySomething**.

   Our intention is to have the Label element start blank and be populated by pressing the button.

4. Select the label in the storyboard, and change the Text attribute to be empty in the Attribute inspector.

   To be able to change the label text programmatically, the label must have an outlet that you can access from the `InterfaceController` class.

5. Control-click the label, and drag it into the assistant editor, releasing when Xcode shows the insertion line.

6. This time select Outlet as the Connection type, and name the outlet **messageLabel**. Update the `saySomething` method to match the following code:

```
@IBAction func saySomething() {
    messageLabel.setText("Hello Wrist!")
}
```

   Now that you can change the label text, let's make the message change between "Hello Wrist!" and "Bye Wrist!" on tapping the button.

7. Add an outlet named `button` so you can programmatically change the button text.

   An easy way to toggle the label text on tapping the button would be to inspect the current text value and change it accordingly.

8. Replace the `saySomething` method with the following code:

```
@IBAction func saySomething() {
    if messageLabel.text == "Hello Wrist!" {
        messageLabel.setText("Bye Wrist!")
    } else {
        messageLabel.setText("Hello Wrist!")
    }
}
```

   Unfortunately this highlights a fundamental difference between regular UIKit elements and those from WatchKit. A `UILabel` has a property named `text` that you can use to set and inspect the label text, whereas WatchKit has only one method: `setText`. If you want to track the state of elements in a WatchKit app, it's up to you to handle it yourself in the extension.

9. Create a Boolean property in the extension:

```
private var sayingHello = true
```

   The `saySomething` method now needs to track the state of the Boolean instead of trying to inspect the label text.

10. Use the `button` outlet to update the button text while you are updating this method:

```
@IBAction func saySomething() {
    if sayingHello {
        button.setTitle("Say Goodbye")
        messageLabel.setText("Hello Wrist!")
        sayingHello = false
    } else {
        button.setTitle("Say Hello")
        messageLabel.setText("Bye Wrist!")
        sayingHello = true
    }
}
```

If you have been exercising patience so far and have not skipped ahead to run the app already, then it is time for your patience to be rewarded.

"I'M SORRY, BUT I DON'T HAVE A WATCH"

As it has done in the past with other iOS devices, Apple has provided the ability to develop apps for the Apple Watch without access to the physical hardware. Although testing against a simulator is never going to be as foolproof as using the real device, it can often be a time-saver in terms of workflow and invaluable when limited access to the physical devices would otherwise slow down development.

The Apple Watch line is quite possibly the most diverse product range that Apple has ever produced. At the time of launch, there were 38 different models available across the Apple Watch, Sport, and Edition product options. The prices range from (relatively) cheap at $349 for the Sport variant up to an eye-wateringly expensive $17,000 for the Edition watches. So how do you safely test all the variations your app could be run on without breaking the bank? Thankfully, although the products may be cosmetically different, the entire range has only two real differences: the 38mm watch and the 42mm watch.

WHAT DO YOU WANT TO TEST?

The first step to running your watch code is to decide what your entry point is going to be. When your app is installed on a physical device, it can be invoked in four ways:

- By launching the app directly from the home screen of the watch
- By displaying a complication on the watch face
- By viewing a notification
- By viewing a glance

The Watch simulator provided with Xcode 7 is capable of testing all these interactions, but it is not always immediately apparent how you might do so. While running your app you can choose Hardware > Home (or press Control-Command-H) to simulate pressing the digital crown, which returns the simulator to a watch face. At this point it is possible to drag down to display the Notification Center, or drag up to display glances, but unfortunately your notifications and glances will not be displayed. Given this, how are you supposed to test your code in the same ways your users will be able to?

CHOOSING YOUR (HOPEFULLY NOT SO EVIL) SCHEME

Fortunately, the iOS App with WatchKit App project template has you covered. While creating the project files, Xcode also created a number of extra schemes that allow you to run your app in a variety of ways. To inspect them, choose Product > Scheme > Manage Schemes from the main menu, and note the four extra schemes that Xcode created (**Figure 1.11**).

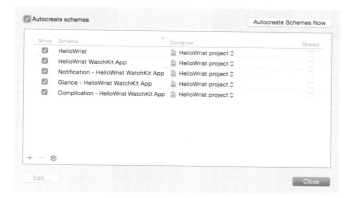

FIGURE 1.11 The Manage Schemes dialog—more schemes than a supervillain convention

The standard iOS app scheme (HelloWrist) is present, as you would expect, but there is also a scheme named HelloWrist WatchKit App, which is created for all WatchKit apps. This is the scheme you need to build and run to execute the app as though it had been launched from the home screen of the watch. This corresponds to the interface controller scene in the Interface.storyboard file (**Figure 1.12**).

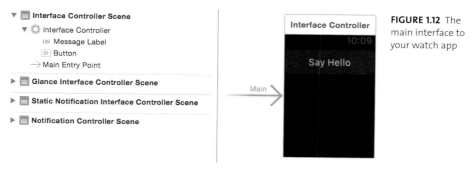

FIGURE 1.12 The main interface to your watch app

Of the three remaining schemes, the first two—Notification - HelloWrist WatchKit App and Glance - HelloWrist WatchKit App—were created because you selected the options Include Notification Scene and Include Glance Scene when you were creating the WatchKit App target (Figure 1.2). These schemes allow you to run the app as though the watch had received a glance or a notification. You can customize the appearance of these views using the Glance Interface Controller Scene (**Figure 1.13**), the Static Notification Interface Controller Scene, and the Notification Controller Scene (**Figure 1.14**).

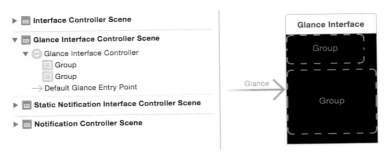

FIGURE 1.13 The Glance Interface Controller Scene

FIGURE 1.14 The Notification Interface Controller Scenes

NOTE: Chapters 8 and 9 delve into the details of how to work with glances and notifications, respectively.

The final scheme—Complication - HelloWrist WatchKit App—was created in response to enabling the Include Complication option when choosing the project options (Figure 1.2). This scheme allows you to run the simulator to test your complication. This is a simpler proposition than it may sound—it simply launches the simulator directly to a watch face on which you can configure your complication to be displayed. Creating and testing your complications is examined in detail in Chapter 7.

ACCESSING THE WATCH SIMULATORS

Choosing a simulator for running your iOS app requires that you open the scheme selection menu and choose a simulator from the list of options currently available to you. It stands to reason that the Watch simulators can be found in the same place:

1. Click the device portion (the right side) of the scheme selection button to view the list of simulators (**Figure 1.15**).

   Unfortunately, although there are plenty of iPhone and iPad simulation options presented, there are no Watch simulation options. That is because we currently have the HelloWrist App scheme selected, and the target for that scheme is an iOS app. To see the Watch simulators we need to select a different target.

2. Click the scheme portion (the left side) of the scheme selection button to display the list of available schemes.

3. Select one of the four HelloWrist WatchKit App schemes to switch to a scheme with a WatchKit app target.

   The device portion of the scheme selection button will change to indicate that running the selected scheme will launch both iPhone and Watch simulators. It's not possible to launch a Watch simulator in isolation, so the selection will include iPhone and Watch simulator combinations (**Figure 1.16**).

FIGURE 1.15 With an iOS scheme selected, the Watch simulators are not available to select.

FIGURE 1.16 The iPhone and Apple Watch simulator combinations

4. Select the simulator combination that you want to launch.

   The default configuration includes iPhone 6 and 6 Plus, as well as 38mm and 42mm Apple Watch options. These should be enough to satisfy most test requirements, but if you really need to, you can create more combinations in the Devices section of Xcode.

   The Watch simulator shares some of the limitations of the iOS simulator. You cannot run the same app in both an iPad and iPhone simulator at the same time, and you cannot display both the 38mm simulator and the 42mm watchOS simulators at the same time. Also, you cannot run the watchOS simulator along with the iPad simulator—the Apple Watch has an intimate relationship with iPhones but cannot be used with iPads. Not even simulated ones.

TRYING OUT HELLOWRIST!

You've shown a commendable amount of patience, and now it's time to actually run your app.

1. Select the HelloWrist WatchKit App scheme from the scheme portion of the scheme selector button.

2. Click the Run button to launch the Watch app.

3. This will spawn the iOS app in a process called Simulator, and the watchOS app in a process called Simulator (Watch). The iOS simulator won't run an active app, but it is available for the Watch simulator to communicate with.

Your app should be prompting you to "Say Hello" (**Figure 1.17**). Tap the button, and say hello to your future in watchOS development.

FIGURE 1.17 Someone wants to say hello...

WRAPPING UP

You've come to the end of your initial tour of WatchKit. In many ways it's remarkably similar to regular old iOS development, but it has just enough caveats and new ways of doing things to justify buying a book on the subject. Lucky you!

In the next chapter, we'll take a look at the layout of a WatchKit App project template. We'll also discuss how you can go about adding a watchOS companion app to your existing iOS projects.

CHAPTER 2

Anatomy of a watchOS App

Although a watchOS app may seem like a miniature version of an iOS app, the underlying architecture is subtly different. It isn't essential to know the difference, but it can help in understanding how your watchOS app works and performs.

APPS AND EXTENSIONS

A major limitation of the first generation of watchOS apps was that they could not run their code directly on the device. To circumvent this limitation, Apple allowed a watchOS app to run its code in the background on the user's iPhone, by taking advantage of iOS extensions.

For the second generation of watchOS apps, Apple has retained the same extension-based execution model but with the distinction that the extension now runs on the watch instead of on the iPhone. In most respects the code that now runs on the watch is the same as that which ran on the iPhone, but with some changes to the APIs and to the performance characteristics.

When you created an iOS App with WatchKit App project in Chapter 1, it included a number of extra elements in your project that you might not have encountered before. There are some additional targets and schemes, but perhaps the most obvious differences are the addition of two new file groups in the Project Navigator: WatchKit App and WatchKit Extension.

TIP: We're aware that we use the terms WatchKit and watchOS in a seemingly interchangeable fashion in this book. We've tried to match the terminology that Apple has used in any specific dialog or documentation.

WHAT IS A WATCHKIT APP?

A WatchKit app is the binary application that gets executed on your watch. The main responsibility of the app is to load the user interface, and for that reason the storyboard file that represents your app is located within the WatchKit App file group. This group is also the ideal place to include images and other resources that will be used within your user interface. Although storyboards themselves can contain a degree of conditional logic, the WatchKit App file group is limited to relatively static content. The layout of the storyboard scenes can be controlled through code, yet there is no code in the WatchKit App file group. To remedy this, during the compilation process the app bundle will be augmented with another bundle: the WatchKit Extension file group.

WHAT IS A WATCHKIT EXTENSION?

A WatchKit extension is a collection of code and other compiled resources that form the application logic that drives the user interface presented by the WatchKit app. When the app is launched, the extension host can load the app extension and marshal the communications between the user interface and the extension.

Although you can add as many files as you wish to your WatchKit extension, there are a number of files worth noting in the output of the iOS App with WatchKit App project template:

- `InterfaceController.swift`: This is the controller file that is associated with the main interface scene of your storyboard. It implements the `WKInterfaceController` class—the WatchKit equivalent of `UIViewController`—and is explored in detail in Chapter 3.
- `ComplicationController.swift`: This file is used to support a complication on the watch face. It implements the `CLKComplicationDataSource` that is used to provide information to a watch face that includes the complication. It is covered in Chapter 7.
- `Assets.xcassets`: This is a standard Xcode asset catalog file that is pre-populated with a folder for managing the assets associated with complications (Chapter 7). You can use it for storing other image assets beyond complications.
- `GlanceController.swift`: The `GlanceController` class is used to support the glance that the template creates for you. It's a fairly standard subclass of `WKInterfaceController`, and its use is documented in Chapter 8.
- `NotificationController.swift`: The `NotificationController` class is a subclass of `WKUserInterfaceController` and is used to provide extra functionality required by dynamic notification scenes. Notifications are intimately examined in Chapter 9.
- `PushNotificationPayload.apns`: This file is a sample payload for testing notifications. It is also detailed in Chapter 9.

One file that we have not mentioned yet is `ExtensionDelegate.swift`. This file is special because it's the main entry point for your app and is analogous to the `UIApplicationDelegate` in your iOS app. It contains a class named `ExtensionDelegate`, which implements a protocol named `WKExtensionDelegate`. By implementing the protocol, the class assumes three main responsibilities:

- **Stage Change Monitoring:** The lifecycle callback methods `applicationDidFinishLaunching()`, `applicationDidBecomeActive()`, and `applicationWillResignActive()` are defined here. These give you the opportunity to prepare your app as it launches, and tidy up as it's about to shut down.
- **Notification Handling:** Your app can respond to notifications both while it is running and when response action buttons are pressed. This protocol allows you to implement `didReceive...` methods to handle notifications as they come in, and `handleActionWithIdentifier...` methods to respond to notification actions taken when your app isn't running. Refer to Chapter 9 for everything you'll ever want to know about notifications.
- **Handoff Coordindation:** When your app is launched as a result of a handoff event, this protocol provides a method, `handleUserActivity(_:)`, that you can implement to respond to the event. Handoff is explored in Chapter 10.

WHY DO WE NEED THIS CONVOLUTED SYSTEM?

It's hard to know why Apple has presented us with what is seemingly a quite convoluted system. After all, iOS apps bundle the user interface and application logic into the one app, so why doesn't watchOS?

It may simply be that, as we evolve from the extension-on-iPhone model of watchOS 1, we are at a stepping-stone on the way to completely bundled watchOS apps. Alternatively, an extension running within an extension host written by Apple can be more tightly controlled; this provides watchOS with more ways to enforce security and energy efficiency measures.

WATCHKIT APP PROJECT LAYOUT

Adding any additional targets to an iOS app greatly increases the complexity of your Xcode project setup. Adding a WatchKit app goes even further; if you followed the walkthrough in Chapter 1, you noticed that creating a WatchKit app target can lead to an explosion of targets, schemes, and files in your project. These may seem intimidating—after all, you just want to write an app, not get a lesson in (Xcode) project management—but there is a method to the madness.

In Chapter 1 we created a project using the iOS App with WatchKit App template, with the Include Notification Scene, Include Glance Scene, and Include Complication options selected (Figure 1.2). This resulted in the generation of extra file groups and targets for the HelloWrist WatchKit app and for the HelloWrist WatchKit extension (**Figure 2.1**). It also resulted in the generation of four new schemes; one allows you to directly build and run the full WatchKit app, and the other three allow you to run the notification, glance, and complication features directly (**Figure 2.2**).

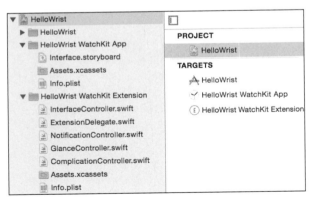

FIGURE 2.1 Project and targets for an iOS App with WatchKit App project

FIGURE 2.2 Schemes for an iOS App with WatchKit App project

You have some control over the number of schemes that are being created; you can dese-lect the Notification, Glance, and Complication options in the template options (Figure 1.2) if you don't need the functionality they provide. Notable by its absence is a scheme that allows you to directly build and run the WatchKit extension; the only options are for building the WatchKit app and the notification, glance, and complication schemes. Your WatchKit Exten-sion target will be built as part of the WatchKit app scheme; the tight integration between app and watch means you should never need to run the extension in isolation.

CREATING WATCHKIT APPS AND EXTENSIONS

We have already established that watchOS apps result in a lot of extra files, schemes, and targets to manage in Xcode, but how do you go about bringing that extra complexity into your life?

Xcode project and target templates come in many flavors and have differing options that affect how much of your app configuration you get for free and how much you need to configure yourself. Your route through this maze is determined by your requirements—and yours alone—but with the following sections we hope to point out some of the options available to you and help you make a decision.

USING PROJECT TEMPLATES

The important thing to remember when creating a watchOS app is that it requires an iOS app in order to live. This has the potential to be confusing; iOS apps have their own set of templates, and attempting to create a standard iOS app project will not furnish you with the artifacts you need to build a watchOS app. Conversely, creating a watchOS-specific app may not necessarily provide an iOS app that meets your immediate requirements.

When you start to create a new app project (using File > New > Project from the Xcode main menu), you should decide whether the watchOS app is the primary focus for your development.

If the iOS app is intended only as a delivery mechanism, or will be very light in features, then you are unlikely to need a particularly complex iOS app, and your logical next move is to select the watchOS section in the template chooser dialog (**Figure 2.3**). Selecting the option iOS App with WatchKit App provides you with a basic iOS app that is functionally equivalent to a Single View application from the iOS project templates.

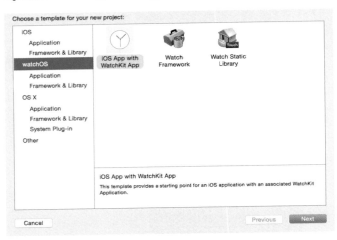

FIGURE 2.3 The watchOS project template selection

NOTE: The other options available in the watchOS section are for creating a framework or a static library. We're not going to cover these here; if you're the kind of developer who wants to create a framework for your watchOS app, you're probably already in the advanced developer category. Thanks for buying the book, though!

When you select an iOS App with WatchKit App template you are presented with a set of options relating to both the iOS and watchOS apps (**Figure 2.4**). They may seem straightforward, but there are a few things to be aware of so we'll run through the options one by one.

- **Product Name:** This is the same as the Product Name option in any normal Xcode project, with the caveat that it is the name of your iOS app only. The watchOS app will be given a name of the form *ProductName WatchKit App*.

- **Organization Name** and **Organization Identifier:** These options are the same as they would be in any Xcode project.

- **Bundle Identifier:** Although not editable, Bundle Identifier is displayed as it is generated from some of the previous options. The significance of the identifier here is that it refers to the iOS target and not the WatchKit App target, which gets its own identifier of the format `ios-bundle-identifier.watchkitapp`.

- **Language:** The Language option can be Swift or Objective-C, and this setting will be applied to the generated code for both the iOS and watchOS targets.

- **Devices:** Unlike a normal iOS project template, the Devices pop-up menu offers only the choice of Universal or iPhone; you can't bundle a watchOS app with an iPad-only app.
- **Include Notification Scene:** Selecting this option creates a scheme, storyboard scene, and source file for including basic notification handling support in your watch app.
- **Include Glance Scene:** Selecting this option creates a scheme, storyboard scene, and source file for including a glance in your watch app.
- **Include Complication:** Selecting this option creates a scheme and source file for including a complication in your watch app.
- **Include Unit Tests** and **Include UI Tests:** Selecting these options adds the necessary configuration to create test targets, though the test targets are only applicable to your iOS app; watchOS doesn't fully support unit or UI testing yet.

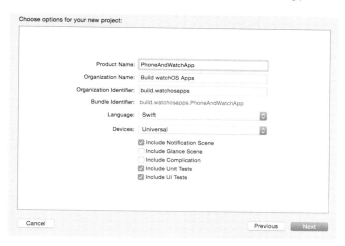

FIGURE 2.4 The template options for the iOS App with WatchKit App project

Maybe you don't want to start with a Single View application for your iOS app and require a bit more in the way of complexity. For example, if your iOS app is intended to be a fully featured app with a companion watchOS app, then you may find the Single View application to be somewhat lacking. Or maybe you could be satisfied with a Single View application but have a requirement to use Core Data; in that case, you will find that the iOS App with WatchKit App project template is lacking a Use Core Data option, which means you may be better served by creating a dedicated iOS app and adding a watchOS target at a later stage.

USING TARGET TEMPLATES

Creating a watchOS app from scratch is simple, but what happens when you already have an iOS app and you want to add a watchOS app to it? You have two main options: Create a new project based on the iOS App with WatchKit App template and painstakingly copy your existing iOS app code across by hand (losing any commit history you might have had on the way); or add a WatchKit App target to your existing iOS app project. Although you may want to do the former (everyone wants a fresh start sometimes!), we definitely recommend the latter.

To add a watchOS app to your existing iOS app project you should select File > New > Target from the Xcode main menu to display the target template chooser dialog. One potentially confusing item is an entry named Apple Watch, under the iOS heading in the left-hand column. Clicking the Apple Watch option reveals more (**Figure 2.5**); this is how you can create an older-style WatchKit app for watchOS 1. At the time of this writing we can't see many good reasons for going down this route, but if you happen to have a stubborn customer base who refuse to upgrade to watchOS 2, this is where your world of pain begins.

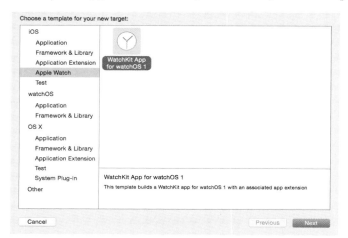

FIGURE 2.5 The WatchKit App for watchOS 1 target template—probably best avoided

For modern watchOS development, select the watchOS section to see the options available to you for creating a watchOS 2 app (**Figure 2.6**). Unlike with the project template options, this time you don't get iOS App with WatchKit App as a choice—instead you get a boring old WatchKit App. At this stage Apple is making the assumption that you already have an iOS app target in your project. If you don't (maybe this is an OS X project), you'll need to go back and create an iOS app target first.

If you select the WatchKit App template and click Next, you are presented with a series of options for the target that are similar to those shown for the iOS App with WatchKit App project (**Figure 2.7**). There are a few differences worth highlighting:

- **Product Name:** In this dialog, Product Name is the name of the watchOS app and can be distinct from the iOS app.
- **Organization Identifier:** This cannot be changed here because Xcode must set to the Bundle Identifier of the companion iOS app.
- **Bundle Identifier:** This also can't be changed but is formed from the Organization Identifier and the Product Name.

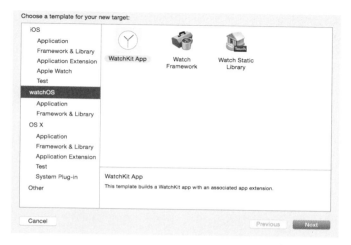

FIGURE 2.6 The watchOS target template selection

FIGURE 2.7 The template options for the WatchKit App target

- **Language:** Interestingly, when creating your WatchKit app target you can choose to use a different language than the one you used when creating your iOS app project. This is good for developers with existing iOS apps that were created in Objective-C but wish to perform ongoing development in Swift.

- **Include Notification Scene**, **Include Glance Scene**, and **Include Complication:** These options, when selected, create the appropriate extra artifacts in your project.

- **Project:** If you are working in a multi-project workspace, this option allows you to select which project the new target should be created within.

- **Embed in Companion Application:** The WatchKit app must be associated with an companion iOS app; if you have only one iOS app in your project, this is an easy choice to make, but if you have more than one iOS app target in your project (or workspace), you have to decide which app will be the official companion. This determines which iOS app the user has to install to get the WatchKit app onto their watch.

NOTE: The iOS App with WatchKit App project template will generate two targets: Product Name WatchKit App and Product Name WatchKit Extension. This is different from the WatchKit App target template, which creates targets named Product Name and Product Name Extension. These subtle naming differences can be confusing, especially if you are following the instructions in this book, where we will often start our examples with the iOS App with WatchKit App project template.

USING OLD-SCHOOL TECHNIQUES

You can, of course, do things the hard way. This is also known as "hand-crafting" or "taking the hipster route." Although there are always some people who think they can do it better themselves, sometimes it *really is* necessary to create targets, schemes, and code without the aid of Xcode. For example, you may have created your WatchKit App target at a time when you thought you wouldn't need a complication with your app, but now you've identified such a need. For those circumstances, we'll cover the manual creation of such project artifacts in the appropriate chapters later in the book: Chapter 7, "Working with Complications," Chapter 8, "Working with Glances," and Chapter 9, "Working with Notifications."

However, what if you need to tweak some settings that the templates created on your behalf? Most of the settings you need to worry about can be found hidden under the settings for the WatchKit App and WatchKit Extension targets. It's rare that you'll need to change these settings too much, but if you find you have a need, make sure you have a recent source control commit to revert to, or a recent backup of your project. Just in case.

WRAPPING UP

This completes our discussion of WatchKit apps and extensions. After the hands-on approach of Chapter 1, this has been quite the theoretical run through the way WatchKit apps are created and configured, but we feel that it is worth knowing how they are organized and behave so you can work with confidence when building them.

The next chapter dives back into WatchKit itself to explore how to work with the APIs that are provided by watchOS to allow you to interact with your watch app.

CHAPTER 3

Implementing Navigation

Apps on the Apple Watch, and the watchOS APIs that we use to work with them, are very obviously siblings of iOS. As you work with the watch, you see lots of similarities in the interface and in the code—but you'll also see significant differences. When the iPhone introduced us to what was then iPhoneOS, it was presented as relying on the same technologies as OS X, but developed in a way that works better on smaller devices. watchOS is like that, but it moves iOS to a new device.

NAVIGATING THE APPLE WATCH

When you're coming to the Apple Watch from other iOS devices, the main differences you'll encounter are in simplification, which only makes sense when you consider that you're dealing with much less space for display and interaction, and much more constrained resources. Strong conventions are even more important than on larger devices. Perhaps in the future there will be scope for the great innovation in UI we've seen in iOS (with its misses as well as its hits), but in these early days of watchOS it's worth looking first to the interface paradigms Apple has provided for us.

And that's not a bad thing. Constraints encourage creativity, and users of these brand-new devices will be helped by learning what to expect.

Chief among those constraints are the four ways available to watchOS apps to present to the user: Apple Watch apps, with their own UIs and interactions; complications, which allow your apps to add their most important, at-a-glance piece of information to the watch face; glances, which show a chosen set of information without allowing for interaction; and notifications, which may or may not allow the user to respond with an action.

We'll spend more time on complications, glances, and notifications in Chapters 7, 8, and 9, respectively, but for now we'll explore some of the capabilities of apps on the watch as we take a tour of the available navigation options.

NAVIGATION TYPES

iOS has given us several different approaches to navigation within an app, some designed by Apple and directly supported in the frameworks (navigation controllers, page view controllers, various modal view controllers, the hidden reverse of the Utility app, tab bars, popovers), and some dreamed up by third-party developers (the stacked cards of Twitter's first iPad app, various kinds of sliding view controllers, and the sometimes fashionable and often controversial burger menu).

On the watch, however, are really only two options:

- Page-based navigation is reminiscent of the scroll view or page view controller-based navigation, such as in Apple's Weather app on iOS.
- Hierarchical navigation is analogous to the drill-down walk of a navigation controller.

What's more, when creating your interface you must decide which of these two options will be the basis for your navigation; an app may use one or the other.

Additionally, an app may present a modal interface, which may include page-based navigation of its own.

It doesn't sound like much, but we think you'll find that it's not as restrictive as it sounds.

PAGE-BASED NAVIGATION

Let's take a quick look at how page-based navigation works in practice.

1. Open Xcode, and create a new project, selecting the Watch OS > Application > iOS App with WatchKit App template.

2. Choose Swift as the language for the project.

> **NOTE:** This book uses Swift, so selecting it as the language for the project will allow you to follow along with the code.

3. Leave the Include Notification Scene, Include Glance Scene, and Include Complication options unselected (unlike in Chapter 1) (**Figure 3.1**). We're not going to be using them in this example. Click Next, and choose where to save your project.

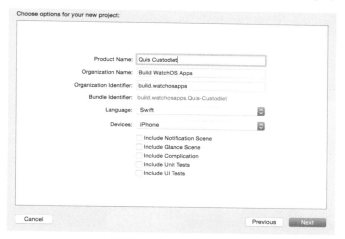

FIGURE 3.1 WatchKit target options

4. Open `Interface.storyboard` from the WatchKit App's group in the Project Navigator. You'll see just one scene, something like that in **Figure 3.2**.

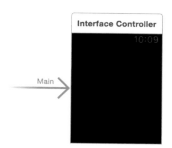

FIGURE 3.2 A lone scene in the storyboard

5. Add another interface controller scene to the storyboard by finding the Interface Controller entry in the Object Library (**Figure 3.3**) and dragging it onto the storyboard next to the existing one.

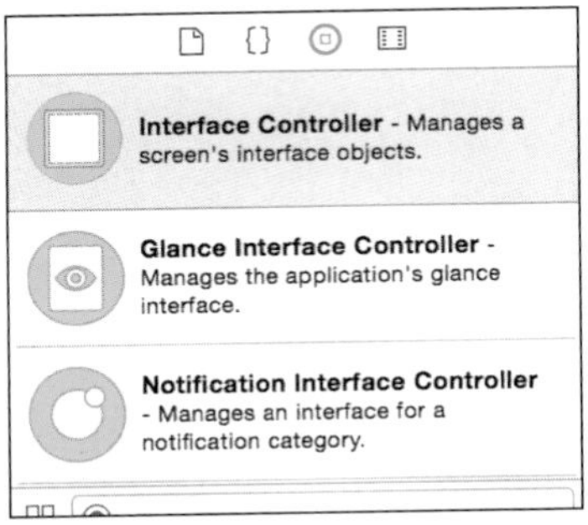

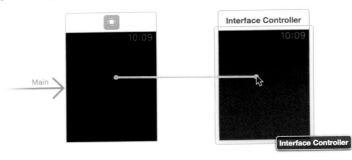

FIGURE 3.3 Xcode's Object Library

6. Control-click and drag from the first interface controller scene to the one you just placed (**Figure 3.4**), then select "next page" from the popup (**Figure 3.5**) that appears when you release your click.

You could run the app now to see how the pages work, but it would be difficult to distinguish the pages.

FIGURE 3.4 Creating a segue relationship

FIGURE 3.5 Selecting the segue

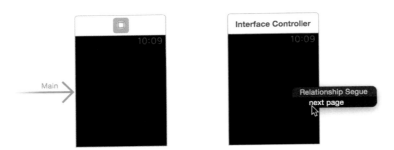

7. Add a couple of labels to your interface controller scenes (perhaps identifying them as shown in **Figure 3.6**—these have Alignment set to Center in both horizontal and vertical directions), then run the WatchKit App scheme in one of the iPhone + Watch simulator pairs.

In the Apple Watch simulator window, you should be able to happily swipe back and forth between your two interface controllers (**Figure 3.7**).

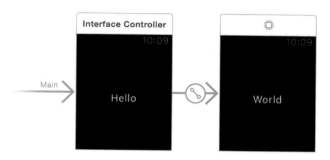

FIGURE 3.6 Storyboard scenes ready to page

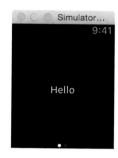

FIGURE 3.7 The first page in the simulator

Swiping between full-screen pages is an interface approach that is very well established on iOS, going all the way back to the original Weather app installed as standard on the first iPhone. You may be well used to working with these interfaces, either by working with UIScrollView yourself or via the UIPageViewController class introduced in iOS 5. When working with WatchKit, you must keep a number of key differences in mind.

- Although you may be accustomed to dynamically providing the pages of your iOS navigation on demand, things are very different when dealing with WKInterfaceControllers as pages: The number of pages, and the classes of the controllers, is provided in advance. This is done either by connecting a chain of scenes in the storyboard, as you've just done, or by calling WKInterfaceController's reloadRootControllersWithNames (_:contexts:) class method. The array of names provided to that method contains NSStrings to match the names of scenes in the storyboard, while contexts is an optional array of AnyObjects. The arrays correspond to each other, with the first context object being passed to the first controller, the second context to the second controller, and so on.

- All the interface controllers represented by the pages are instantiated and initialized at once, before the interface is displayed. Your extension code manages the content displayed in response to events in the WKInterfaceController lifecycle, which you'll learn more about later in this chapter.

- If you want to include more than one interface controller in a modal presentation, they must be handled as page-based rather than in a drill-down hierarchy. This is accomplished with the presentControllerWithNames(_:contexts:) method.

HIERARCHICAL NAVIGATION

The drill-down method through a series of table views, presented in a navigation controller, is possibly the most used approach to navigation on the iPhone—and the master-detail split view, originally seen on the iPad, is often best understood as a variant of this style. On the phone, think of the Music app, browsing albums and then tracks. Or remember browsing in Mail from Mailboxes to Inbox to a thread to a specific email. Even the humble Phone app displays this approach: groups to contacts list to a single contact.

Although table views tend to be a big part of a hierarchical structure, your iOS view controllers can trigger navigation to the next layer however you like. On the watch, you'll probably find navigation being triggered by user interaction with a table row, a button, or perhaps the context menu (more on that later in this chapter).

As with the paged navigation, each screen in the user's journey is managed by a subclass of WKInterfaceController. Navigation up the stack is provided by the system-supplied and -managed back button, just like the standard Back button item of a UINavigationController. You can customize the string displayed by setting the controller's title in the storyboard editor.

To experiment with hierarchical navigation in an app, return to your page-based app and make the following changes:

1. Delete the "next page" segue between the two scenes.
2. Delete the label from the first scene, and replace it with a button.
3. Control-click and drag from the button to the second scene in the storyboard.
4. Select "push" from the popup that appears when you release the click.

The storyboard should now look something like **Figure 3.8**; note the icon, embedded in the segue arrow, that identifies the type of segue, and how it differs from the simple "linked objects" icon that was used for the "next page" segue in Figure 3.6.

FIGURE 3.8 Hierarchical navigation in the storyboard

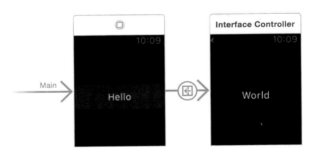

When you run your app, you'll be able to click back and forth between the two screens (**Figures 3.9** and **3.10**). Notice that the back arrow in the second screen is just a small, anonymous arrow. You can add a custom title using the scene's Title property in the storyboard editor, or in code using the WKInterfaceController's setTitle(_:) method. "What's WKInterfaceController?" you ask. This is a good time to find out.

FIGURE 3.9 The button in the Watch simulator

FIGURE 3.10 The second controller in the Watch simulator

THE WKINTERFACECONTROLLER

By now you have figured out that when you're working with WatchKit interfaces you spend lots of time in subclasses of WKInterfaceController. As suggested by the name, this class is somewhat analogous to the UIViewController of iOS, although (as is the case throughout WatchKit) the interface it presents to the developer is much simpler. WKInterfaceController feels a little like the essence of UIViewController in a smaller, lighter package.

Perhaps the most significant way this is achieved is in the very close relationship between WKInterfaceController and UI storyboards. Wherever you might seek to "instantiate" an interface controller, you reference it by its identifier from the storyboard.

We say "instantiate," but even that isn't something you'll ever do directly in code. You might provide the identifier as a member of an array passed to reloadRootControllers WithNames(_:contexts:) or provide it to presentControllerWithName(_:context:), but the system will take it from there.

If you haven't gotten Apple's very large hint by now, take heed: There is no laying out your interface in code, however much fun you might have found that in the past. When preparing interfaces for Apple Watch, your options are to define your interface elements in the storyboard editor or to define your interface elements in the storyboard editor. The future will be storyboarded.

THE CIRCLE OF LIFE

In a manner that will, again, be familiar from UIViewController, the lifecycle of a WKInterfaceController is marked with callbacks. Following a theme with which you are very familiar, the callbacks are many fewer than on iOS.

init()

The init() method is the designated initializer for WKInterfaceController and is ready to be overridden. As you'd expect, your override should always make sure to call super.init(). The init() method is also the first place your approach to controllers will diverge from your experience with UIViewController.

Although UIViewController has the special designated initializer init(nibName:bundle:), the WKInterfaceController has only init(). And as noted previously, you'll never be calling it from your own code. Instead, you can override init() for when it's called by the system. Also, although you might be accustomed to waiting until viewDidLoad() is called before you can access interface elements loaded from a storyboard, by the time init() has been called on your interface controller, the objects referred to by your @IBOutlets are ready and waiting for your attention.

That being said, updating your UI is best done in awakeWithContext(_:).

NOTE: The normal pattern in Swift is to call *super.init()* last in your override. In *WKInterfaceController*, it is that call to *super* that hooks up any *@IBOutlets* in your controller. So you want to make sure to call super before trying to address any interface elements. However, you should still make sure that any non-optional properties are initialized before calling *super.init()*.

awakeWithContext(_:)

Once the interface controller is initialized, its awakeWithContext(_:) method will be called. This is the method from which you are likely to make most of the initial UI updates for the controller.

The context received is typed as an AnyObject? and is provided by the interface controller which passes control to the receiver. As an AnyObject?, the context is whatever you want to pass from one interface controller to the next—or nil if there's nothing needed.

Bear in mind that WKInterfaceController does not have a context property, so if you want to be able to access the received object outside of this method, then your subclass will need to have its own property or properties in which to stash the received information.

willActivate(), didDeactivate(), didAppear(), AND willDisappear()

WKInterfaceController has a set of lifecycle callbacks that are reminiscent of UIViewController's methods viewWillAppear(), viewDidAppear(), viewWillDisappear(), and viewDidDisappear(). The WKInterfaceController versions are usually called exactly when you'd expect:

- willActivate() is called before the interface controller's UI is displayed on the watch screen.
- didDeactivate() is called when the interface controller's UI has been removed from the screen.

You should do as little work as possible in these methods. For example, it may seem logical to perform your UI updates in willActivate(), much as you might employ viewWillAppear(_:) in UIViewController, but the documentation stresses that as much as possible should be done at initialization, with only necessary last-minute updates performed in this method. Note as well that some time may pass between the call to willActivate() and the interface appearing onscreen.

Once didDeactivate() has been called on your interface controller, the system considers it inactive—and may deallocate it at any time to reclaim resources. In case this happens, you should perform any necessary cleanup here, including any state-persistence your app needs. The key word here is *necessary*. Any work in this method should be kept as quick as possible.

One further nuance is that by the time didDeactivate() has been called and the interface controller is regarded as inactive, the system will not act on any attempts to update the controller's UI, including the values of controls. This will be the case until the next time the controller receives a call to its willActivate() method.

- didAppear() is called just after the interface controller's interface has been displayed on the screen.

- willDisappear() is called shortly before the interface controller's interface is removed from display.

As these methods coincide closely with the display and removal of your interface controller's UI, they are a good place to perform tasks like the configuration of UI animations.

SUPPORTING NAVIGATION

The methods on WKInterfaceController related to navigating between controllers can be grouped as follows:

- Methods that directly drive hierarchical navigation
- Methods that help manage page-based navigation
- Methods to support storyboarded navigation managed with segues
- Methods to present interface controllers modally
- Methods related to interactions in table views

NAVIGATING IN A HIERARCHY FROM CODE

As demonstrated earlier in this chapter, the hierarchical navigation on Apple Watch is very similar in approach to using a UINavigationController on iOS. The methods used to navigate between interface controllers have a straightforward equivalence to the ones you know and love so well from the larger devices.

- pushControllerWithName(_:context:) is used to push a new interface controller to the top of the navigation stack—note again that the controller is referenced by the name it has been assigned in your storyboard file.

- popController() and popToRootController() behave exactly as you would expect, to trigger navigation back through the stack of previous interface controllers.

In addition to using the storyboard editor to set the interface controller's title, and so control the text shown by the back button, the controller has the method setTitle(_:), which you can use to update the back text at run time.

To try working with these transitions from code, you can replace the storyboard-based push segue of our earlier hierarchical navigation with an action method in our custom controller code.

Notice that when your project was created, Xcode added an InterfaceController.swift file to the WatchKit Extension group in the Project Navigator (**Figure 3.11**). This is also set as the custom class of the interface controller in the first scene that was added to the storyboard (**Figure 3.12**).

FIGURE 3.11 The WatchKit Extension group in the Project Navigator

FIGURE 3.12 The custom class in the storyboard editor

1. Add the following code to the InterfaceController class in InterfaceController .swift:

```swift
@IBAction func helloTapped() {
    pushControllerWithName("World", context: nil)
}
```

2. Delete the push segue from the storyboard file.

3. Find the InterfaceController custom class in the storyboard editor's sidebar (**Figure 3.13**), then Control-click and drag from the button to that class in the list.

4. Select helloTapped from the popup that appears.

5. Select the second scene in the storyboard editor, and set its identifier to the string **World** (**Figure 3.14**).

6. Run the app. It should behave exactly as it did before—only without the segue in the storyboard!

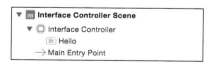

FIGURE 3.13 The custom class in the storyboard sidebar

FIGURE 3.14 The interface controller identifier

CREATING PAGE-BASED NAVIGATION FROM CODE

When experimenting earlier with page-based navigation, we mentioned briefly that we are not limited to setting up chains of paged interface controllers in the storyboard. Although all controllers still have their interface defined in the storyboard file, it is possible to forgo connecting them in order there, and rather load the set of pages in code. You could do this with the initial interface controller of your app, to set up the pages at load, or you could do this at any time in response to received data—whether it's information that your app's collection of controllers needs to be changed, or in response to a user interaction.

The method for re-creating the pages is the class method on WKInterfaceController `reloadRootControllersWithNames(_:contexts:)`, which instantiates and initializes a whole new collection of interface controllers and uses it to replace any current collection.

The other method available for interacting with the page-based navigation from code is `becomeCurrentPage()`, which an interface controller can call on itself to be animated into view.

RESPONDING TO SEGUES

Where segues are used in the storyboard to define navigation, the methods `contextForSegueWithIdentifier(_:)` and `contextsForSegueWithIdentifier(_:)` will be called, with the returned context objects passed to the incoming interface controllers' `awakeWithContext(_:)` methods. These methods allow up-to-date data to be passed to the incoming controller or controllers.

CREATING A MODAL PRESENTATION

If your Watch app needs to present one or more interface controllers modally, you may define the presentation in the storyboard or in code. If you are performing the presentation explicitly in code, use the method `presentControllerWithName(_:context:)` to present a single controller, but use `presentControllerWithNames(_:contexts:)` to present a paging navigation between interface controllers. (Note again the method `contextsForSegueWith Identifier(_:)` for handling presentation of multiple interface controllers.)

In either case, a call to `dismissController()` will end the modal presentation.

TOUCHING ON TABLE VIEWS

Table views may be employed as they often are on iOS—as part of the navigation in an app. In this case, there is the very familiar-looking method `table(_:didSelectRowAtIndex:)` and two table view-specific segue methods, `contextForSegueWithIdentifier(_:inTable:row Index:)` and `contextsForSegueWithIdentifier(_:inTable:rowIndex:)`. Chapter 4 explores table views and their interactions in detail.

THE CONTEXT MENU

So far we've skipped over an important part of the interface controller's standard user interface.

When the user performs a force touch on the interface of a `WKInterfaceController`, that interface controller's context menu (something like that in **Figure 3.15**) will be displayed. (This is the only way a third-party app can respond to a force touch, because there is currently no public API for its detection.)

FIGURE 3.15 Interface controller context menu

The context menu can show a maximum of four options, each of which is displayed as an image (either a custom image from your WatchKit app's bundle or one from the set of standard icons provided by WatchKit) with a short title below it. The options may be defined either in the storyboard or in code in the interface controller, and in either case a tap on the option will send an action message to the interface controller.

To experiment with the context menu, return to the example app from earlier in this chapter.

1. Add another interface controller scene to your watch app's storyboard, drag in a label, and give it an identifier of **Info**.

2. Find the Menu object (**Figure 3.16**) in the Object Library, and drag it onto the first interface controller in your app. Note that when you release the drag, there will be no sign of the menu on the storyboard canvas, but it will appear in the storyboard editor's left sidebar (**Figure 3.17**).

The menu is created with a single menu item already in place.

FIGURE 3.16 Menu object

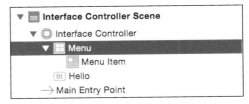

FIGURE 3.17 The menu in place

3. Select the menu item, and give it a title and image of **Info**, as in **Figure 3.18**.

FIGURE 3.18 Menu item configuration

4. Make the menu item trigger a navigation to your new interface controller by adding the following method to InterfaceController.swift:

```
@IBAction func contextInfoTapped() {
    pushControllerWithName("Info", context: nil)
}
```

5. Connect the action of the menu item to that method, then run the app.

6. Activate an interface controller's context menu in the simulator by clicking and holding in the Apple Watch window.

   After a moment, the context menu will appear. Clicking the menu item will trigger the navigation to your new interface controller.

   We're going to add one more item to the context menu, but this time we'll do it from our interface controller in code.

7. Open InterfaceController.swift again, and add the following method:

```
func contextMoreTapped() {
    presentControllerWithNames(["World", "Info"], contexts: nil)
}
```

8. Add the following method at the top of the InterfaceController class:

```
override init() {
    super.init()

    addMenuItemWithItemIcon(.More, title: "More", action:
Selector("contextMoreTapped"))
}
```

9. Run the app.

10. Activate the context menu.

    You should see another option: More.

11. Click the More menu item, and the eagle-eyed will spot the use of modal presentation of paged navigation back and forth between two interface controllers.

AND SO MUCH MORE

Because WKInterfaceController is a core class in watchOS, you will find that a great deal of what you need to do in your code will happen in—or not far removed from—its subclasses. The excitement and opportunity presented, especially with the release of watchOS 2, include:

- Alerts (Chapter 4)
- Interface animations (Chapter 6)
- Integration with other platforms via the Handoff APIs (covered in Chapter 10 along with other cross-device communication topics)
- Responding to the user's interaction with notifications (Chapter 9)
- Audio recording and media playback (Chapter 12)
- Accepting user input (Chapter 11)

WRAPPING UP

This chapter has been a quick overview of the navigation options available to your WatchKit app, with a longer look at some of the navigation-specific API provided by WKInterfaceController. We have explored enough to be able to instantiate a whole gang of interface controllers and hook them together with a variety of navigational approaches for use in different ways.

Yet all the interface controllers we could come up with would end up being pretty boring and useless without ways of communicating with the user: presenting information and detecting interaction. Chapter 4 surveys the UI controls available in WatchKit and gives some examples of their use.

CHAPTER 4

Exploring Controls

iOS has always had a place for innovative custom UIs, but it's often a good idea to start with the standard controls provided by the platform. On Apple Watch, standard controls are (for now) the only option—but as we take a tour of the available interface elements, you'll see that there's still plenty to work with on the new platform.

HOUSE RULES

As we take a look through the Object Library and the APIs, almost everything has a similar and direct analog available on the larger iOS devices. But let's pause for a moment and review some small but important differences in the Watch environment (which we are sure will be no trouble to an intelligent, creative, and insightful developer such as you, dear reader).

- The user interface and the controls it contains are defined during development using the storyboard editor. In contrast to iOS, you can't create the UI in code. If you are one of those developers who prefer to avoid the visual editor, then you'll find it's time to dip your proverbial toe in its waters.

- Even so, some properties of the controls can be set at run time (how else would you update a label to give your user information that you didn't have at build time?), but only some. Others can be set only in the storyboard editor. We'll identify which properties on each control can be dynamically updated as we examine each.

- Where values can be set to controls, they cannot be read by your Watch app. For example, you can set a switch to on from your interface controller, but you cannot read from it whether it is on or off. Instead, you must wire up the switch's change event to an @IBAction method in your controller and keep track of state changes in a property.

This might sound like the Watch presents an even more restrictive environment than we're used to as developers for iOS platforms, but as you saw when exploring the available navigation options (Chapter 3), you *can* do a lot with what's available.

WATCHKIT CONTROLS

All interface objects (what we refer to as "controls") in WatchKit are subclasses of WKInterfaceObject. Apps are limited to using and configuring the standard controls, so we can't work with our own subclasses of WKInterfaceObject—or of any of its subclasses (which are the controls in the following sections). Any configuration is done in the storyboard editor or via @IBOutlet properties in your interface controllers.

WKInterfaceObject provides common methods for hiding and showing the control, changing its size, and setting its accessibility attributes. We'll refer to hiding, showing, and changing size methods as you learn about the available controls, and we'll look in detail at the accessibility options in Chapter 6.

SIMPLE DISPLAY CONTROLS

The following controls are for *displaying* data to the user. They do not accept user interaction.

LABELS

Where would we be without labels in our user interfaces? The humble label is the first option to display text to the user in any iOS app, and it's the first option in your Watch app as well.

The WKInterfaceLabel is analogous to UILabel and is configurable in some of the same ways: text (of course), text color, font, minimum scale and maximum number of lines (to handle long text values), and alignment. Additionally, text color can be set at run time with the label's setTextColor(_:) method. The text displayed by the label can be updated with the setText(_:) and setAttributedText(_:) methods. The latter, as you'd expect, allows configuration of the text's style.

WKInterfaceDate and WKInterfaceTimer (**Figures 4.1** and **4.2**) are two special label classes that are a new idea to WatchKit.

FIGURE 4.1 WKInterfaceDate

FIGURE 4.2 WKInterfaceTimer

WKInterfaceDate always displays the current date, the current time, or both. The storyboard editor is used to configure the format of the displayed date–time information, using setTextColor(_:), setTimeZone(_:), and setCalendar(_:), which are available at run time. This control makes it trivial to display the current date and time in your app.

WKInterfaceTimer is equally specialized. It manages, displays, and updates a countdown timer, with the format and displayed units configurable in the storyboard editor. The Enabled check box in the Timer (**Figure 4.3**) specifies whether the timer starts counting down immediately when the interface is initialized.

FIGURE 4.3 The timer's Enabled setting

The timer label is managed programmatically using its setDate(_:), setTextColor(_:), start(), and stop() methods. Once started, the timer will count down to its target date without any further management from your app.

> **TIP:** Your app receives no notification or callback when the timer reaches zero. If your app needs to take any action when the timer is up, you should run an NSTimer object set to the same target date. Remember that your interface control has no way to communicate with the code running in your WatchKit extension.

IMAGES

The WKInterfaceImage is used to display an image, or an animation made up of a series of images, in your Watch app's interface. Use the storyboard editor to configure the initial image, its content mode, the tint color for template images, and whether the control is able to animate. At run time, a number of methods are available to set the image or images, to set the tint color, and to start and stop animation.

As has been the case since the early days of the web (on iOS and other platforms), the humble image control is a very powerful tool for setting the look and feel of your app, communicating information, or even adding a little whimsy or delight for the user. We'll spend significant time in Chapters 5 and 6 looking at how to get the best out of WKInterfaceImage.

MAPS

The WKInterfaceMap control (**Figure 4.4**) takes much of the pain out of displaying a map to the user. Its output is essentially a specialized image—the map is not interactive. However, you can configure it to launch the Maps app to the location in the map control—simply set it to Enabled in the storyboard editor.

FIGURE 4.4 WKInterfaceMap

The Enabled property is the only configuration available in the storyboard editor—all other configuration must be made at run time from your interface controller.

The area covered by the map is set either with its setVisibleMapRect(_:) method or with setRegion(_:). Which you use depends on how your app defines its areas—with an MKMapRect or with an MKCoordinateRegion. In either case, the map control adjusts the area it displays and its zoom level to make sure the area specified is visible.

It is also possible to add image annotations to the map (addAnnotation(_:withImage: centerOffset:) and addAnnotation(_:withImageNamed:centerOffset:)) or to add pins (addAnnotation(_:withPinColor:)). The method removeAllAnnotations() does what it says, clears the map of annotations.

NOTE: Remember that the map will not display if the user's phone doesn't have a network connection. As with the Maps apps on iPhone and on the Watch, map data is downloaded as needed.

INTERACTIVE CONTROLS

Displaying information to the user is, of course, only half the story. WatchKit offers buttons, switches, and sliders for all your users' tapping needs.

BUTTONS

`WKInterfaceButton` is a tappable control that should be connected to an `@IBAction` method in an interface controller. The signature of this method is slightly different from the equivalent on iOS, taking no parameters:

```
@IBAction func buttonTapped()
```

The other notable difference is that a button can contain multiple other interface objects, acting as a group (see the "Control Groups" section later in this chapter for a discussion of `WKInterfaceGroup`), as well as the expected single text label. This is configured using the Content property in the storyboard editor.

You can configure buttons with different fonts, text colors, background colors, and background images, as well as with the title text itself. You may also enable or disable the button. These properties can be set programmatically as well as in the storyboard—title color and font being managed via the `setAttributedTitle(_:)` method, whereas the background is updated using the `setBackgroundColor(_:)`, `setBackgroundImage(_:)`, `setBackgroundImageData(_:)`, and `setBackgroundImageNamed(_:)` methods. **Figure 4.5** shows examples of how a button can be configured.

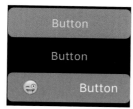

FIGURE 4.5 Examples of differently configured buttons

SWITCHES

`WKInterfaceSwitch` is a control that displays the familiar on/off switch with a label beside it. The class and its properties manage both the switch itself and the label for you (**Figure 4.6**).

Because it's not possible to query controls for their state, the switch's action method takes the following form:

FIGURE 4.6 A switch and its title

```
@IBAction func switchSwitched(value: Bool)
```

When the method is called, your interface controller should stash the state of the switch in a property if necessary. When creating the switch in the storyboard editor, you may configure its initial state, the color of the switch's On state, whether it is initially enabled, and the text, color, and font for the switch's label.

At run time you can use setTitle(_:) or setAttributedTitle(_:) to update the switch's label, setOn(_:) and setEnabled(_:) to update its state and whether it's active, and setColor(_:) to update its On color.

SLIDERS

WKInterfaceSlider allows the user to select a value within a defined range—think of the volume slider in iPhone's Music app or the volume control in the Watch's Now Playing glance (**Figure 4.7**).

FIGURE 4.7 The slider in the Now Playing glance

The minus and plus buttons visible in Figure 4.7 are provided by default. They can be replaced with custom images, which must be part of the WatchKit App bundle when distributed.

The value of the slider is represented as a Float and is delivered to your interface controller via an action method with the following signature:

```
@IBAction func sliderSlid(value: Float)
```

As with the switch control, your interface controller should store the state value as necessary.

The slider presents quite a number of configuration options, most of which must be managed in the storyboard editor:

- The value of the slider is initially set in the storyboard and can be updated at run time with the setValue(:_) method.
- The minimum and maximum possible values.
- The number of steps the slider recognizes between those two values. This can also be set in code with setNumberOfSteps(_:).
- Whether the slider displays as a continuous, solid bar or as a row of segments.
- The color of the slider bar, also configurable with the setColor(_:) method at run time.
- Custom min image and max image for the slider's minus and plus buttons.
- Whether or not the slider is enabled. You can update this state at run time with setEnabled(_:).

MOVIES

Your app can play video via a `WKInterfaceMovie` control. This control displays a poster image and a play button for the video file (**Figure 4.8**); tapping the play button plays the video in a modal presentation.

FIGURE 4.8 A `WKInterfaceMovie` control

We'll demonstrate using `WKInterfaceMovie` when exploring the media capabilities of Apple Watch in Chapter 12.

STRUCTURAL CONTROLS

A `WKInterfaceController`'s user interface is arranged quite differently from a view hierarchy on iOS in that it takes a series of controls and flows them down the screen. If you've ever written HTML for a webpage, this might feel familiar. As with HTML, there are options (although not nearly as many as on the web) for managing this flow by using some structure controls.

CONTROL GROUPS

`WKInterfaceGroup` is an interface object designed to contain other interface objects, and although it may not sound very exciting (it's a box!), this control enables a great deal of customization for how its members are displayed (**Figure 4.9**).

FIGURE 4.9 An interface group in the storyboard

Figure 4.10 shows the configuration options available for an interface group. A group can display a background of a solid color or an image—the image can even be animated! If used, the background has a default corner radius of 6 points. Modifying the group's edge insets and spacing will vary how much of the background is visible around and between items in the group. The interface group's layout can also be configured to flow its contained items horizontally or vertically.

FIGURE 4.10 Interface group configuration

The properties that can be updated at run time are

- Background color, with setBackgroundColor(_:).
- Background image, with setBackgroundImage(_:), setBackgroundImageData(_:), and setBackgroundImageNamed(_:).
- Corner radius, with setCornerRadius(_:).
- Background image animation can be controlled with methods that mirror those on WKInterfaceImage: startAnimating(), startAnimatingWithImagesInRange(_: duration:repeatCount:), and stopAnimating().

SEPARATORS

After the whirl of options available on an interface group, WKInterfaceSeparator is delightfully simple. It's a horizontal line to separate controls, and you can set its color in the storyboard editor and in code via its setColor(_:) method. That's it.

TABLES

Working with table views is the bread and butter of many iOS developers. WKInterfaceTable is different enough from UITableView that we'll take some time to work with it and its API.

1. In Xcode, create a new iOS project, and add a WatchKit App target.

2. In the WatchKit App's storyboard, add a table to the interface controller scene (**Figures 4.11** and **4.12**).

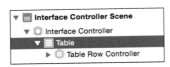

FIGURE 4.12 The table in the interface controller scene

FIGURE 4.11 The table in the storyboard editor

3. Add the source file for a class named RowController to the WatchKit extension. It should be a subclass of NSObject (**Figure 4.13**).

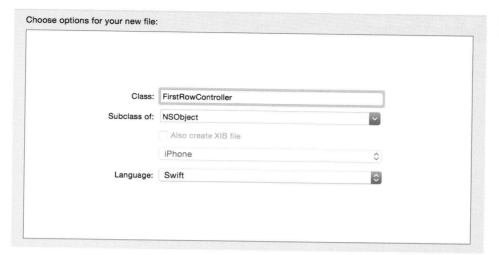

FIGURE 4.13 Creating a row controller

4. Update the contents of RowController.swift to the following:

```swift
import WatchKit

class RowController: NSObject {
    @IBOutlet weak var listLabel: WKInterfaceLabel! {
        didSet(oldValue) {
            listLabel.setTextColor(UIColor.greenColor())
        }
    }
}
```

5. In the WatchKit App's Interface.storyboard, select the table's table row controller in the left sidebar. Open the Identity inspector and set the table row controller's Class setting to RowController (**Figure 4.14**). The Module setting will update automatically.

FIGURE 4.14 Setting the table row controller's class

6. Open the table row controller's Attribute inspector, and set its Identifier to RowController.

7. Add a label to the row controller's group, and connect it to the row controller's `listLabel` property (**Figure 4.15**).

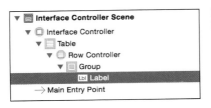

FIGURE 4.15 The interface controller's hierarchy of interface objects

8. Replace the contents of `InterfaceController.swift` with the following:

```swift
import WatchKit
import Foundation

class InterfaceController: WKInterfaceController {
    @IBOutlet weak var listTable: WKInterfaceTable!
}
```

9. Connect the table in the storyboard to the `@IBOutlet` you have just defined.
10. Add the following two methods to the `InterfaceController` class:

```swift
override func awakeWithContext(context: AnyObject?) {
    super.awakeWithContext(context)
    updateTableItems()
}

func updateTableItems() {
    let listOfThings = [
        "Apple", "Banana", "Pear", "Orange", "Lemon",
        "Guava", "Melon", "Starfruit", "Grape"
    ]
    let numberOfThings = listOfThings.count

    listTable.setNumberOfRows(numberOfThings, withRowType: "RowController")

    for i in 0..<numberOfThings {
        let rowController = listTable.rowControllerAtIndex(i) as!
RowController
        rowController.listLabel.setText(listOfThings[i])
    }
}
```

11. Add the following method to the same class:

```
override func table(table: WKInterfaceTable, didSelectRowAtIndex rowIndex:
Int) {
    let rowController = listTable.rowControllerAtIndex(rowIndex) as!
RowController
    rowController.listLabel.setTextColor(UIColor.redColor())
}
```

12. Run the WatchKit App, you should see a list of fruit (**Figure 4.16**). Tapping a row will turn its label red.

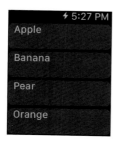

FIGURE 4.16 The table in the Watch simulator

This example demonstrates the basics of setting up and populating a WKInterfaceTable. Note the following details of using a table:

- The table is populated all at once when the data is available. This is in contrast to the approach taken on iOS, where the UITableView asks its data source for each cell to display in turn as needed.

- Access to an individual row, perhaps to update some property of its UI, is simple using rowControllerAtIndex(_:).

- The idea of a "row controller" is implemented in two parts. First, in the storyboard, the row controller is created and its UI is defined. Then, it's necessary to create a custom class (RowController in our example) to associate with that UI. Instances of this class are how you interact with the interface items of a given row. The table identifies the row controller types by their Identifier properties and instantiates them according to their Class settings.

In this example, we have used only a single type of row in the table. However, you can define multiple row controllers on a table by increasing its Rows attribute in the storyboard editor. Interface controller code can then reference the different row controller types by their differing Identifier attributes.

> **TIP:** In the storyboard, a table's Rows attribute represents the number of different row controllers, whereas the actual number of rows in the table at run time is provided by your interface controller.

Three methods on `WKInterfaceTable` allow you to specify which row types to use:

- `setNumberOfRows(_:withRowType:)`, the method used in the example, specifies the number of rows in the table and assigns the same row type to each of them.
- `setRowTypes(_:)` takes an array of strings that are the identifiers for the row controllers. The array should contain one string for each row that should be displayed in the table.
- `insertRowsAtIndexes(_:withRowType:)` takes the identifier of the row controller to use for the inserted rows.

In each case, as seen in the example, you access the row controller object for a given row using the table's `rowControllerAtIndex(_:)` method.

It's possible to add and remove table rows without re-creating the row set for the whole table. This is done using the methods `insertRowsAtIndexes(_:withRowType:)` and `removeRowsAtIndexes(_:)`. The interface controller can trigger a scroll to a specified row by calling `scrollToRowAtIndex(_:)` on the table.

Finally, it's possible to define segues in the storyboard that are triggered by taps on table rows. (This will be familiar to you if you've ever configured a `UITableView` to trigger a segue on iOS.) When one of these segues is triggered, the table's interface controller receives one of the table segue callbacks asking for the context to be received by the incoming interface controller's `awakeWithContext(_:)` method. These callback methods are `contextForSegueWithIdentifier(_:inTable:rowIndex:)` and `contextsForSegueWithIdentifier(_:inTable:rowIndex:)`. Which is called depends on the target and type of the segue, the latter being the method called when transitioning to a modal presentation of paged interface controllers.

PICKERS

One of the features of Apple Watch most talked about when it was announced was its digital crown, which provides a smooth, intuitive hardware interface for the user to scroll onscreen content. Developer access to the digital crown's scrolling action is via the `WKInterfacePicker` control.

`WKInterfacePicker` allows your app to define a series of options (represented by instances of the class `WKPickerItem`), providing text, an image, or both for each. The user selects the picker by tapping it. They can then use the digital crown to scroll through the available options, and then tap the control again to select the current option.

> **TIP:** Interacting with pickers in the Apple Watch simulator is delightfully intuitive. Simply click the picker to give it focus (if it is not already focused), then use your normal scrolling action via the trackpad or mouse to simulate the movement of the digital crown.

There are three types of picker your app can use:

- The List picker (**Figure 4.17**) displays a list of options and allows the user to scroll through them and select one. Each item may have an accessory image, a title, both an accessory image and a title, or a content image.

- The Stacked picker animates through a virtual stack of cards, displaying one at a time onscreen, with a whimsical transition between items. Each item should be assigned a content image.

- The Image Sequence picker cycles through a series of images according to the user's scrolling of the digital crown, displaying one at a time. The images are supplied via the picker items' contentImage properties. This picker type differs from the behavior of the Stacked picker in that the transition isn't animated. If the picker's focus highlight (the green outline visible in Figure 4.17) is disabled and the sequence of images is constructed with care, this option might give you all kinds of ideas for custom UI. (See Chapter 6 for another approach to using a picker to control an animation: with its setCoordinatedAnimations(_:) method.)

FIGURE 4.17 A List picker with a focus highlight

Note that the Stacked and Image Sequence pickers (**Figures 4.18** and **4.19**) look identical. The difference is in the transition—or lack of transition, in the Image Sequence picker—between the items.

FIGURE 4.18 A Stacked picker with a focus highlight

FIGURE 4.19 An Image Sequence picker with a focus highlight

Each type of picker is configurable in two ways in the storyboard editor:

- The Focus property of the picker in the storyboard editor controls whether the picker is outlined to show when it is in focus (responding to digital crown input), whether it shows its caption in addition to its focus ring (**Figure 4.20**), or whether there is no indication that the picker has focus.

- The Indicator property specifies whether or not the picker gives an indication of its current display in the list of items. The indicator can be seen in Figure 4.17, and is reminiscent of `UIScrollView`'s scroll indicators on iOS.

FIGURE 4.20 A List picker with a caption

As with other controls, `WKInterfacePicker` has a `setEnabled(_:)` method to set whether or not it is available for the user to interact with. It can be given focus programmatically with a call to its regally named `focusForCrownInput()` method.

The picker's items are set via its `setItems(_:)` method, which accepts an array of `WKPickerItem` instances. The currently selected item is specifiable by its index, via the `setSelectedItemIndex(_:)` method. Each picker item has the following properties available for configuration:

- `contentImage` is available to all three types of picker: it's the only property used by Stacked and Image Sequence pickers, and if it's set in the `WKPickerItems` to be consumed by a List picker, then the other properties should not be set.
- `title` is the text used by a List picker.
- `accessoryImage` is the small image used by a List picker, displayed next to its title.
- `caption` is the text used in the picker's caption area, if it's enabled (Figure 4.20).

NOTE: The images accepted by `WKPickerItem`'s image properties are of the type `WKImage`. These can be created from instances of `UIImage` by calling `WKImage`'s `init(image:)` initializer.

Finally, to let your app respond to the changing selection of the picker, the picker can send an action method to its interface controller. The method takes the form `@IBAction func pickerAction(index: Int)` and receives the index of the picker item selected by the user.

ALERTS

It's possible to display an alert, with options for the user, in much the same way as using `UIAlertController` (or the older, deprecated API `UIAlertView`) on iOS. Although alerts don't involve subclasses of `WKInterfaceObject`, we include them here because they are a natural fit in our tour of UI controls.

An alert is triggered with a call to WKInterfaceController's method presentAlertControllerWithTitle(_:message:preferredStyle:actions:). The actions parameter takes an array of WKAlertAction instances.

To see the alerts in action, carry out the following steps:

1. Create a new iOS App with WatchKit App project (File > New > Project).

2. In the WatchKit App's Interface.storyboard, add a button as shown in **Figure 4.21**.

FIGURE 4.21 The DANGER! button

3. Update your InterfaceController.swift file to have an empty implementation, as follows:

```
import WatchKit
import Foundation

class InterfaceController: WKInterfaceController {

}
```

The button will be updated depending on the option chosen by the user when the alert is presented.

4. Add the following enum and property inside (since Swift allows nested types, and this enum is of interest only inside the class—yay!) the curly brackets of the InterfaceController class:

```
enum ButtonState {
    case OutOfDanger, Danger, Exploded
}

var buttonState = ButtonState.Danger
```

5. Create the following @IBAction and @IBoutlet in InterfaceController, and connect both to the button in the storyboard:

```
@IBOutlet var dangerButton: WKInterfaceButton!
```

```
@IBAction func dangerTapped() {
    presentAlertControllerWithTitle("Danger!",
        message: "What will you do?",
        preferredStyle: .Alert,
        actions: alertActions())
}
```

We then need to define the actions for the alert.

6. Define the method referenced in the previous call:

```
func alertActions() -> [WKAlertAction] {
    return [
        WKAlertAction.init(title: "Deal with it",
            style: .Default) {self.buttonState = .OutOfDanger},
        WKAlertAction.init(title: "Ignore it",
            style: .Cancel) {self.buttonState = .Danger},
        WKAlertAction.init(title: "Explode it",
            style: .Destructive) {self.buttonState = .Exploded}
    ]
}
```

Next, the button needs to be updated according to the value of the buttonState property. The time to do this is in the willActivate() method.

7. Add the following code to the interface controller:

```
override func willActivate() {
    super.willActivate()
    updateButton()
}
```

```
func updateButton() {
    switch buttonState {
    case .OutOfDanger: outOfDanger()
    case .Danger: danger()
    case .Exploded: exploded()
    }
}
```

8. Add the following three methods to set the different button states:

```
func outOfDanger() {
    dangerButton.setTitle("Phew")
    dangerButton.setEnabled(false)
}

func danger() {
    dangerButton.setTitle("DANGER!")
    dangerButton.setEnabled(true)
}

func exploded() {
    dangerButton.setTitle("BOOM!")
    dangerButton.setBackgroundColor(.redColor())
    dangerButton.setEnabled(false)
}
```

TIP: The InterfaceController class here uses an enumeration to track the state of the button and update the UI accordingly because the interface controller will be deactivated while the alert is shown. This means the button will not respond to the calls to its setters in the alert handlers, and needs to be updated when willActivate() is called on the controller. To save future-you some debugging pain, you might want to remember this moment.

9. Run the app and tap the button. You should see the alert appear, as in **Figure 4.22**.

FIGURE 4.22 An alert, asking the important question

The `preferredStyle` parameter in the call to `presentAlertControllerWithTitle(_:message:preferredStyle:actions:)` in step 5 is a case of the `WKAlertControllerStyle` enumeration. The available cases are

- `Alert` dispays a simple, flexible alert with a variable number of actions. This is the style used in the example.
- `SideBySideButtonsAlert` accepts only two actions and displays their buttons side by side (**Figure 4.23**).
- `ActionSheet` accepts either one or two custom actions and comes with a standard Cancel button in its top corner (**Figure 4.24**).

As an exercise, we suggest you try modifying the previous example to display alerts matching those in Figures 4.23 and 4.24.

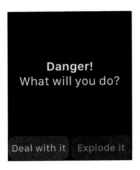

FIGURE 4.23 An alert of style `SideBySideButtonsAlert`

FIGURE 4.24 An alert of style `ActionSheet`

USER INPUT

You might have noticed that none of the interface objects is anything like our old friends `UITextField` or `UITextView` from iOS. Textual input on the Watch is a *very* different proposition from other devices. We'll look at it in detail in Chapter 11.

WRAPPING UP

This chapter skimmed over all the interface controls available from WatchKit. Knowing the blocks from which you build your user interface is only part of the story. Designing UI for the Watch is a very different prospect from doing so for larger devices. Read on to Chapter 5 to learn how to effectively combine these pieces in your app.

PART II

Creating Apps

Designing Your App's User Interface

Every platform has its own idioms, the ways of presenting content and performing actions that users of that platform come to expect over time. Some of these conventions may be set by the platform's vendor (for example, the use of tab bar controllers and navigation controllers in iOS, as demonstrated by Apple right from the launch of iPhone), while others come from third-party developers and designers, gain traction, and become popular across the platform (the pull-to-refresh interaction on iOS, for example, was first implemented and used by a third-party developer).

The conventions of a platform change and develop over time. Some elements endure, whereas others turn out to be gimmicks that hinder rather than help. Sometimes the platform's owner decides it's time for a change (what did you think the first time you saw the look and feel of iOS 7?). Sometimes the community insists.

Apple Watch is a very young platform, and few conventions have been established or user expectations set. It's an exciting time when the world is your digital rotary input mechanism.

You're not all on your own, though. The best place to start when deciding how to take advantage of the platform is, of course, the Apple Watch "Human Interface Guidelines" (HIG), published by Apple at http://bit.ly/bwa-hig. Every developer working in watchOS should get to know those guidelines *very* well. In this chapter, we're not going to repeat what's in the HIG, but we will highlight some of the developing best practices on the platform.

THINKING ABOUT DESIGN

In comparison with the rest of the Apple ecosystem, Apple Watch provides a drastically different way for users to interact with your software. The watch is, of course, closest in philosophy and in size to iPhone, but it still requires a change in thinking and approach as you design your apps. Every aspect of an app's design, be it visual layout, interaction design, information architecture, even use of color, is very different in this little window on your wrist.

Consider:

- Apple Watch is smaller than iPhone. Much smaller. (Well, obviously. You're glad you bought this book, aren't you, for insights like that one?) In terms of how much and what can be onscreen at a given time, and of the size of your tapping digit against the screen, there's just less of it.

- iPhones have bigger screens than the Apple Watch. The iPhone's screen is great for long periods watching out for fave notifications from Twitter or browsing your library of cat-fail GIFs, but Apple Watch excels at the short, sharp, focused interaction. Don't expect to be too comfortable reading through your ebook library on your wrist.

- Being small, but being a class of device that you expect to always be there and always be ready when you need it, the watch is very frugal with its resources—which all, eventually, comes down to power. Talking to the network costs power, having the screen lit up costs power, performing any computation costs power, so the less time spent doing any of these things, the better.

- Apple Watch introduces physical, tactile ways to connect with the user that are new to the Apple ecosystem: the Taptic engine (discussed in Chapter 14), force touch, and the digital crown.

- Many of us might have our phones with us pretty much all the time, but your watch is right there strapped to your wrist. There's no need to fish around in your pocket or purse. Just lift your arm a little and look down. The watch brings—and expects—a whole new immediacy to the use of software.

This all provides us with an interesting set of challenges: how to focus on the quick, simple interaction while still providing a beautiful and graceful experience? How to be immediate and responsive to the user, minimizing lag, while being careful and economical with system resources? How to show off as a developer without the opportunity to create awesome new custom controls? Maybe we can help with that.

MEETING THE CHALLENGE

Some pieces of information, developing best practices, techniques, and tips can help you provide the best experience possible for the user. These are based on the foundation provided by the HIG and will be useful as you work and flourish within the constraints of the platform.

"PHENOMENAL COSMIC POWER, ITTY-BITTY LIVING SPACE"

Apple Watch comes in two sizes: 42mm and 38mm (or, as we like to call them, Small and Smaller). Those numbers, which may seem arbitrary, are conventional sizes to watch makers, and refer to the height of the watch. The display on the 42mm watch is 312 pixels wide by 390 pixels tall, while that of the 38mm watch is 272 pixels wide by 340 pixels tall.

That's not a lot of room, even on the larger watch. A number of techniques and principles will help you make the most of the space available.

WALL-TO-WALL USER INTERFACE

If you look at an Apple Watch while its display is off, you might notice that it's quite difficult to tell where the screen itself ends and the black bezel of the device begins. This is a great advantage when laying out your user interface. **Figure 5.1** is a screenshot taken from the Music app running on a 42mm Apple Watch. Notice how much of the width of the screen is filled by the table rows.

FIGURE 5.1 Screenshot of the Music app

This layout looks tight in the screenshot. If you're anything like us, then your hands are probably itching to add some margin around the edges. But when run on the device, this UI looks completely natural. The black of the watch face around the screen provides the needed margin, leaving the full size of the screen itself available to UI elements.

Of course, to take advantage of this bonus visual space, your app will need to keep to the watchOS standard of a black background. That said, with current hardware and software, you'd need to have a very good reason not to: It would take significant effort to provide a colored background for your app's display. Doing so would be a major break from the current design language of watchOS, and on an OLED (organic LED) display such as that of the Apple Watch, black pixels consume no power, leading to longer battery life for the user.

CONTENT BEFORE CHROME

If you've been developing software for Apple platforms for more than a couple of years, then we're sure you have an opinion on gradients in title bars. Or green felt. Or what about brushed metal? Pinstripes? Cheerful blue pills for buttons? We could go on. These are all examples of the evolving design language used on iOS and OS X over the years, and they all have one thing in common: They take up space on the screen. (They all have other things in common, as well, starting with where you might think each falls in the spectrum of good taste—but let's not dwell on the past!)

Of course, when we say "chrome" we don't just mean the nonfunctional aspects of what's onscreen. Compare **Figure 5.2** with **Figure 5.3**. The first shows the Maps app running on an iPhone 6, while the second shows the Maps app on the Apple Watch. On iOS, there is plenty of screen space to expose much of the app functionality in persistent UI: search, current location, the info menu, and more. On the other hand, almost all the available screen space on the watch is given over to the map itself. Most functionality is accessed via the context menu or via Siri.

FIGURE 5.2 Maps running on an iPhone 6

FIGURE 5.3 The watchOS Maps app

AS MUCH AS YOU NEED—AND NO MORE

Complementary to the principle of *content before chrome* is that of paring content down to the absolute minimum needed for your app to perform its function for the user. **Figure 5.4** shows a contact card from the watchOS Phone app. Almost none of the information available in the equivalent screen on iOS is displayed on the watch.

FIGURE 5.4 Screenshot of the watchOS Phone app

A key principle here is to carefully consider the use cases for your watchOS app, bearing in mind the following:

- Apple Watch is not suited to lengthy perusal of huge chunks of data. In fact, its display will go to sleep after only a few seconds of inactivity, leaving the wearer with very little time to contemplate the variety of options you give them. Fewer possibilities will make for a more effective interaction.

- Some of the most essential features of smartphones (especially iPhone) are their immediacy and convenience when compared with more traditional computing devices, and Apple Watch emphasizes these even more. In order to play to these strengths, you will need to identify the key information to present to your user, and the key actions they might then take with your app. Look again at Figure 5.4. The contact's name and image (if one is set) are the key pieces of information for quick identification, and two big buttons enable the most common actions: make a call or send a message.

- Of course, some apps require a fuller navigational structure to provide all the value they can for the user (see Chapter 3 for the options). In these cases, you will need to decide which approach or approaches are most appropriate. Does paging between controllers make sense, to divide up chunks of functionality? Or are you presenting structured data that would be best handled in a drill-down hierarchy? Would the scrolling provided via the digital crown help the user as they try to get into your app, find what they need, and get out again?

- Getting data to the watch is costly. It is time consuming, via the Bluetooth link to the host iPhone. Using those radios to send and receive drinks up available power, as does the computational work of processing input and output. Users don't enjoy discovering that their hot new app is also the reason they need to charge their device by lunchtime.

We're not saying that your app shouldn't do anything—if we were, we could all just go home now. All the potential that Apple Watch presents for wonder, delight, and utility would be wasted if we were afraid to make our apps *do* anything because of something we read in a book. However, designing great software is every bit as much about deciding what to leave out as it is about deciding what to put in.

TAP TARGETS, FAT FINGERS, AND SMALL SCREENS

Back in the mists of time, at the Dawn of the iPhone SDK, Apple recommended that all tap targets in an iPhone app be at least 44pt square—the size they had identified as the minimum that could be tapped accurately with a fingertip. With the release of Apple Watch, the screens we're tapping may be smaller, but our tapping digits are as big and inaccurate as ever. You might even find that trying to tap at a little screen on your wrist makes for even less coordination and accuracy, so it's useful to think about what controls the user will absolutely need in your app, and whether it is more useful to make them bigger targets than it is to have them all onscreen at the same time.

Figure 5.5 shows the watchOS screen displayed when an alarm is going off. Consider the circumstances in which users encounter this interface: An alarm is going off, and they need to silence it quickly and easily. Nice big buttons make this as simple as possible, which is a definite plus if your alarm has just gone off during an orchestral performance.

FIGURE 5.5 Screenshot of Apple Watch's alarm screen

In the excitement of developing your watch app, make sure to test it on a physical device on your wrist—and to do so in the kind of situations where you imagine it might be used, be that when you're walking down the street or when you're lounging on your couch.

BRINGING A LITTLE COLOR

With the standard black background and the limited scope for visual flourish, the use of color is a key way to establish the character and identity of your app.

Each app can specify a global tint color, which is used by the OS to set, for example, the color of the text in the Watch's status bar while your app is running (**Figure 5.6**) or the color of the app name text in a short-look notification.

FIGURE 5.6 Screenshots of the Music app, World Clock app, and Weather app

To set the global tint color for your app in Xcode:

1. Select the app's `Interface.storyboard`.
2. Open the File inspector.
3. Set the global tint color using the color selector (**Figure 5.7**).

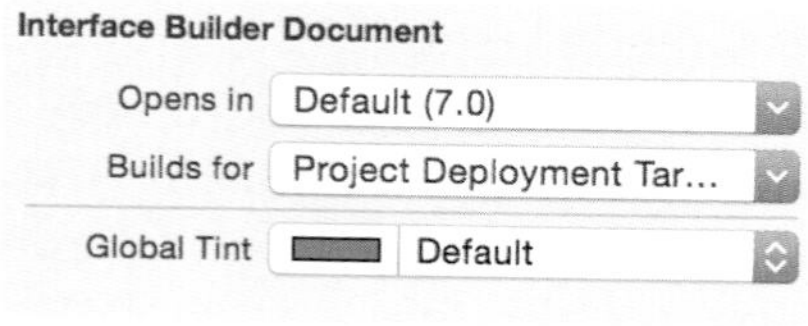

Interface Builder Document

Opens in	Default (7.0)
Builds for	Project Deployment Tar...
Global Tint	Default

FIGURE 5.7 Setting an app's global tint color

Rather than take up valuable screen space with your logo or other branding, Apple recommends using the global tint color of your app to reflect the product's identity. This is good advice—it's a simple, effective approach. Consider also the other places where the color could be introduced: button text or backgrounds, table row backgrounds, or other small interface elements. Look, for example, at the city location markers in the World Clock app in Figure 5.6. The app's identifying color is used in such a small visual element, yet it is prominent enough that it strengthens the identity of the app as a whole.

BE PREPARED

Waiting can be a frustrating experience. Waiting on a device that was meant to provide instant and immediate convenience is an even more frustrating experience. A poorly placed "Please Wait…" or an activity spinner blocking the UI can be enough to turn a user right off your app and send them to the delete button. Yet sometimes, especially when accessing remote resources, a wait is inevitable. So what is a developer to do?

READINESS

Do what you can to make sure your app has the data it needs in advance of when the user expects it. You might find limitations to your ability to predict the future, but sensible background loading and caching of data can greatly reduce the wait time when the user launches your app. See Chapter 10 for how to load data from the network and transfer it between the watch and its host iPhone.

THE IMPRESSION OF READINESS

Perhaps your app is such that it's not practical or possible to have everything preloaded and ready for users whenever they come along. In that case, all is still not lost. If data is your thing, is there a minimal, or approximate, data set that you can use, and then refine once the app is active? Alternatively, is there an idle state that the user interface can display while being fully set up?

Our eyes and our minds are very willing to receive suggestion and to be lulled into satisfaction. A spinner might appear only for a second or two before being replaced with a fully active and interactive UI, but those seconds will *seem* much shorter to the user if they are spent looking at a nearly ready UI that then becomes ready.

GESTURE AND TOUCH

The range of available gestures is one of the defining characteristics of a touch-based interface. If you've spent much time as a user of iOS devices, you'll have encountered a tremendous range of gestures—some more useful and usable than others: taps with varying numbers of digits, double taps, triple taps, pinches, swipes, long presses, rotations... they've all been put to myriad uses.

The watchOS, as you probably expect by now, has fewer options available: taps to trigger actions on controls (for example, the tap of a button), swipes for exploring content and for triggering navigation, and the force touch to trigger a `WKInterfaceController`'s context menu. Add in the occasional use of the digital crown to control zoom level (as in the Maps app, for example), and those are the possibilities.

From the developer's point of view, the gestures themselves are understood and received only via watchOS controls and interface controllers, with the recognition and response to the gestures themselves being the business of the operating system. Unfortunately, there is no equivalent of the various `UIGestureRecognizer` subclasses available on iOS. The smaller screen sizes of Apple Watch do not leave enough room (literally) for the variety and experimentation that has been seen on the larger devices, enforcing a standard approach to touch and gesture.

WRAPPING UP

Several points in this chapter have made reference to the differences between watchOS and iOS—and, in particular, to the more restrictive environment offered by the watch. We encourage you to view these differences positively and to approach the constraints creatively. Apple Watch is a new platform in the Apple ecosystem, and this is the first time many of us have developed software for the new category of "wearable" devices. These are still the early days of learning and internalizing the patterns and conventions of the platform, and users' understanding and expectations will only develop and become more flexible over time.

We have been quite opinionated in this chapter and have sought to present current understanding of best practice in designing for watchOS. Remember, though, that the magic exists not only in knowing when to follow the rules, but also in knowing when to break them. So experiment, play, and see where your taps and swipes can take you!

CHAPTER 6

Building Your App's User Interface

There is a lot to remember when planning and designing the user interface of any app, and if it's done right then it can be the work that turns a mediocre app into a good one—or a good app into one that is truly great! But the planning is still only part of what needs to be done. Even the best ideas are meaningless until they're put into practice. In this chapter, we will take a tour of the tools and techniques that are available to get an interface up and running and ready to interact with.

LAYING OUT THE USER INTERFACE

When it comes time to actually create the user interface of your app, you will do so in Xcode's storyboard editor. This is familiar territory for many iOS developers, but the controls are positioned on the storyboard in a way that is quite different from what you may be used to. Whereas on iOS you may place controls wherever you like in a view—defining their positions either in absolute terms or by defining layout constraints to control their positions relative to other objects—when laying out an interface for a watchOS app, you are essentially describing a list of interface elements that will then be placed in the interface controller's view in the order in which they are listed.

To see how this works in practice, open Xcode and do the following:

1. Create a new project by selecting File > New > Project and choosing iOS App with WatchKit App.

2. Select `Interface.storyboard` from the WatchKit App group in the Project Navigator.

3. Drag a Label object from the Object Library onto the interface controller scene in the storyboard.

   Note that wherever on the scene you drop the label, even if you drag it around, it will end up positioned as in **Figure 6.1**.

4. Drag and drop two more labels onto the scene. They will position themselves in a tight column in the upper-left corner of the view, as in **Figure 6.2**.

FIGURE 6.1 The label in the storyboard scene

FIGURE 6.2 Three labels in a scene

This demonstrates the main principle of UI layout for watchOS: As you add interface elements in the storyboard editor, they are added to the end of the interface controller's scene. If you were to continue merrily dragging labels (or other objects) from the Object Library and dropping them into the scene, you would see that the scene itself will start to grow in height to accommodate the extra objects. This translates to a vertical scroll when the interface is displayed. Please take a moment to enjoy the thought of not having to manage the vertical size of a scroll view's content.

If you select one of the labels in the scene, the Attributes inspector will show the options available for controlling its layout (**Figure 6.3**). These are the layout controls used for controlling the configurable size and layout options for any interface object.

FIGURE 6.3 The storyboard layout options for a label

Under the View heading are three items you can configure:

- The Alpha setting is a number between 0 and 1 that controls the transparency of the object. The setting 0 is completely transparent (and therefore invisible), and 1 is completely opaque.

- Selecting the Hidden option will hide the object. Try selecting a label and selecting the Hidden check box. Note that the remaining objects in the interface will reflow to fill the space left by the hidden item; this is in contrast to the behavior on iOS, where a hidden object still participates in the layout system and so still occupies its space.

- The Installed check box appears to have the same effect as the Hidden option: Deselecting Installed makes the selected object disappear (it is no longer "installed" in the view). However, there is a key difference. An object that is hidden in the interface still exists, whereas one that is not installed is never instantiated. If you have an @IBOutlet to an interface object, it can be shown and hidden at runtime, and that outlet will continue to reference the object, even if it is initially hidden. Any interface object that is not installed will never be connected to an @IBOutlet and so cannot be controlled from your code. You will discover shortly why this is useful.

The options under the Alignment heading control the placement of the object in two dimensions (**Figure 6.4**):

- In the Horizontal dimension, the options are Left, Center, and Right. These are straightforward and behave as you might expect, setting the object to hug the left or right edge of its container (either the main view of the interface controller or a containing interface group) or to keep itself centered.

- In the Vertical dimension, the available options are Top, Center, and Bottom. These are a little more complex than the Horizontal setting and provide rough control over the ordering of the objects in the flow of the layout. Those items configured to be positioned to Top come first in the layout, followed by those configured to Center, and finally the objects that have been configured to be placed at the Bottom come last.

The best way to understand how the Alignment options interact is to add a few more labels to the storyboard scene, change the text and colors of the labels so you can differentiate them, and start experimenting. Believe us when we say that it takes longer to describe the behavior than it does to get the feel of it in practice—it's pretty intuitive.

FIGURE 6.4 Labels aligned around an interface

The third set of layout options is under the Size heading. You can set three possible behaviors independently in the Horizontal and Vertical dimensions:

- Size To Fit Content is the default behavior. As the name suggests, the interface object will size itself to be big enough to display everything it contains, but no bigger. For example, a label will expand to show its text, or an interface group will grow along with its contents.

- If you select the behavior Relative to Container, two new fields appear (**Figure 6.5**). The first input takes a number between 0 and 1, which is a factor applied to the size of the containing view or group. For example, if a label is set to have its width Relative to Container, and this input is set to 0.5, then the label will be one half the width of its container. The second input is labeled Adjustment and takes an absolute value expressed in points. As the label suggests, this is a value that will be added to the size calculated by applying the factor above it. A negative value will result in a reduction in the final calculated size. With these options, it is possible to configure an interface object to have, for example, a width that is three quarters (0.75) of the width of its container, minus another 10 points.

- The third possible sizing behavior is to define a Fixed size. When selecting this behavior for a dimension, one additional input appears (**Figure 6.6**). This input takes a number that is used as the size, in points, at which the interface object is fixed in that dimension. These dimensions can also be set and changed at runtime, using the WKInterfaceObject's setWidth(_:) and setHeight(_:) methods.

FIGURE 6.5 Options for Relative to Container sizing

FIGURE 6.6 Options for Fixed sizing

Using these options gives you a great deal of flexibility in laying out your app's user interface, and it's very straightforward to manage. Sizing interface objects to their content and making sure that the interface doesn't get mangled as content length changes can all be taken care of by the OS.

GROUPING INTERFACE OBJECTS TOGETHER

In Chapter 4, we briefly mentioned the power of the WKInterfaceGroup control. It is worth getting to know a little better.

1. Return to your Xcode project from earlier in this chapter, or create a new one to work with. In Interface.storyboard, update the layout to contain six labels, each placed Top-Left and edited so that you can tell them apart. See **Figure 6.7** for how we've done it.

2. Drag a Group object to the scene, and drop it above the top label (**Figure 6.8**).

3. Now drag the first three labels into the group (**Figure 6.9**).

FIGURE 6.7 A rainbow of an interface

FIGURE 6.8 A group added to the scene

FIGURE 6.9 Labels added to the group

You can use these interface objects to experiment with how the group and its configuration affect the layout of the interface. Make sure the group is the selected interface object, and open the Attributes inspector (**Figure 6.10**).

FIGURE 6.10 Interface Group configuration options

The first options under the Group heading are the ones that control the layout of the group's members.

- Layout has two possibilities: Horizontal and Vertical. This determines how the group's members will flow; they can be added one after the other either across the group or down the group. Note that if the group's members are too wide to be displayed in a horizontal layout, they will not flow onto a new line. Rather, the group will clip horizontally. When laying out vertically, however, the group will grow as necessary.

- Insets can be set to Default or Custom. If you select Custom, four inputs display: one for each edge of the group. These inputs take absolute point values, which cannot be negative. The values are used to pad the dimensions of the group, providing clear space around its edges. Note, again, that if a group is set to lay out horizontally, then the combination of its padding and the widths of its members can lead to clipping (**Figure 6.11**).

FIGURE 6.11 Clipping in an interface group with insets

- The Spacing between the members of a group can either be left to its default or have a custom value (in points) set. In a Horizontal group, this also introduces the possibility of clipping.

As with other interface objects, you can set alignment and sizing behaviors for groups. Consider also that you can nest interface groups, and you will discover how they can be combined to provide a great deal of control over some quite complex interfaces.

HANDLING THE DIFFERENT SCREEN SIZES

As mentioned, Apple Watch is available in two screen sizes: 38mm and 42mm. The screens differ not only in their physical size but also in their point dimensions. Your app may be such that you don't need to make any adjustments to your user interface to accommodate the differences in screen size, or you may decide that some adjustments are necessary. This differentiation is handled in the storyboard editor.

Figure 6.12 shows the options available for an instance of WKInterfaceLabel. Note that many of the options are preceded by a small plus icon (+). Clicking this icon displays the menu shown in **Figure 6.13**.

Selecting, for example, the Apple Watch 42mm customization as a configuration option adds an alternative input for that option (**Figure 6.14**), allowing you to specify a different value that will be applied specifically when your app runs on a 42mm device.

When an alternative has been added, it can be removed again by clicking the small × beside it.

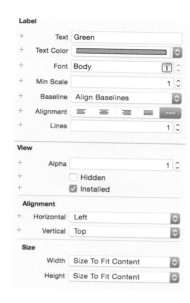

FIGURE 6.13 Screen size customization options

FIGURE 6.12 A label's options in the storyboard editor

FIGURE 6.14 An alternative configuration for a 42mm watch

Alternative configurations are applied by giving preference to the more specific option. When there are no alternatives, the value supplied is that for a device of any screen size. Where an alternative has been supplied for the size of device on which the app is running, it is the one that is used. (If you have used adaptive UI and size classes for layout on iOS, this behavior is familiar to you.)

This, by the way, is where the previously mentioned Installed attribute comes into its own. By specifying whether or not an object is installed for a given screen size, you can define whole chunks of interface that aren't even instantiated on a certain size of device.

Finally, where you have defined different layout attributes for different screen sizes, it is possible to view the interface in the storyboard editor as if it were one or the other. To do so, click the Any Screen Size indicator at the bottom of the editor window. The menu that displays (**Figure 6.15**) allows you to select which layout to display.

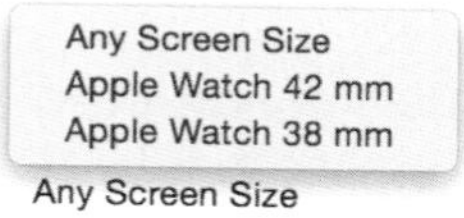

Any Screen Size
Apple Watch 42 mm
Apple Watch 38 mm

Any Screen Size

FIGURE 6.15 Previewing different layouts in the storyboard editor

IMAGES AND ANIMATION

Images have been a secret weapon in interface design for a long time. Many times we've looked at an inventive—or flashy—bit of UI work and wondered, "How did they do *that?*" and gone on to discover that carefully applied image assets (a gradient here, a simulated shadow there, a subtle bit of visual noise in the background) have been a vital ingredient. Images are a way to accomplish much with little.

But as Peter Parker's uncle was known to say, "With great power comes great responsibility," and it is the responsibility of the developer to be frugal with the resources available to a user's device. watchOS allows us to delight with images, stills and animation, but asks us to do so as efficiently as possible.

CONTENT VS. CHROME

Broadly speaking, there are two ways to use an image in an app (and this applies whether the image is a single still frame or a sequence presented as an animation).

- As mentioned, images can be used to provide a range of flourish and embellishment in the user interface, from the subtle to the ostentatious. We often refer to this aspect of the interface as part of the "chrome"—those elements that surround the content presented, rather than being part of the content themselves.
- Conversely, images can be part of the content of the app. This doesn't necessarily mean only the images in, for example, a photo sharing or browsing app. We consider images content if their presentation is in some way part of the purpose of the app.

watchOS enables both uses of images and animation, but it is wise to remember our earlier principle of remaining as lightweight and uncluttered as possible. We suggest sticking to images as content, and thinking very carefully about the costs and benefits before doing otherwise.

GETTING IMAGES ONTO THE WATCH

You have two ways to make images available to your watch app. The first and simplest way is to include the images in an asset catalog in your app's bundle. Of course, this is a bit restrictive; is your app one where every image it might need to display can be anticipated, prepared in advance, and shipped along with the app?

The alternative, of course, is to obtain the image data at runtime. This will probably mean either asking the user to select an image from the photo library on their phone or downloading an image from the Internet. In either case, importing an image from outside your watch app means communication with the host iPhone, with the associated costs in time, power, and bandwidth.

Whichever way your app obtains and accesses its images, you should bear a few principles in mind:

- watchOS, like iOS before it, likes to deal with PNGs. PNG (Portable Network Graphics) is an image format that provides pretty effective compression, is lossless, provides some support for transparency, and is widely supported. We suggest defaulting to PNG when you have a choice of image formats, except when you have a specific reason to do otherwise (such as when, for example, a file such as a large photograph would be better handled in a lossy format like JPEG).

- As with iOS apps, it is best to work with image files that, as far as is possible, are already sized appropriately for their use. There are two reasons for this. First, files that are larger than needed take up unnecessary space in the device's limited storage (and, if being transferred wirelessly, consume bandwidth too). Second, and more noticeable to your users, large images require more memory to display and take more processing cycles to move around the screen. If you've ever made the mistake of throwing full-resolution photographs into a UICollectionView, then you know what we mean. If not, then please learn from the mistakes of (at least one of) your authors.

- When shipping image assets with your app, use Xcode's asset catalog feature to package them. Not only does this provide a useful structure for the image assets in your project, but it also makes it very easy to provide and manage alternative image files for the two different watch sizes. When loading images using the various imageNamed(_:) methods and passing the name assigned to the image in the asset catalog, the system will take care of loading the correct one.

- If using images as icons in the user interface, the asset catalogs' Render As Template Image setting (**Figure 6.16**) is a convenient option. When this mode is selected, you can use the image control's setTintColor(_:) method to change the color of the image when it is displayed. This is most effective with line-art icons like those commonly used in iOS tab bars.

FIGURE 6.16 The Render As Template Image option

DISPLAYING IMAGES

You can display an image in watchOS in two ways: Your interface can include a WKInterfaceImage control that shows the image, or the image can be set as the background image on another control (such as a WKInterfaceButton or, commonly, a WKInterfaceGroup) using one of the setBackgroundImage... methods. Both approaches allow for single images or for multiple images together running as an animation.

WatchKit deals with images mostly as instances of the UIKit class UIImage, which can encapsulate still and animated images. (The exceptions to this are images intended for use in a `WKPickerItem`, which must be supplied as instances of `WKImage`—see the "Pickers" section in Chapter 4.) `UIImages` can be instantiated by loading an image or images from a file or by supplying the data as `NSData`.

WatchKit controls that take images or background images provide three methods to do so:

- `setImage(_:)` and `setBackgroundImage(_:)` accept a `UIImage` argument, which may contain multiple frames of an animation.
- `setImageData(_:)` and `setBackgroundImageData(_:)` accept an instance of `NSData`. If your app already has the PNG or JPEG data available (from, say, a download operation), then using these methods provides better performance than loading and decoding a file.
- `setImageNamed(_:)` and `setBackgroundImageNamed(_:)` take a string that contains the name of an image in the app's bundle. The file will be loaded and the image data used.

Which of these methods you end up using depends on whether the images are bundled with your app, downloaded for immediate use, or downloaded and stored for later.

CONTROLLING ANIMATION

Two kinds of animation are available in watchOS: Image-based animations, as described earlier, display a sequence of images over a specified time, and interface animations provide the ability to animate select properties of interface objects. Let's walk through an example of these techniques. (To follow along with this example, download a zip archive of the animation's images from http://bit.ly/bwa-assets.)

1. In Xcode, create a new project based on the iOS App with WatchKit App template, and give it a name of your choice. Don't include the Glance, Notification, and Complication options.

2. Open the `Assets.xcassets` asset catalog in the WatchKit Extension group. (Note that the other groups in the project also contain a file named `Assets.xcassets`. Make sure you've opened the one belonging to the WatchKit Extension.)

3. Select the image files `spinner0@2x.png` through `spinner11@2x.png`, and drag them into the left column of the asset catalog view. You should end up with a list like that in **Figure 6.17**.

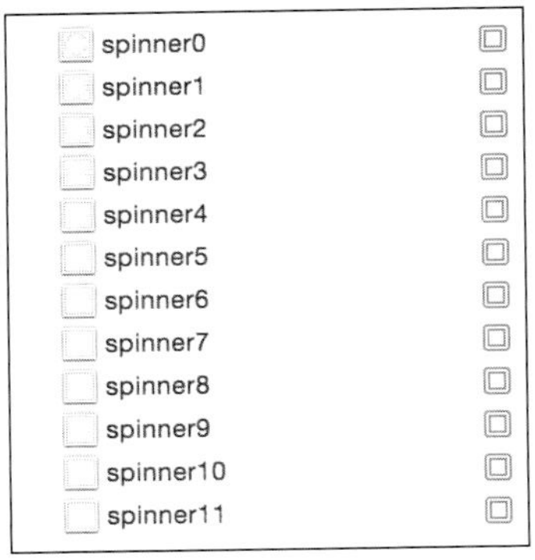

spinner0
spinner1
spinner2
spinner3
spinner4
spinner5
spinner6
spinner7
spinner8
spinner9
spinner10
spinner11

FIGURE 6.17 Animation frames in the asset catalog

4. If the `spinnerX` images aren't selected, Command-click them all to make sure you have them selected. Then, in the Attributes inspector, select the Apple Watch check box under Devices, and deselect the Universal check box (**Figure 6.18**).

FIGURE 6.18 Image Devices settings in the asset catalog

5. Work through the spinner images, ensuring that each image is assigned to the 2x slot in the asset catalog (**Figure 6.19**).

FIGURE 6.19 Image assignments in the asset catalog

6. Open the WatchKit App's `Interface.storyboard`, and add an Image object and a Button object to the interface controller (**Figure 6.20**). Set the image's horizontal alignment to Center.

FIGURE 6.20 The image and button in the storybard scene

7. Open `InterfaceController.swift` from the WatchKit Extension group, and replace its contents with the following:

```
import WatchKit
import Foundation

class InterfaceController: WKInterfaceController {
    @IBOutlet var spinnerImage: WKInterfaceImage!
```

```
        @IBOutlet var button: WKInterfaceButton!

        @IBAction func buttonTapped() {

        }
    }
```

8. Return to Interface.storyboard, and connect the image and button to their outlets and action.

9. Add the following method to the InterfaceController:

```
override func awakeWithContext(context: AnyObject?) {
    super.awakeWithContext(context)
    let spinnerAnimation = UIImage.animatedImageNamed("spinner",
    → duration: 2)!
    spinnerImage.setImage(spinnerAnimation)
}
```

10. Update the InterfaceController's buttonTapped() method to read as follows:

```
@IBAction func buttonTapped() {
    spinnerImage.startAnimating()
}
```

11. Run the app, then tap the button, and you should see the spinner animating. Delightful, but it won't stop! For that to happen, you need to modify the code a bit.

    Just as it isn't possible to query WKInterfaceObject subclasses for their state (Chapter 4), the interface controller cannot query the WKInterfaceImage to see if its animation is currently running. This means you have to add a property to the controller.

12. Make the following changes to InterfaceController.swift, adding a property and updating the implementation of buttonTapped():

```
private var animating = false

@IBAction func buttonTapped() {
    if animating {
        spinnerImage.stopAnimating()
        button.setTitle("Spin")
        animating = false
    } else {
        spinnerImage.startAnimating()
        button.setTitle("Freeze")
```

```
            animating = true
        }
    }
}
```

13. Run the app, and try tapping the button a few times.

    Note the behavior of the animation when it is stopped: It immediately resets to the last frame in its sequence.

    You can add a bit of color now and use an interface animation to do so.

14. Add the following to `InterfaceController`:

```
private func updateButtonToStopped() {
    let goColor = UIColor.init(red:4/255, green:222/255, blue:13/250,
    → alpha:0.28)

    button.setBackgroundColor(goColor)
    button.setTitle("Spin")
}


private func updateButtonToGoing() {
    let stopColor = UIColor.init(red:250/255, green:17/255, blue:79/250,
    → alpha:0.34)

    button.setBackgroundColor(stopColor)
    button.setTitle("Freeze")
}
```

15. Modify `buttonTapped()` to read as follows:

```
@IBAction func buttonTapped() {
    if animating {
        spinnerImage.stopAnimating()
        animating = false
        animateWithDuration(0.2, animations: updateButtonToStopped)
    } else {
        spinnerImage.startAnimating()
        animating = true
        animateWithDuration(0.2, animations: updateButtonToGoing)
    }
}
```

16. Add the highlighted line to awakeWithContext(_:):

```
override func awakeWithContext(context: AnyObject?) {
    super.awakeWithContext(context)
    let spinnerAnimation = UIImage.animatedImageNamed("spinner",
    → duration: 2)!
    spinnerImage.setImage(spinnerAnimation)
    updateButtonToStopped()
}
```

17. Run the app, and try the button.

You see it make a smooth transition between its "Spin" and "Freeze" states.

Using WKInterfaceController's animateWithDuration(_:animations:) method is as simple as that. And, we must admit, this example gives an impression of the extent of its capabilities too. The animations parameter takes a closure containing the changes to be animated. Not all properties of a WKInterfaceObject can be animated. Those method calls that can be animated are:

- setAlpha(_:)
- setWidth(_:) and setHeight(_:)
- setHorizontalAlignment(_:) and setVerticalAlignment(_:)
- setBackgroundColor(_:)
- setContentInset(_:) on a WKInterfaceGroup

Changes to properties that cannot be animated will be applied without a transition.

PICKER-LINKED ANIMATION

Apple Watch's digital crown provides another control for animation, and an interesting one. A picker can have any number of animations associated with it, via its setCoordinatedAnimations(_:) method. The method parameter is an array of objects that conform to the WKImageAnimatable protocol—which, of course, includes WKInterfaceImage.

As the user scrolls through the picker's items, any coordinated animations update in parallel with the picker's current position in its array of items. The frames of the animation are automatically apportioned according to the number of items in the list. Where there are more frames than items, the animation will proceed by multiple frames per item. If there are fewer frames than items, then the picker must progress by multiple items to move to the next frame.

This technique is easy to work with and powerful. Return to the spinner project from the previous section, and make the following changes:

1. In Interface.storyboard, delete the button from the Interface Controller scene. Add a Picker object to replace the button, and make sure that it is styled as a List with a Focus Style setting of None, and that its Indicator is Disabled (**Figure 6.21**). You will be adding empty items to the picker, and these settings ensure that it has no visible user interface of its own.

The picker must be present in the interface to receive updates from the digital crown, but it won't be visible—so it doesn't matter where it is placed. However, other controls will need to be fitted around it. In this case, for neatness, we put it at the bottom of the scene (**Figure 6.22**).

FIGURE 6.22 The image and picker in the storyboard scene

FIGURE 6.21 Interface configuration for an invisible picker

2. Open InterfaceController.swift, and add the following @IBOutlet and method:

```
@IBOutlet var picker: WKInterfacePicker!


private func setupPicker() {
    var items: [WKPickerItem] = []
    if let itemCount = spinnerAnimation.images?.count {
        for _ in 1...itemCount * 2 {
            items.append(WKPickerItem())
        }
    }

    picker.setItems(items)
    picker.setCoordinatedAnimations([spinnerImage])
    picker.focus()
}
```

3. Connect the picker in the storyboard scene to the new @IBOutlet.
4. Delete the animating variable and the methods buttonTapped(), updateButtonToStopped(), and updateButtonToGoing(). Also delete the button's @IBOutlet.
5. Replace awakeWithContext(_:) with the following, noting the extraction of spinnerAnimation to a lazy property:

```
lazy var spinnerAnimation: UIImage = UIImage.animatedImageNamed("spinner",
→ duration: 2)!
```

```
override func awakeWithContext(context: AnyObject?) {
    super.awakeWithContext(context)

    spinnerImage.setImage(spinnerAnimation)
    setupPicker()
}
```

When the interface controller is prepared for display, the invisible picker is activated by the call to its focus() method in setupPicker(). Scrolling with the digital crown will then update the animation.

THE SETTINGS INTERFACE

An oft-neglected part of an app's user interface is how settings and preferences are exposed to the user. iOS provides an easy-to-use API to make simple settings available through the system Settings app, which includes screens for installed apps. watchOS has a very similar capability, with the app-specific settings accessed via the Watch app on the host iPhone.

As with iOS, settings are accessed programmatically via the NSUserDefaults API. However, there are some differences in how the defaults are managed for a watchOS app:

- The watchOS app has its own settings bundle, separate from that of the iOS app. It is up to you to create this bundle, and it should be named Settings-Watch.bundle.

- To allow the settings bundle to be shared between the two devices, it must belong to an App Group container, with the iOS app and WatchKit extension having the App Group capability and belonging to the same container. The Root.plist file in Settings-Watch.bundle should include the key ApplicationGroupContainerIdentifier, with the matching value set to the container's identifier.

- Code in the WatchKit extension can read values from the settings bundle but cannot write values.

- On iOS it's common to use the object returned by NSUserDefaults.standardUserDefaults() to read and write values in the app's settings bundle, but the container-based approach needed by watchOS means that the user defaults object is obtained via a call to NSUserDefaults.init(suiteNamed:), passing the identifier of the App Group container.

- The data in the user defaults will be available only to your WatchKit extension when running on an actual device—not on the simulator. See Chapter 13 for a guide to deploying to the hardware.

The settings to show in the host phone's Watch app are defined by editing the Root.plist file in Settings-Watch.bundle. The example property list shown in **Figure 6.23** produces the settings shown in **Figure 6.24**.

Key	Type	Value
▼ iPhone Settings Schema	Dictionary	(3 items)
ApplicationGroupContainerIdentifier	String	group.build.watchosapps.In-A-Spin
Strings Filename	String	Root
▼ Preference Items	Array	(2 items)
▼ Item 0 (Text Field - Book Title)	Dictionary	(4 items)
Type	String	Text Field
Title	String	Book Title
Identifier	String	title
Default Value	String	Build watchOS Apps
▼ Item 1 (Toggle Switch - Show	Dictionary	(4 items)
Type	String	Toggle Switch
Title	String	Show Index
Identifier	String	show_index
Default Value	Boolean	YES

FIGURE 6.23 An example settings Root.plist

FIGURE 6.24 Settings displayed in Watch.app

Accessing these settings from the WatchKit extension is as simple as using code like the following:

```
if let userDefaults: NSUserDefaults = NSUserDefaults.init(suiteName:
→"group.build.watchosapps.In-A-Spin") {
    let showIndex = userDefaults.boolForKey("show_index")
    let bookTitle = userDefaults.stringForKey("title")
}
```

The combination of defining options in the settings bundle's property list file and accessing them via NSUserDefaults makes for a very convenient way to manage simple settings for your apps.

ACCESSIBILITY

In recent years, Apple's systems have gained a reputation for excellent accessibility features that meet the needs of a wide range of users. This is especially true of iOS, even though it is a platform that does away with most physical controls and relies very heavily on visual cues for interaction. Many of the accessibility features of iOS are also present in watchOS, making the Apple Watch an impressively accessible device.

Most of the accessibility features of the operating system require no special effort on the part of app developers. Features such as Zoom, Mono Audio, Grayscale, and the extra on/off labels on switches will just work for your app when enabled by the user. Others, such as VoiceOver and Dynamic Type support, may require a little effort on your part when developing the app. However, Apple has done an excellent job of making these technologies easy to adopt.

WHY ACCESSIBILITY?

As developers, we don't often talk in terms of the ethics of the software that we build, but perhaps the first reason to spend time on the accessibility of your apps is an ethical one. Making our software accessible and usable to as many people as possible, regardless of any accommodation they need, is a good thing to do. From a more pragmatic point of view, the more people *can* use your app, the more people *will* use your app. And when the cost of making your app accessible via the technologies available in the OS is so low, the benefit looks even greater.

The first task, then, is to think about how your app displays information and makes interactions available to the user. For example, if your app uses color to convey meaning (see the red and green of the button in the animation example in the "Controlling Animation" section of this chapter), is that meaning also clear to users who perceive color differently or who have their watch set to display in grayscale? Is the same meaning communicated in some other way as well? Does your app rely on audio cues? Can it use the Taptic engine as well, to provide a tap on the user's wrist?

These are simple yet important principles. A little advance thought can have a substantial impact.

DYNAMIC TYPE

The Dynamic Type system was introduced to iOS in version 7 and is available in watchOS. It allows developers to identify the use of a piece of text, and have that text sized according to the user's system-wide preference for text size.

In watchOS, this system is made available via `UIFont` and `UIFontDescriptor`. For example, a font can be instantiated with the class method `preferredFontForTextStyle(_:)`, which will return the font for the passed style in the user's current preferred size. The styles are:

- `UIFontTextStyleHeadline`
- `UIFontTextStyleSubheadline`
- `UIFontTextStyleBody`
- `UIFontTextStyleFootnote`
- `UIFontTextStyleCaption1`
- `UIFontTextStyleCaption2`

The equivalent method on `UIFontDescriptor`, `preferredFontDescriptorWithText-Style(_:)`, returns a font descriptor that can be used when instantiating a font.

You can use these fonts in, for example, constructing an attributed string to set to an interface label. It is also possible to apply these styles to a label via the Font Style selector in the storyboard editor (**Figure 6.25**).

Using this system to style the text your app displays gives the user control over the text size in your app, allowing them to increase or decrease it as necessary.

FIGURE 6.25 Using text styles in the storyboard editor

VOICEOVER

VoiceOver is the most well-known accessibility system in iOS and watchOS, and it is the one that requires the most effort from the developer—but that's still not very much.

VoiceOver is a screen reader and alternative set of gestures that users can use to navigate an app's interface. When VoiceOver is activated, a single tap selects an element of the interface, and any associated accessibility information is read out loud. The user may then double tap to activate the control. Flicking left and right with one finger moves the VoiceOver focus through the interface, and sliding one finger around reads aloud the information for each control as your finger passes over it. Many other gestures are available with VoiceOver, including some alternatives, but the ones mentioned are the basic ones. The best way to get to know it is to go to the Settings app on your Apple Watch, open the Accessibility section, and activate VoiceOver.

VoiceOver relies on interface objects being identified as accessibility elements. Labels and interactive controls are identified as such by default; images, for example, are not. You configure this in an object using the method `setIsAccessibilityElement(_:)`, which is available on all subclasses of `WKInterfaceObject`. Objects with this set to `false` are invisible to VoiceOver.

Each object then has a series of properties to expose different data to VoiceOver, set with the following methods:

- `setAccessibilityLabel(_:)` sets the string that is used to describe the object to the user. If none is set, the system uses the title of the object (or text, in the case of a label); the title is often a sensible default, which means that in many cases your buttons, labels, and table rows will have the correct accessibility label already!

- `setAccessibilityHint(_:)` allows you to provide a string that describes what the element *does*. For example, a good accessibility hint for a button might be "Makes the widget go ding." This phrase should be as brief as possible while still being sensible; it should start with a verb ("Does this"), and it should include neither what the element *is* nor *how to activate it* (don't say, "Button you tap to make the widget go ding").

- `setAccessibilityValue(_:)` allows you to update a changing value on a control that has one. For example, it could be the value associated with a slider or with the state of a switch.

- `setAccessibilityTraits(_:)` allows you to provide context for the other accessibility information by providing a bitmask of traits such as Static Text, Search Field, Button, Link, Plays Sound, Updates Frequently, Causes Page Turn, and many others. See the documentation for the full list of available traits.

Additionally, there is a method, `setAccessibilityIdentifier(_:)`, that does not expose additional information to the user. Rather, it allows you to set an identifier that your app can use.

As noted, `WKInterfaceImage` objects default to *not* being active as accessibility elements. If you use an image to communicate information that your user needs, your app may enable it as an accessibility element and set the various properties listed earlier as necessary. To provide even more flexibility, the method `setAccessibilityRegions(_:)` allows you to define multiple accessibility elements in a single image.

One final thing to consider is sensible and useful grouping of elements. If, for example, you have an interface group containing many labels that make little sense in isolation, it may be better to disable the contained labels as accessibility elements and instead make the group the accessibility element, with appropriate label, hint, and traits.

Using the principles and APIs described here, we hope you find that with only a little thought and care it is very straightforward to make your Apple Watch app fully accessible to all users.

WRAPPING UP

In this chapter, you've seen some of the tools and techniques that you can use to assemble a user interface for an Apple Watch app. The diverse library of standard controls can go a very long way, and there is potential to do even more with the creative use of images and animation and the availability of the digital crown—all while still keeping apps completely accessible.

In complications, glances, and notifications, Apple Watch provides opportunities to put these tools to use outside the app itself. Read on through the next chapters to learn more.

CHAPTER 7

Working with Complications

If the release of the Apple Watch does not go down in history for revolutionizing the field of wearable computing, at the very least it will go down in history for inspiring countless bloggers to pretend that they've always known what a watch complication was.

In this chapter, we will bring you up (or down) to the level of the bloggers by explaining what a complication is, why your users might want you to add one to your app, and how you might go about doing so.

INTRODUCING COMPLICATIONS

Watches started life with a simple purpose—to help people tell the current time in terms of hours and minutes. Although the internals of a watch that solely tells the time can be tiny and complex, telling time is considered the *simplest* function that a watch can perform. Anything else—a date indicator, a stopwatch, a calculator function—is considered a *complication*. Despite the fact that the standard Apple Watch faces actually include numerous complications, Apple, in its inimitable fashion, decided to co-opt the name *complication* to describe any additional widgets that can be configured to slot into designated areas around the rest of the watch face.

Although there were numerous Apple-supplied complications in watchOS 1, it's only with the introduction of ClockKit (a new framework included in watchOS 2) that it's now possible for third-party developers to include their own complications as part of their Watch app.

As one of those third-party developers, you have an amazing opportunity to get data from your app directly onto the face of your users' watches. It might seem like the equivalent of a notification or a glance, but this is something way more. Notifications need you to push the data to the user, and glances need the user to initiate a request for information. A complication is a part of your app that is always right there on their watch face and can be kept up to date through the magic of timelines and time travel—without having to reach a speed of 88mph.

TIMELINES AND TIME TRAVEL

Although it may sound like some sort of magic, or like Apple has achieved some feat from the realms of science fiction, the ability to provide up-to-the-minute data for your complication is actually just some very clever software engineering and data caching.

Each complication on a watch face needs to have up-to-date data at the precise moment the user raises her wrist to look at her watch. Rather than continuously fetching data on request, a complication expects the associated app to provide a timeline of data, such as a sequence of calendar appointments or predicted temperatures at intervals throughout the day. Your app will be requested to provide up to three different types of information: for the current time, for the future, and for the past.

The most important information is that for the current time. You don't have to provide data for the future or the past—it may not even be possible to do so—but if you do provide future data, it can allow your complication to display information without resorting to repeated requests to your app every time the current information becomes outdated.

A further advantage of providing past and future data is that it allows the user to take advantage of the Time Travel feature of watchOS 2. Time Travel can be achieved by turning the digital crown while viewing the watch face; the watch will emit a brief tap, and Time Travel mode will be indicated on the screen (**Figure 7.1**).

FIGURE 7.1 Time Travel: It's like we're living in the future.

Rotating the digital crown clockwise goes forward in time (appropriately enough), and it scrubs through the timeline of future data that apps have provided to their complications. Whenever future data is not available, the complication is shown as disabled while in Time Travel mode. Rotating counterclockwise goes backward, of course, through the data time-line for the complications. Again, if historical data is not available, the complication will be shown as disabled.

You don't have to support Time Travel with your complication (and depending on your app, you may not even be able to), but it is a delightful feature of the Apple Watch in general, and worth supporting if you can.

COMPLICATED ARRANGEMENTS

If you have browsed the available faces on an Apple Watch, you have seen a number of different complications that may, from a high level, seem like a complete mishmash of styles. Fortunately, they actually break down into just five main families, some of which have their own customizations, which can be broken down into data layouts.

FAMILIES

The complication families are broadly grouped by the watch faces that they are primarily associated with, and each of those watch faces dictates different form factors that are possible. You do not have to support all the families—and we encourage you not to abuse the space that has been made available to you—but bear in mind that the more families you support, the more chance you have of getting your complication onto a relatively sparse, but invaluable, piece of real estate.

Modular

The Modular watch face lends its name to two families: Modular Small and Modular Large. **Figure 7.2** shows an example Modular watch face.

The highlighted area in the Modular Large complication in Figure 7.2 (left) is the single, large, and horizontally oriented rectangle that dominates the middle of the Modular face. Its size and orientation make it particularly suitable for displaying relatively intensive textual information.

FIGURE 7.2 Modular Large (left) and Modular Small (right) complications

The remaining complications on the Modular face are all examples of the Modular Small complication family (including a calendar, stopwatch, moon phase indicator, and sunrise/sunset indicator). They share a rounded rectangular shape (as highlighted in the screenshot on the right), and as a result Modular Small complications can be used interchangeably in the four available spaces on the Modular watch face.

Utilitarian

Although it may sound like a sci-fi cult, the Utilitarian complication families are named for their inclusion in the Utility watch face (**Figure 7.3**) as well as in the Mickey, Chronograph, and Simple faces. Unfortunately, for reasons known only to them, Apple seems reluctant to let developers customize the "Mickey butt-wiggle/foot-tap," which is arguably the best complication there is. Our personal idea for Morse code–style message delivery through Mickey's foot taps is currently on the shelf.

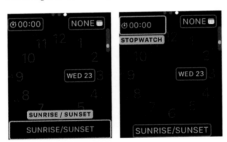

FIGURE 7.3 Utilitarian Large (left) and Utilitarian Small (right) complications

The line of information on the bottom of the face (the sunrise/sunset time) is the sole Utilitarian Large complication slot available. It is well suited to data that needs to be formatted with a reasonable amount of width, but don't worry if your data output is a bit on the narrow side, because the complication data will be sensibly centered.

The Utility face features two other parcels of screen space that can accommodate a complication—at the upper-left and upper-right corners, meeting at the center of the screen. This complication type is named Utilitarian Small, and you are not restricted to using the entire width of the space available to you. You can use simple icons that will be pushed to the far-left or far-right side of their respective spaces.

NOTE: The Utility face (and others) actually features a fourth complication when you enter its customization mode. It corresponds to the date display in Figure 7.3. We won't consider it here because it can show only the date (in a number of styles) or be turned off. It's not yet open to third-party developers.

Circular

The Circular family is not named for a watch face, and is a bit of a misnomer considering that it occupies a space that is actually a rectangle (**Figure 7.4**). They can be displayed on the Color watch faces.

FIGURE 7.4 Circular complications on a Color watch face

In the four corners of Figure 7.4, you can see four examples of the Circular complication in action. Although they appear in similar positions to the Utilitarian Small complications, they do not have the same flexibility to occupy a rectangular shape; they can take only the form of a square and are best suited to round graphical complications.

DATA LAYOUTS

The complications you've seen so far have varied by the watch face they can be configured with, but also in the presentation of their data. Each of the families can be subdivided into a number of data layouts; you need to choose the layout that best suits your data and specify that layout when writing the code to support your complications. The full range of complication families, their available data layouts, and the template identifiers you can use to reference them in code are shown in **Table 7.1**.

TABLE 7.1

FAMILY	LAYOUT	TEMPLATE IDENTIFIER
Modular Large	Standard Body	CLKComplicationTemplateModularLargeStandardBody
	Tall Body	CLKComplicationTemplateModularLargeTallBody
	Table	CLKComplicationTemplateModularLargeTable
	Columns	CLKComplicationTemplateModularLargeColumns

continued on next page

continued from previous page

FAMILY	LAYOUT	TEMPLATE IDENTIFIER
Modular Small	Simple Text	CLKComplicationTemplateModularSmallSimpleText
	Simple Image	CLKComplicationTemplateModularSmallSimpleImage
	Ring Text	CLKComplicationTemplateModularSmallRingText
	Ring Image	CLKComplicationTemplateModularSmallRingImage
	Stack Text	CLKComplicationTemplateModularSmallStackText
	Stack Image	CLKComplicationTemplateModularSmallStackImage
	Columns Text	CLKComplicationTemplateModularSmallColumnsText
Utilitarian Large	Flat	CLKComplicationTemplateUtilitarianLargeFlat
Utilitarian Small	Flat	CLKComplicationTemplateUtilitarianSmallFlat
	Square	CLKComplicationTemplateUtilitarianSmallSquare
	Ring Text	CLKComplicationTemplateUtilitarianSmallRingText
	Ring Image	CLKComplicationTemplateUtilitarianSmallRingImage
Circular	Simple Text	CLKComplicationTemplateCircularSmallSimpleText
	Simple Image	CLKComplicationTemplateCircularSmallSimpleImage
	Ring Text	CLKComplicationTemplateCircularSmallRingText
	Ring Image	CLKComplicationTemplateCircularSmallRingImage
	Stack Text	CLKComplicationTemplateCircularSmallStackText
	Stack Image	CLKComplicationTemplateCircularSmallStackImage

With more than 20 different options to present your data in a complication (including tabular layouts, open and closed rings, and images), all that remains to be done is to choose the variations you want to support and introduce some complications to your life. Rather than display all the available styles here, we encourage you to browse the existing complications supplied by watchOS and find the styles that best suit your data.

ADDING COMPLICATIONS

So you've decided that life isn't simple enough and you want to introduce some complications. How you include a complication in your app depends on when you decide you want to do it. As you'll see here, and in later chapters for glances and notifications, it's always easier to include a complication when you are creating your watchOS app than it is to retrofit it to one. It's worth giving careful consideration to your project needs at creation time.

INCLUDING A COMPLICATION IN A NEW APP

You can start from scratch and create a complication in a new iOS and watchOS app in one fell swoop, but you can also include a complication when creating a new watchOS target if your iOS app already exists.

CREATING A PROJECT AND APP WITH A COMPLICATION

Here are the steps to create a complication when you create your project and app.

1. From the Xcode main menu, select File > New > Project.
2. In the new project template chooser dialog, select watchOS > iOS App with WatchKit App (**Figure 7.5**).

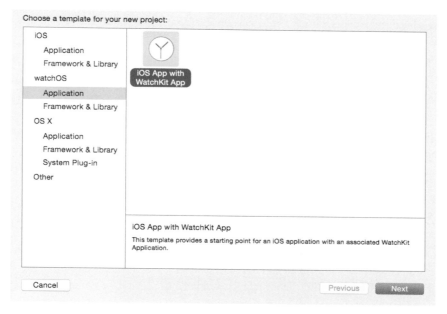

FIGURE 7.5 The project template chooser dialog

3. Click Next to choose the template.
4. In the template options dialog, set Product Name to **I Said What?** and ensure that the Include Complication option is selected (**Figure 7.6**).

FIGURE 7.6 watchOS project settings with Include Complication selected

Choose options for your new project:

Product Name:	I Said What?
Organization Name:	Build watchOS Apps
Organization Identifier:	build.watchosapps
Bundle Identifier:	build.watchosapps.I-Said-What-
Language:	Swift
Devices:	Universal

☐ Include Notification Scene
☐ Include Glance Scene
☑ Include Complication
☐ Include Unit Tests
☐ Include UI Tests

Cancel   Previous   Next

5. Click Next to confirm your options.

6. Choose a location in which to save the project—we'll leave it to you to decide where—and click Create to finish the process.

Now that you've created a project with a complication, we'll take a short diversion to look at the file artifacts and configuration associated with complications. This is important so that you can work with them, and also understand how to create them by hand or to disable them if you no longer want to include one in your app.

CONFIGURING THE COMPLICATION

Unlike glances and notifications, complications, when added to your project, don't make a change to the `Interface.storyboard` file that defines your app interface. This may seem unusual, but glances and notifications are displayed as complete, self-contained views that your app needs to specify and control. Complications, on the other hand, are displayed on the watch face and can be supplied by many different apps, so it is watchOS that needs to manage them. You just get to supply the data and resources that they rely upon.

Like many modern Apple frameworks, the data needs to be supplied by a data source. As part of the project template, a file named `ComplicationController.swift` is created in the WatchKit Extension file group. This file is strangely named, because it does not inherit from `WKInterfaceController`, as the class name `ComplicationController` suggests. Instead, it implements a protocol named `CLKComplicationDataSource`; it's this protocol that defines the data source methods that your code must implement in order to render your complications on the watch face. We'll take a closer look at the methods that need to be implemented to satisfy this protocol later in this chapter.

You'll need to include image resources if the complication templates you decide to use include images. To make this easier for you, the project template adds a complication set to the Assets.xcassets file in the WatchKit Extension file group. The complication set contains three image groups—one each for the Circular, Modular, and Utilitarian families—and each image group takes two size variations for the 38mm and 42mm watch sizes (**Figure 7.7**). We'll add some image resources in the "Including Image Assets" section later.

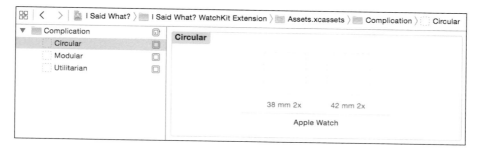

FIGURE 7.7 The Circular complication image asset group

The final changes made by the project template to enable complication support can be found in the settings for the WatchKit Extension target. For this sample project, we would like to support only Modular Large, and here is how you can achieve this.

1. Click the I Said What? project group in the Project Navigator to open the Settings editor.

2. Select the I Said What? WatchKit Extension target in the Settings editor.

3. Open the General settings tab.

4. Scroll down to view the Complications Configuration settings group (**Figure 7.8**).

5. Deselect the complication families until only the Modular Large family remains selected (Figure 7.8).

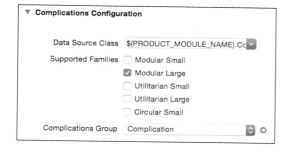

FIGURE 7.8 The Complications Configuration section of the target settings

While you are here, it is worth exploring the configuration settings in this group:

- **Data Source Class:** This setting is a combined text-entry field and popup menu. Clicking the popup menu control presents a list of the classes found in the WatchKit Extension target that implements the CLKComplicationDataSource protocol. Pick a class from the list, or type the name of one directly into the text field, in order to tell watchOS the class it should use as a data source.

In the project template, it is set to $(PRODUCT_MODULE_NAME).ComplicationController by default. If you are setting it yourself, be aware that Xcode can sometimes drop the $(PRODUCT_MODULE_NAME) portion. This will cause your app to have problems finding the data source, so make sure to replace it if necessary.

- **Supported Families:** This setting is a series of checkboxes that represent the five different complication types. By default, they are all enabled, but you can disable specific checkboxes to indicate to watchOS that you do not wish to support that complication family.

- **Complications Group:** The final setting is a standard popup menu that, when clicked, presents a list of complication sets found in asset groups contained within the WatchKit Extension target. By default, it's set to use the complication set within Assets.xcassets in the WatchKit Extensions file group, but if you want to include a different set of images, you can select them here.

TIP: The Data Source Class and Supported Families settings are mirrored within the Info.plist of the WatchKit Extension target. This could be useful if you have a complex build system and wish to change these settings for specific builds (for example, paid and free versions of your app). The Complications Group setting is held within the main project settings and is not so easily changed at build time.

If you added complication support when you created your project, you can also use these settings to disable that support. Remove the Data Source Class setting or deselect all the Supported Families options to stop your app from offering complications.

ADDING A COMPLICATION TO AN EXISTING APP

Sometimes it is hard to predict exactly what you'll need in your app when you are creating the project, and it's highly likely that at some stage you'll need to add complication support to an existing watchOS app that doesn't have one. Although it isn't as easy as selecting a checkbox, it still isn't too difficult to achieve.

1. From the Xcode main menu, select File > New > Project.
2. In the new project template chooser dialog, select watchOS > iOS App with WatchKit App (Figure 7.5).
3. Click Next to choose the template.
4. In the template options dialog, set Product Name to **Simple Life** and ensure that the Include Complication option is *not* selected (**Figure 7.9**).
5. Click Next to confirm your options.
6. Choose a location to save the project, and click Create to finish the process.

    You are now the proud owner of a complication-free project named Simple Life. Let's make it more complicated by adding a data source class.

FIGURE 7.9 watchOS project settings with Include Complication deselected

Choose options for your new project:

Product Name: Simple Life
Organization Name: Build watchOS Apps
Organization Identifier: build.watchosapps
Bundle Identifier: build.watchosapps.Simple-Life
Language: Swift
Devices: Universal

☐ Include Notification Scene
☐ Include Glance Scene
☐ Include Complication
☐ Include Unit Tests
☐ Include UI Tests

Cancel   Previous   Next

7. In the Project Navigator, click the WatchKit Extension file group to select it.

8. From the Xcode main menu, select File > New > File.

9. In the new file template chooser dialog, select the watchOS > Source category, click the WatchKit Class template to select it, and click Next to continue (**Figure 7.10**).

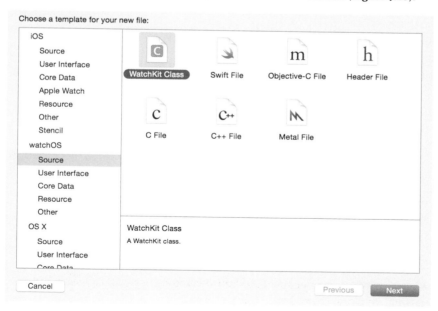

FIGURE 7.10 The new file template chooser dialog showing the WatchKit Class template

Choose a template for your new file:

iOS
  Source
  User Interface
  Core Data
  Apple Watch
  Resource
  Other
  Stencil
watchOS
  Source
  User Interface
  Core Data
  Resource
  Other
OS X
  Source
  User Interface
  Core Data

WatchKit Class   Swift File   Objective-C File   Header File

C File   C++ File   Metal File

WatchKit Class
A WatchKit class.

Cancel   Previous   Next

10. In the new file options dialog, set the Class name to `ComplicationDataSource`, and click Next to continue (**Figure 7.11**).

   Apple named this class `ComplicationController`, but we want to acknowledge its true purpose in life.

11. In the save dialog, navigate to the Simple Life WatchKit Extension folder, ensure that the Target for the new file is set to Simple Life WatchKit extension, and click Create to finish creating the new file.

12. Update the newly created `ComplicationDataSource.swift` file to import the ClockKit module (more on this framework very soon), and add `CLKComplicationDataSource` as a protocol.

```
import WatchKit
import ClockKit

class ComplicationDataSource: NSObject, CLKComplicationDataSource {

}
```

   This causes the `ComplicationDataSource.swift` file to report an error; it implements a protocol that it doesn't completely conform to yet. We're not worried about that right now, but if you want to populate it, see the section "Providing Timeline Entries" later in this chapter.

   You now need to create an asset catalog entry that you can set as the Complications Group setting.

13. In the WatchKit Extension file group, select the asset catalog named `Assets.xcassets`.

14. From the Xcode main menu, select Editor > Add Assets > New Watch Complication.

    This creates a new complication set named Complication, and completes the process of artifact creation. All that remains is to configure the WatchKit Extension target settings to reference the artifacts.

15. In the Project Navigator, click the Simple Life project folder to open the Settings editor.

16. Click the Simple Life WatchKit Extension target to view its settings, and scroll down to the Complications Configuration section.

17. Set the Data Source Class setting to `$(PRODUCT_MODULE_NAME).ComplicationDataSource`.

18. Select one or more complication families for the Supported Families setting.

19. Set the Complications Group setting to Complication.

It's time you updated your résumé to say that you're a traditional watchmaker; you have just handcrafted a complication.

INCLUDING IMAGE ASSETS

Given the lack of space in any of the complication templates, it can be very difficult to convey a lot of information. The old adage "a picture is worth a thousand words" is rarely as appropriate as it is here. Many of the standard watchOS complications include images to help include as much data as possible.

Although it may be tempting to just throw a collection of images into your project, using just any old images in your complication will result in unexpected behavior. This is because Apple wants the complications to have a very uniform look and feel, and this is a lot harder to achieve if every developer has a different color scheme.

To prevent this, the images provided by your complication are expected to use a monochrome image with varying alpha levels that can then be rendered into any color scheme that watchOS chooses. The best way to achieve this is to create a black and white grayscale image and use an image conversion tool to convert the grayscale into different levels of transparency. **Figure 7.12** shows a comparison between a grayscale image and the same converted image. We've created some images that you can use without having to get into image manipulation.

FIGURE 7.12 The monochrome image (left) and the alpha-channel image (right)

1. Download the compressed modular file from bit.ly/bwa-modular-assets, and decompress the file.

   Once you have your images, you can include them in the asset catalog file named `Assets.xcassets` in the WatchKit Extension folder. As shown earlier (Figure 7.7), this asset catalog comes prepopulated with a group named Complication that contains three predefined image assets (for Circular, Modular, and Utilitarian complications). Each of the assets can supply images for 38mm and 42mm watch form factors.

2. In the Project Navigator, open the WatchKit Extension file group, and click the file named `Assets.xcassets` to open it.

3. Click the Complication group in the asset catalog editor to expand it, then click the Modular image asset to select it (**Figure 7.13**).

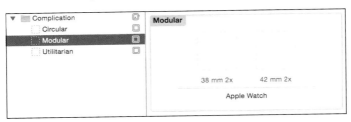

FIGURE 7.13 The empty Modular image asset

4. In the Finder, navigate to the folder where you downloaded the image assets, or locate your own assets if you wish to use them.

5. Drag the file named `modular-38mm.png` into Xcode, and drop it onto the image well named 38 mm 2x (**Figure 7.14**).

FIGURE 7.14 Adding an image to the asset catalog

6. Repeat step 5 for the file named `modular-42mm.png`, and drop it onto the image well named 42 mm 2x.

   The image assets are now included in the project and can be loaded into a `UIImage` using their path within the asset catalog. For example:

```
let asset = UIImage(named: "Complication/Modular")
```

   The `UIImage` class will choose which of the two images to use based on the size of the device the code is actually running on.

CLOCKKIT

Working with complications requires that you dive into a new framework introduced in watchOS 2: ClockKit. It is ClockKit that defines the CLKComplicationDataSource protocol that your app must implement in order to support complications. As you start to implement this protocol, you'll quickly need to start pulling in other classes and types from ClockKit, including some interesting new classes for dealing with text and images.

First, though, you'll look at the data source itself in the context of creating your sample app named I Said What? The purpose of this app is simple; it provides a complication to tell you what you said on Twitter exactly one year ago.

Working with the CLKComplicationDataSource protocol will feel familiar to you if you have dabbled even briefly with table views on iOS (and specifically with the UITableViewDataSource protocol). It's a comprehensive protocol that provides a lot of flexibility, but with that flexibility comes a degree of complexity. Fortunately, the default project template contains most of the protocol methods pre-implemented. We will work through them, filling them in as we go and giving extra details where necessary.

TIMELINE SETTINGS

Before the data source can provide entries for your timeline, you need to provide some basic information to ClockKit so that subsequent requests for data make sense. For example, if your complication can't provide information for times in the future, you can indicate this and spare future requests for future timeline entries.

In the case of our example app, because the data will be one year old, you do have both future and past information. You communicate this to ClockKit through the required protocol method getSupportedTimeTravelDirectionsForComplication(_:withHandler:). Happily, the default implementation in the template covers this already, but we will replicate it here to discuss some general techniques that apply to most of these protocol methods.

```
func getSupportedTimeTravelDirectionsForComplication(complication:
→ CLKComplication,
    withHandler handler: (CLKComplicationTimeTravelDirections) -> Void) {
    handler([.Forward, .Backward])
}
```

Two parameters are common to many of these methods:

- complication: This parameter is a reference to an instance of a CLKComplication class. The parameter is passed in so that you can ask to which family the complication belongs. CLKComplication has just one property (family), which returns a CLKComplicationFamily enum indicating whether the complication is ModularSmall, ModularLarge, UtilitarianSmall, UtilitarianLarge, or CircularSmall.

- handler: This parameter is a reference to a closure that is passed to the method by ClockKit. It's your responsibility to call this handler at the end of the method and pass it the appropriate information. The type of information to be passed to the handler varies between the protocol methods, but the signature of the protocol method will give you the necessary guidance in each instance.

NOTE: If you support more than one type of complication, you should use the family property on CLKComplication to let you construct custom responses for each family you support. In our sample project we have indicated that we only support the Modular Large family, so we have skipped any family-specific handling for the sake of brevity.

In the previous sample, we are calling the handler with a set of supported directions ([.Forward, .Backward]) that our complication supports. If you wanted to support time travel only to the past, you would pass .Backward; to support time travel only to the future, then pass .Forward; or to indicate no time travel support at all, pass .None.

When a specific time travel direction has been indicated as supported, your data source will then be asked to specify exactly how far forward or back it can go. You can indicate your supported dates by implementing the methods getTimelineStartDateForComplication(_: withHandler:) and getTimelineEndDateForComplication(_:withHandler:). The handler parameter for both methods can be passed an optional NSDate. The date specified indicates the point beyond which the complication should be dimmed during Time Travel; supplying the current time is another way to say that Time Travel is not supported in the specified direction, whereas passing nil indicates that there is no limit to Time Travel capabilities in this direction.

For your app, you want to support 12 hours of past timeline entries and 6 hours of future timeline entries.

1. Update the methods as follows:

```
func getTimelineStartDateForComplication(complication: CLKComplication,
    withHandler handler: (NSDate?) -> Void) {
    let twelveHours = NSDate(timeIntervalSinceNow: -12 * 60 * 60)
    handler(twelveHours)
}
```

```
func getTimelineEndDateForComplication(complication: CLKComplication,
    withHandler handler: (NSDate?) -> Void) {
    let sixHours = NSDate(timeIntervalSinceNow: 6 * 60 * 60)
    handler(sixHours)
}
```

If your complication deals with sensitive data, then you need to consider whether your complication should be displayed when the watch has not been unlocked. To disable your complication from being displayed when the watch is locked, pass the HideOnLockScreen value to the handler in the protocol method getPrivacyBehaviorForComplication(_:withHandler:). If your data is not sensitive, then you can return ShowOnLockScreen instead. For our sample app, we would like to respect the privacy status of the original Twitter account, so you will programmatically determine which option to return.

```
func getPrivacyBehaviorForComplication(complication: CLKComplication,
    withHandler handler: (CLKComplicationPrivacyBehavior) -> Void) {
    let privateAcct = TwitterAccount.isPrivate()
    handler(privateAcct ? .HideOnLockScreen : .ShowOnLockScreen)
}
```

> **NOTE:** The ClockKit documentation states that the getPrivacyBehaviorForComplication(_:withHandler:) method is required, yet the protocol definition specifies it as optional. In matters of privacy, it is always best to be explicit, so we recommend that you always implement this method for the security of your users.

You need an implementation for the TwitterAccount type that you used in the previous code.

2. Create a Swift file named TwitterAccount.swift in your WatchKit Extension file group, and add the following code:

```
struct TwitterAccount {
    static internal func isPrivate() -> Bool {
        return true
    }
}
```

You'll use this fake data source for the purposes of example only, and you will flesh it out as you progress through the chapter.

You have now implemented most of the configuration that you need to tell ClockKit in what directions you support Time Travel and for how long. Now you need to start providing ClockKit with the data to display.

COMPLICATION TIMELINE ENTRIES

When ClockKit asks your data source for timeline entries, it expects to receive collections of `CLKComplicationTimelineEntry` objects. These are a combination of a date and the data for the timeline from that date onward. The data is represented by a `CLKComplicationTemplate` subclass that corresponds to a complication family and the layout it uses. The full list of subclasses can be seen in Table 7.1 earlier in the chapter.

Each template subclass has its own very specific set of properties that correspond to the type of data it is capable of displaying. For our example, we would like to utilize a large complication on the Modular watch face to show a portion of a tweet in the body area, along with the exact time and date it was posted in the header area. To do this you can use the `CLKComplicationTemplateModularLargeStandardBody` complication template. Creating one is very simple, but attempting to set a time and date directly into the header and the tweet text in the body unveils the new concept of *providers*.

Rather than deal directly in text strings and images, ClockKit instead demands that you use a set of provider types that are more capable of adapting their content to the confines of a complication. ClockKit defines two main provider types: `CLKImageProvider` and `CLKTextProvider`, though it provides a number of subclasses of `CLKTextProvider` that you should use in preference.

For our complication template, you need a provider capable of formatting a date string, another to present the tweet text, and a third to display an icon to represent the app. For these you can use a `CLKDateTextProvider`, a `CLKSimpleTextProvider`, and a `CLKImageProvider`. The following code shows how these providers could be created; we'll use this code later in the chapter to implement the functionality in our example app.

```
let tweetDate = NSDate(timeIntervalSinceNow: -365 * 24 * 60 * 60)
let dateProvider = CLKDateTextProvider(date: tweetDate, units: .Year)
let textProvider = CLKSimpleTextProvider(text: "An entertaining tweet")
let image = UIImage(named: "Complication/Modular")!
let imageProvider = CLKImageProvider(onePieceImage: image)
```

In this example, we have used the simpler form for creating the image provider that takes a single image. If you want more control over how your image interacts with complication color changes, you should take a look at the alternative `init` methods in the Apple documentation.

With the providers created, they can be combined in the creation of the `CLKComplicationTemplateModularLargeStandardBody` complication template:

```
let complication = CLKComplicationTemplateModularLargeStandardBody()
complication.headerTextProvider = dateProvider
complication.body1TextProvider = textProvider
complication.headerImageProvider = imageProvider
```

Once a complication template has been created, the actual complication timeline entry can finally be created. Along with the complication template, you need to supply a date that represents when the timeline entry becomes valid:

```
let timelineEntry = CLKComplicationTimelineEntry(
    date: NSDate(),
    complicationTemplate: modularLargeComplication)
```

This gives you a timeline entry that has a starting point of right now, but you may be wondering how to define the end of a timeline entry—after all, a calendar appointment would have an end time as well as a start time. Timeline entries are valid from their starting point until the starting point of the next timeline entry supplied by your data source.

This may mean that the source of your data (for example, a calendar API) may not map directly onto complication timeline entries. You may wish to represent non-appointment time in your complication by displaying the text "Free." To do this, you need to map each calendar appointment into two timeline entries: one to represent the start of the appointment, and one to represent the end of the appointment. It can take a little time to get your head around the idea, but a little pen-and-paper planning can go a long way in helping to map your existing data onto a timeline.

PROVIDING TIMELINE ENTRIES

You now know how to create a timeline entry so that you can supply one on request, and the CLKComplicationDataSource protocol contains a collection of related methods that you can implement to provide the entries when ClockKit decides that your complication needs more information.

When working with other data sources, such as those for requesters like table or collection views, you are probably used to a pattern whereby you tell the requester how many items you have, and it asks you for them one by one as needed. ClockKit takes a different approach and can make three different types of request:

- Supply a *current* timeline entry.
- Supply a collection of timeline entries *before* a given date; these form your past data.
- Supply a collection of timeline entries *after* a given date; these form your future data.

The reason for doing it the ClockKit way is straightforward: If you don't support Time Travel, you need to supply only the current entry request, and you need to implement the past and future requests only if you support those directions. ClockKit may request past and future data multiple times with varying before/after dates—it does this to request more data in the appropriate direction if it needs it.

GETTING THE DATA

When ClockKit is preparing to update your complication for display on the watch face, it executes the getCurrentTimelineEntryForComplication(_:withHandler:) method implemented by your CLKComplicationDataSource. This is a required method, so it must be implemented, though your implementation can return an optional timeline entry. If you decide to return nil, ClockKit takes this as an indication that you're having trouble getting the data, and does not ask for more. We'll discuss the implications of this later, in the "Budgeting" section.

You worked through the theory behind constructing a timeline entry in the previous section, so you'll use this knowledge to create and return an entry. First, though, let's create a helper method just to make timeline entry creation a bit quicker.

1. Open the file named ComplicationController.swift, and add the following method:

```
func createTimelineEntryOnTweetDate(tweetDate: NSDate, currentDate: NSDate,
    tweetText: String) -> CLKComplicationTimelineEntry {

    let units: NSCalendarUnit = [.Year, .Month, .Day]
    let dateProvider = CLKDateTextProvider(date: tweetDate, units: units)
    let textProvider = CLKSimpleTextProvider(text: tweetText)

    let image = UIImage(named: "Complication/Modular")!
    let imageProvider = CLKImageProvider(onePieceImage: image)

    let complication = CLKComplicationTemplateModularLargeStandardBody()
    complication.headerTextProvider = dateProvider
    complication.body1TextProvider = textProvider
    complication.headerImageProvider = imageProvider

    return CLKComplicationTimelineEntry(
        date: currentDate, complicationTemplate: complication)
}
```

2. Implement the protocol method with the following code:

```
func getCurrentTimelineEntryForComplication(complication: CLKComplication,
    withHandler handler: ((CLKComplicationTimelineEntry?) -> Void)) {
```

```
    let tweetDate = NSDate(timeIntervalSinceNow: -365 * 24 * 60 * 60)
    let timelineEntry = createTimelineEntryOnTweetDate(tweetDate,
        currentDate: NSDate(), tweetText: "An entertaining tweet")
    handler(timelineEntry)
}
```

If you have the ability to display future or past timeline entries and have indicated that your complication will do so, ClockKit will make further requests for this information using the getTimelineEntriesForComplication(_:beforeDate:limit:withHandler:) and getTimelineEntriesForComplication(_:afterDate:limit:withHandler:) methods. They both work in the same way, so we'll just talk about the beforeDate variant for now. The methods take a number of parameters:

- complication: This parameter is the same as in the other method calls—it contains a reference to the complication so that you can determine what family it is and tailor your response accordingly.

- beforeDate: This is an NSDate object specifying a time and date that represents the most recent point in time for which ClockKit currently has entries. When you provide timeline entries, they must occur *before* this date in the timeline.

- This may seem strange; you could just give every possible timeline entry prior to the current date, so why specify a date? ClockKit specifies a date because it may call this method multiple times and the date will allow it to ask for different segments of your timeline. Subsequent calls will include the date of the last entry in the previous response so that it can grab another batch of entries from the timeline.

- For the companion future timeline method, afterDate represents the last point in time for which ClockKit has entries. Your response should contain only entries that occur *after* this date in the timeline.

- limit: This parameter is an integer that indicates the maximum number of timeline entries that you should supply to ClockKit. This is another essential component in the time budgeting process for your complication, designed to prevent you from spending too long preparing a large number of timeline entries that are not needed immediately.

- handler: As per the other data source method calls, this is the handler that you should call at the end of the method to signal ClockKit that you are finished. You execute the handler with an optional array of CLKComplicationTimelineEntry objects. The array should contain entries that are no closer together in time than a minute and in chronological order up to the limit specified. Returning nil or an empty array is your way to tell ClockKit that you have no more data, so there is no point in requesting any more right now.

Having discussed how the method works and the parameters involved, you can now attempt to implement it and generate some past timeline entries. First, though, we need a quick way to generate some sample data.

3. Update the `TwitterAccount.swift` file to include a line that reads `import Foundation`, then add the following method to the `TwitterAccount` struct:

```
static func tweetsBeforeDate(date: NSDate) -> [(date:
→ NSDate, text: String)] {
    var tweets: [(date: NSDate, text: String)] = []
    for i in 1...5 {
        let interval = arc4random_uniform(UInt32(i * 10))
        let timelineDate = date.dateByAddingTimeInterval
        → (-1 * Double(interval) * 60)
        let tweetText = "My tweet at \(timelineDate)"
        tweets.append((timelineDate, tweetText))
    }
    return tweets
}
```

The method is very simple and adds five tweets with increasingly older dates.

4. Update the `getTimelineEntriesForComplication(_:beforeDate:limit:withHandler:)` method in the data source to take advantage of the `tweetsBeforeDate(_:)` method:

```
func getTimelineEntriesForComplication(complication: CLKComplication,
    beforeDate date: NSDate, limit: Int,
    withHandler handler: (([CLKComplicationTimelineEntry]?) -> Void)) {

    let entries = TwitterAccount.tweetsBeforeDate(date).map {
        (date: NSDate, text: String) -> CLKComplicationTimelineEntry in
        let tweetDate = date.dateByAddingTimeInterval(-365 * 24 * 60 * 60)
        return createTimelineEntryOnTweetDate(tweetDate, currentDate:
            date, tweetText: text)
    }
    handler(entries)
}
```

NOTE: We haven't taken the trouble here to limit the number of entries we return for this very simple example. While experimenting with small numbers of entries, it is unlikely to cause problems, but it is worth sticking to the value of the `limit` parameter for production code.

PLACEHOLDER TEMPLATES

When users of your app are configuring their watch face, they will want to see your complication with some representative data so that they can see how it would look should they use it. This might sound like an afterthought, but if your complication doesn't convey just how useful an addition it will be in your users' daily lives, then it is less likely that they will want to add it to their watch face.

ClockKit generously gives you the opportunity to supply a presentation template for display when the user is scrolling through the range of complications available to them. This is just a normal CLKComplicationTemplate but should be configured with static data. Your data source will be asked for this only occasionally, so the data you supply should be applicable to more than just the instant it was requested.

The method you should implement to support this is getPlaceholderTemplateFor Complication(_:withHandler:). As per most of the data source methods, you will be supplied a complication parameter to determine the complication family to work with, as well as a handler that should be executed at the end of the method, with the template as a parameter.

For the example application, add the following method to the ComplicationController class:

```
func getPlaceholderTemplateForComplication(complication: CLKComplication,
    withHandler handler: (CLKComplicationTemplate?) -> Void) {

    let tweetDate = NSDate(timeIntervalSince1970: 499138500)
    let units: NSCalendarUnit = [.Year, .Month, .Day]
    let dateProvider = CLKDateTextProvider(date: tweetDate, units: units)

    let tweetText = "Drove Delorian. Traveled in time."
    let textProvider = CLKSimpleTextProvider(text: tweetText)

    let image = UIImage(named: "Complication/Modular")!
    let imageProvider = CLKImageProvider(onePieceImage: image)

    let placeholder = CLKComplicationTemplateModularLargeStandardBody()
    placeholder.headerTextProvider = dateProvider
    placeholder.body1TextProvider = textProvider
    placeholder.headerImageProvider = imageProvider

    handler(placeholder)
}
```

TESTING COMPLICATIONS

Once again, we have made you wait a long time to actually try out the code you have written. This is the point on your personal timeline when you finally get to see your complication in action.

If you created your complication with a new project (or target) template, then you will already have the test scheme that you need to start testing your complication—feel free to jump ahead to the "Running the Test Scheme" section. If you manually created your complication (possibly by following the steps in the earlier section "Adding a Complication to an Existing App"), then you will need to set up a test scheme.

CREATING THE TEST SCHEME

Thankfully, the process for creating a test scheme is not an arduous one. If you still have the Simple Life project from earlier, you can follow along with these steps:

1. From the Xcode main menu, select File > Product > Scheme > New Scheme.

2. In the scheme creation dialog, set the Target to **Simple Life WatchKit Extension**, and replace the generated Name setting with the more concise **Complication** (**Figure 7.15**).

FIGURE 7.15 Scheme creation settings for the Simple Life complication

3. Click OK to finish creating the scheme.

4. From the Xcode main menu, select File > Product > Scheme > Edit Scheme to open the scheme you just created.

5. Select the Run action, and open the Info tab.

6. Click the Executable popup menu, and select Simple Life WatchKit App.app.

   This will cause additional options to appear below the Executable popup menu.

7. Click the Watch Interface popup menu, and select Complication (**Figure 7.16**).

8. Click Close to save the changes.

FIGURE 7.16 The scheme settings required to test a complication

RUNNING THE TEST SCHEME

Now you're ready to actually start testing the complication.

1. Click the scheme selector popup menu to display the full list of available schemes (**Figure 7.17**).

FIGURE 7.17 Scheme selection popup menu showing the Complication test scheme

2. Click the complication test scheme to select it; ours is named Complication - I Said What? WatchKit App, but yours may be named something else (if, for example, you created it yourself).

3. Click the Run button to start testing the complication.

Xcode should build your app, then launch the Watch Simulator to the watch face. Unfortunately, it doesn't go to the trouble of configuring the watch face to display a complication, so you'll need to do that yourself.

As with a real device, you need to force touch the watch face to start configuring it.

4. In the simulator, press Command-Shift-2 to switch the simulator's Force Touch Pressure mode to Deep Press.

5. Click the watch face to enter configuration mode.

6. Press Command-Shift-1 to switch the Force Touch Pressure mode to Shallow Press.

7. If necessary, swipe left or right until you find the Modular watch face.

8. Click the Customize button to edit the Modular watch face.

9. Swipe from right to left to move into the complication configuration screen (**Figure 7.18**).

10. Click the large complication in the center of the watch face—this is the Modular Large complication family—and change the selected complication until it shows the I SAID WHAT? WATCHKIT APP complication (**Figure 7.19**).

   You can change the complication by two-finger scrolling with a trackpad, or by using the up and down arrow keys on the keyboard.

FIGURE 7.18 The complication configuration screen

FIGURE 7.19 Your complication when selected

TIP: If you don't like the I SAID WHAT? WATCHKIT APP name that is presented, you can change it by navigating to the General settings tab for the I Said What? WatchKit App target. Expand the Identity section and update the Display Name field.

11. Confirm your selection by pressing Command-Shift-2 and clicking the screen with a force touch.

12. Press Command-Shift-1, and click the Modular face to return to the watch face.

   The Modular watch face will be displayed, and your complication will be displayed. Witness its magnificence (**Figure 7.20**).

FIGURE 7.20 The I Said What? complication in action

Now that you have the complication running in the watch simulator, it would be nice to try out the Time Travel feature. To step back in time, use the down arrow key on the keyboard, or use a downward scroll gesture on your mouse or trackpad (**Figure 7.21**).

FIGURE 7.21 A historic tweet. Purely in terms of time, not significance.

You should be able to navigate through multiple "historic" tweets; however, when you go beyond 12 hours in the past, the complication will dim. This is because you told ClockKit that you intended to supply only 12 hours of past timeline entries with your implementation of the getTimelineStartDateForComplication(_:withHandler:) method.

If you try to go forward in time, you'll notice that the complication data does not change past the current timeline entry. This is because you haven't yet implemented the getTimelineEntriesForComplication(_:afterDate:limit:withHandler) method. You have two choices for how to handle this: either implement the method or change the getSupportedTimeTravelDirectionsForComplication(_:withHandler:) method to return .Backward only.

If there's one thing we've learned about time travel, it's that meddling with the past can break future timelines, so we'll leave that decision to you.

TRIGGERING COMPLICATION UPDATES

You know *how* ClockKit gets the timeline entries from your data source, but *when* does it make those requests? And what happens if your data changes? Fortunately, ClockKit has a number of mechanisms for scheduling updates, as well as for requesting updates on demand.

UPDATE METHODS

The simplest way to get ClockKit to check back with you for additional timeline entries is to tell it when you next think you'll have the information it requires. When the various timeline entry request methods have finished, ClockKit will call the getNextRequestedUpdateDateWithHandler(_:) method on your data source. When calling the handler, you can supply a date object that specifies a point in time after which you would like to provide more timeline entries.

In your complication, you said you would supply 6 hours' worth of data, so it makes sense to have your data source be queried again after 6 hours. To do this, you would implement the method as follows:

```
func getNextRequestedUpdateDateWithHandler(handler: (NSDate?) -> Void) {
    let sixHours = NSDate(timeIntervalSinceNow: 6 * 60 * 60)
    handler(sixHours);
}
```

Of course, you can't always be sure that the data you currently have will always be valid. There will be occasions when your user makes a change in their app (either on the watch or the phone) or when a push notification alerts you to the fact that the data has changed. You don't want your user to have an out-of-date complication, so it's vital that you have a way to tell ClockKit that the timeline entries it currently has may be outdated or need to be supplemented.

To do this, ClockKit provides you with a way to contact the complications server and ask it for references to any active complications your app currently has. You can instruct the server to either reload the entire timeline or simply extend the current timeline for a specific complication instance. You should be aware that if a user has configured multiple instances of your complication on the current watch face, you'll have multiple complication references to deal with. The following example shows how you could extend the existing timeline:

```
let server = CLKComplicationServer.sharedInstance()
let complications = server.activeComplications
for complication in complications {
    server.extendTimelineForComplication(complication)
}
```

In some circumstances you may realize that your entire timeline has become invalid, and simply extending the existing data will not be enough to remove the stale information. ClockKit provides a separate method on the complication server that you can use to force a reload of the entire timeline: reloadTimelineForComplication(_:).

We mentioned earlier that if you return nil from the getCurrentTimelineEntryForComplication(_:withHandler:) method, ClockKit would stop asking for future data. You can get yourself back on the request list by calling the reloadTimelineForComplication(_:) against the CLKComplicationServer.

Using this method is a somewhat drastic measure, and it's important that you use it with restraint. If you fail to do so, you might soon find out that your time budget will be exhausted.

BUDGETING

We're all used to budgeting in various aspects of our lives, but what exactly do we mean by budgeting when it comes to complications? Simply put, your data source gets only a certain amount of time with which to respond to requests from timeline entries. If ClockKit determines that you have exhausted your time budget, it will stop asking you for more entries.

The purpose of budgeting is to encourage developers to respond promptly to timeline entry requests. Prompt responses make the complication usage more fluid—especially when engaging in Time Travel—and reduce CPU usage and therefore power consumption. Power is a precious resource on the Apple Watch, and anything that can reduce consumption is a good thing.

Now that you know what happens if your complication data source misbehaves, you'll be on your best behavior, but what happens if your data source takes longer than expected on a few occasions and your time budget is exhausted? Is that it for your complication?

Fortunately not; your budget is reset every day, so even if you have a bad time one day and run out of budget, you'll still get a chance to run again tomorrow. Just be careful, though; if it happens too frequently it may be a sign that your data source is badly written or that your data is just not suited to being displayed as part of a complication.

Of course, the big question is this: How much time do you get in your daily budget? Unfortunately, Apple is not telling, so you'll just have to be on your very best behavior! Don't you understand how Apple works by now?

WRAPPING UP

If you feel exhausted, you are not alone. For something so insignificant and simple looking, complications can be very complicated. We think it has been worth it, though. A well-designed complication can display enough of your app's information to keep your user informed about your app without your user having to go in search of it. You might think it a bad thing, but trust us—your users will thank you for it.

In the next chapter, we take a look at a more detailed way for users to see a summary of your app information: glances.

CHAPTER 8

Working with Glances

If you were to look up the word *glance* in the OS X dictionary application, you would see that the first definition (to "take a brief or hurried look") is followed by an example usage: "Ginny glanced at her watch." Glances and watches are inextricably linked; the size and position of a wristwatch makes it ideal to glance at for quick information. It seems fitting then that Apple has used the word as the name for this feature.

WHAT IS A GLANCE?

Whereas a normal glance is a quick look at anything, a *glance* in Apple Watch terms is a short summary of information provided by an app that can be accessed quickly by swiping upward from the main watch face. Glances are displayed as a horizontal sequence of pages that bears a resemblance to a basic `UIPageViewController` layout in iOS. Once the sequence is accessed, the user can swipe from side to side to switch between the glances that they have configured for display (**Figure 8.1**).

FIGURE 8.1 A sequence of three glances from Apple-supplied apps

The content provided in a glance is intended to be a quick summary of your Watch app. It is restricted to a single screen of information; nothing happens when attempting to swipe upward, swiping downward dismisses the glances completely, and swiping sideways switches between glances. This limitation may provide something of a challenge to modern developers, providing an experience that may seem closer to the early days of mobile web browsers and WML (Wireless Markup Language) decks than to the expansive apps they are used to developing on iOS.

Not only is screen real estate in short supply, but so is the level of interaction you can offer to the user. Your glance is not a place to load with buttons as a jumping-off point for different parts of your app. Although you can customize and even animate and update the information in your glance, it is sadly lacking in the customizability that you might take for granted elsewhere in WatchKit. You do have one option available to you, however—tapping anywhere in the glance will take you straight to the corresponding Watch app.

A glance seems similar in concept to a notification; both are intended to convey a small amount of pertinent information for your app. However, the delivery of this information has a fundamental difference: A notification is delivered to the user as a push model, whereas a glance is, in effect, a pull of information.

Notifications can be delivered to the Watch through local channels (such as calendar or timer alerts) or from a remote source (such as a push notification service). This means that you as a developer have a degree of control over when the notification is displayed. You may be in control of the push notifications being sent to the user's phone, or you may have configured the local notifications. Regardless of how the information is being sent to the device, you are in control of the content and the timing of the delivery.

Glances are different in that they are completely user-driven. You have no say as to when users of your app will raise their wrists and swipe upward to start viewing glances. As a result, you cannot accurately predict when a glance will happen and prepare the information to be displayed in advance. This has an effect on how you develop your glance; the lack of foresight means you need to produce your glance quickly so that the user gets the information when they are ready, not when you are.

MANUFACTURING A GLANCE

A glance is a combination of artifacts, such as a storyboard scene to present the UI and source files to control the data that is presented to the user in the storyboard scene. You need to add these to your project and set them up appropriately for your Watch app to properly furnish a glance. You can add a glance to your project in two ways: You can either add one while creating the initial Watch app target or add one to an existing target.

CREATING A GLANCE IN A NEW PROJECT

To add a glance to a project as you are creating a new project, you need to ensure that the Include Glance Scene option has been selected in the iOS App with WatchKit App target options dialog. You did this in Chapter 1, but you may not have realized at the time the significance of selecting the option, so we'll repeat it here to refresh your memory.

1. Create a new project by selecting File > New > Project from the Xcode main menu.
2. In the project template selection dialog, navigate to the watchOS Application category, select the iOS App with WatchKit App template, and click Next.
3. Name the project **GlanceCommander**, and ensure that the Include Glance Scene option is selected in the template options (**Figure 8.2**).

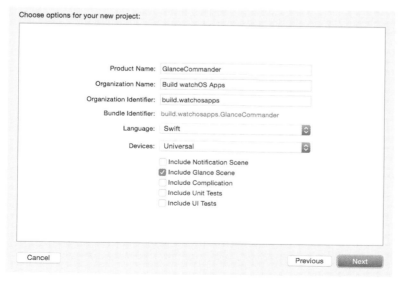

FIGURE 8.2 WatchKit App target options with the Include Glance Scene option selected

4. Click Next.

5. Choose a location on disk, and click Create to save your iOS app project, which includes a WatchKit app target with a glance.

This is the easiest way to create a glance, because the iOS App with WatchKit App project template sets up everything for you. It's definitely worth taking the time to create the glance when you create your project if you need a glance as part of your Watch app.

ADDING A GLANCE TO AN EXISTING PROJECT

If you have a change in requirements and need to add a glance to an existing Watch app, it is still possible to get in on the action, although with a few more hoops to jump through. The following walkthrough assumes you have an existing project that contains a WatchKit app target.

1. Open your existing project containing a WatchKit App target.

2. In the Project Navigator, select the file group containing the WatchKit extension.

3. Select File > New > File from the Xcode main menu.

4. In the new file template selection dialog, choose watchOS > Source > WatchKit Class, and click Next.

5. Adjust the new file template options so that the file is named `GlanceController` and is a subclass of `WKInterfaceController` (**Figure 8.3**), then click Next.

FIGURE 8.3 Creating a glance controller class by hand

Choose options for your new file:

Class:	GlanceController
Subclass of:	WKInterfaceController
Language:	Swift

Cancel · Previous · Next

6. Choose a location in which to save the new file, and ensure that the target is set to the WatchKit extension (**Figure 8.4**)

FIGURE 8.4 Select the WatchKit extension as the target for your glance controller.

7. Click Create to finish the process.

At this point you have a basic controller class that is capable of supporting the glance scene that you will create in the Watch app storyboard file.

8. In the Project Navigator, expand the file group containing the WatchKit App, and click the `Interface.storyboard` file to open it in Interface Builder.

9. Open the Object Library, and find the Glance Interface Controller option (**Figure 8.5**).

FIGURE 8.5 The glance interface controller in the Object Library

10. Drag the glance interface controller onto the storyboard canvas.

11. Ensure that the new glance scene is selected, open the Identity inspector, and enter `GlanceController` as the custom class (**Figure 8.6**).

Everything is ready from a code perspective, but one aspect of the new target template isn't quite matched yet; you still need to create a scheme so that it's possible to directly execute and test the glance.

FIGURE 8.6 The Custom Class setting for the glance scene

12. From the Xcode main menu, choose Product > Scheme > New Scheme.

13. In the Target menu, choose the target that corresponds to the WatchKit app, and give the scheme a name that identifies it as relating to a glance (**Figure 8.7**).

    We have named our scheme "Glance - GlanceEpidemic WatchKit App" to keep it consistent with the Apple naming conventions, but you are free to choose something shorter if you wish.

FIGURE 8.7 Settings for creating a scheme capable of running a glance

14. Click OK to create the scheme.
15. From the Xcode main menu choose the Product > Scheme > Edit Scheme command.
16. Select the Run action in the left panel, then select the Info tab, and change the Watch Interface pop-up menu from Main to Glance (**Figure 8.8**).

FIGURE 8.8 Changing the Run options to execute the scheme as a glance

17. Repeat step 15 for the Profile action, then click Close to save the changes.

    Although it's somewhat more complex to set up glances this way, it does have the added advantage of giving you a better understanding of how the glance (and the components that compose it) integrate into your project. It also gives you the opportunity to slap a hipster statement like "artisanally created" on your app website. After all, you just handcrafted your glance.

DEVELOPING THE GLANCE

Now that your app contains a minimal glance, the next step is to decide what it should look like, what to put in it, and how to keep it up to date.

VISUAL CUSTOMIZATION

The visual appearance of your glance is defined by what you can squeeze into the confines of the glance scene you created. The scene is a small rectangle, just 312 by 390 pixels for the larger watch size, and 272 by 340 pixels for the smaller watch. Combined with the lack of scrolling, these screen sizes mean that every pixel counts, and only the most critical information can be accommodated.

LAYOUT OPTIONS

When you first view a new glance interface controller scene in Interface.storyboard, it may contain either two empty group (WKInterfaceGroup) elements or a cornucopia of controls (**Figure 8.9**). Although it may be tempting to delete them and give yourself a blank canvas to work with, it's not so easily done. It's not possible to delete these elements, and they cannot be resized or moved. This is somewhat limiting, but the empty groups can be populated with other controls, allowing you to personalize your app.

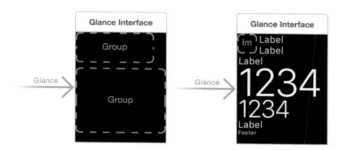

FIGURE 8.9 The default glance layout containing two group elements

Additionally, it is possible to choose from a collection of preset layouts that can be selected independently for the upper and lower portions of the glance. To access the presets, select the glance scene in Interface Builder and open the Attributes inspector (**Figure 8.10**). You can click the Upper and Lower groups to present a set of alternative layouts that provide enough variety to cover many app designs (**Figure 8.11**). When the canned layouts provided do not suit your design, you can customize them by using included subgroups.

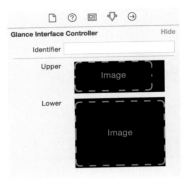

FIGURE 8.10 The predefined Upper and Lower groups in the default glance scene

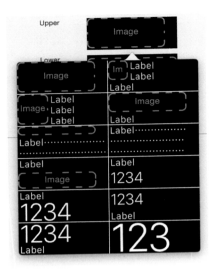

FIGURE 8.11 The preset customization options for the glance groups

STRICT CONTROLS

A fundamental limitation of glances is that they are restricted to a single interaction, in the form of a tap. Tapping the glance launches the full Watch app, although without any context; you can't know if the user tapped a specific control.

To reinforce this limitation, Apple does not support the use of some controls in a glance scene. Adding any of these restricted elements causes Xcode to display an error in the Log Navigator, and you'll be unable to compile and run your application (**Figure 8.12**). On the list of prohibited controls are buttons, pickers, movies, sliders, and switches.

FIGURE 8.12 Adding an interactive element to a glance is an illegal configuration.

Not so strictly controlled are maps and tables, though both come with big limitations. Maps (as discussed in Chapter 4) are restricted to a non-interactive view of a specified location. Unlike the Apple-supplied Maps glance, you cannot pan or zoom a map control in your own glance. Even tapping the map will not cause the map app to open. Instead, your app will be invoked as though you'd tapped anywhere else in the glance.

Similarly, you can take advantage of the table row controller to help you with presenting tabular data, but you are restricted to showing static data that will fit on the limited amount of space available to you. Any attempts by the user to scroll the table will result in a tap being registered by the glance, and the full Watch app will launch.

Given that you cannot use interactive controls to directly invoke part of your glance, there is no value in creating actions in the glance controller to handle interactions. You can still insert outlets to get programmatic interaction with elements such as labels and images that cannot be manipulated by the user.

THE GLANCE COMMANDER

As a practical example of glance user interface creation, you're going to start creating a small glance with an express purpose: let a glance commander tell you whether an activity should be stopped or is safe to continue. If you're not a fan of the six-piece band Electric 6, we apologize for this otherwise seemingly foolish example.

The glance commander UI is a simple one containing the name of the app and two elements indicating the current status. The active element will appear larger and colored, whereas the inactive element will be smaller and gray. To manually duplicate this behavior, open the GlanceCommander project that you created in the "Creating a Glance in a New Project" section, and follow these steps:

1. Expand the GlanceCommander WatchKit App group in the Project navigator, and select the Interface.storyboard file to open the storyboard.

2. Select the glance scene in Interface Builder, and open the Attributes inspector to display the Upper and Lower group templates (Figure 8.10).

3. Change the Upper group to display a small label on top and a larger label on the bottom. Leave the Lower group as a plain group (**Figure 8.13**).

4. Double-click the first label to change the text from Label to **Glance**. Change the text in the second label from Label to **COMMANDER**.

5. Set the Min Scale value to **0.6** in the Attributes inspector to make sure the label fits horizontally within the containing group.

6. Open the Object Library, locate the Table element, and drag it onto the lower group in the glance scene (**Figure 8.14**).

FIGURE 8.13 The Upper and Lower groups for the glance commander

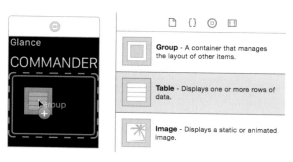

FIGURE 8.14 Dragging a Table element to the lower group

7. In the Attributes inspector, increase the number of Prototype Rows for the table to **2**.

   If the Table element is not selected after adding it in the previous step, you may need to use the document outline to select it. You can show the document outline by choosing Editor > Show Document Outline from the main Xcode menu.

8. Select the first table row controller, and set the Identifier to `GlanceCommandActive` in the Attributes Inspector.

9. Select the second table row controller, and set the Identifier to `GlanceCommandInactive`.

   To introduce some color and enlarge the active row so that it stands out some more, you need to make modifications to the groups contained within the table rows.

10. Select the group in the first table row so that the configurable attributes are displayed in the Attributes inspector (**Figure 8.15**).

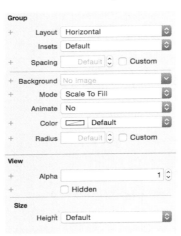

FIGURE 8.15 Configurable attributes for the Group element

11. Change the Height setting from Default to Fixed.

12. In the new field that appears, change the value to **60**.

13. Select the group in the second table row.

14. Change the Color setting to the Dark Gray Color preset.

15. Change the Height setting from Default to Fixed, and this time set the value to **40**.

    We now want to add some controls to the two table rows, as well as perform some basic styling.

16. In the Object Library, find the Label element, and drag one to the first table row.

17. Select the label in the first table row so that the configurable attributes are displayed in the Attributes inspector (**Figure 8.16**).

18. Change the Text field from Label to Active.

19. In the Font drop-down menu, choose the Headline option.

20. Change the Alignment control to the Centered option.

21. Under the Size section, set both the Width and Height options to Relative to Container.

22. Repeat steps 16 through 21 to make the changes for the second table row (changing the Text setting from Label to Inactive), resulting in a layout like that shown in **Figure 8.17**.

FIGURE 8.16 Configurable attributes for the Label element

FIGURE 8.17 A basic Active/Inactive configuration

Later, when using the glance, we want the ability to change the label text as well as the color of the groups. We also want to be able to specify the type and order of the table rows to be displayed, so you need to create some outlets to your glance controller, a subclass of WKInterfaceController.

WORKING WITH WKINTERFACECONTROLLER

A glance that is completely configured through a storyboard is useless to the user of your app. To be useful on more than one occasion it's important that the glance is capable of being updated with fresh data. As you might expect, this requires a companion controller, and a glance scene uses exactly the same type of WKInterfaceController as a standard interface scene.

CUSTOMIZING YOUR COMMANDS

When you first open your example glance, you don't know yet what the glance commander is going to instruct you to do. You also don't have any meaningful information to show the user, because you need to populate the table with inactivate rows. To access the table, we need to have an outlet through which you can programmatically control it.

1. Select the glance scene in Interface Builder, and click the Assistant button in the toolbar, ensuring that the assistant editor is displaying the GlanceController class.

2. Control-click the table element in the scene, and drag the mouse pointer across to the GlanceController class. Release the click when the Insert Outlet instruction appears where you want the outlet to be created.

3. In the popover that appears, name the outlet **commandTable**, and click Connect (**Figure 8.18**).

   To allow customization of the table rows, you need to define a class that you can use to connect to some outlets. Chapter 4 covers this in greater detail, so this will be a whistle-stop tour with the express purpose of getting set up for the next section.

FIGURE 8.18 Create the table outlet in the GlanceController class.

4. Right-click the GlanceCommander WatchKit Extension group in the Project Navigator, and select New File.

5. In the new file template chooser, navigate to watchOS, select Source, and select the WatchKit Class template. Click Next to continue.

6. Name the class GlanceCommand, and ensure that it is a subclass of NSObject and that the language is Swift. Click Next to continue.

7. Choose a location to save the file, and ensure that the target is set to GlanceCommander WatchKit Extension. Click Create to finish.

8. Replace the contents of the new file with the following code:

```
import WatchKit

class GlanceCommand: NSObject {
    @IBOutlet weak var group: WKInterfaceGroup!
    @IBOutlet weak var label: WKInterfaceLabel!

    func activateStop() {
        updateWithText("STOP!", UIColor.redColor())
    }

    func deactivateStop() {
        updateWithText("STOP!", UIColor.darkGrayColor())
```

```
        }

        func activateContinue() {
            updateWithText("CONTINUE!", UIColor.greenColor())
        }

        func deactivateContinue() {
            updateWithText("CONTINUE!", UIColor.darkGrayColor())
        }

        private func updateWithText(text: String, _ color: UIColor) {
            label.setText(text)
            group.setBackgroundColor(color)
        }
    }
```

Now, let's use the new class.

9. Open the Interface.storyboard file, and in the document outline select the Glance-CommandActive table row controller.

10. Open the Identity inspector, and enter GlanceCommand as the Custom Class (**Figure 8.19**).

11. Open the assistant editor, and ensure that the GlanceCommand.swift file is displayed as the counterpart.

12. In the document outline, expand the GlanceCommandActive table row controller.

13. Control-click the Group element, and drag the pointer over the @IBOutlet definition for the WKInterfaceGroup (**Figure 8.20**).

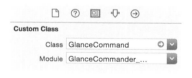

FIGURE 8.20 Connect the Group element to the group outlet.

FIGURE 8.19 Set the Custom Class for a table row controller to GlanceCommand.

14. Connect the Label element to the WKInterfaceLabel outlet.

15. Repeat steps 9 to 14 for the GlanceCommandInactive table row controller.

CONTROLLING THE GLANCE

Now that you have access to the glance from your controller, you can start to think about how you can manipulate the interface and, just as importantly, *when* you can manipulate the interface. Glances are intended to be very quick interactions, and this needs to be accounted for in their programming. Your priority will *always* be to make the user wait for as little time as possible to get information. If your glance is populated primarily by the app running on your watch, the wait should be quick. If, on the other hand, your glance requires information from the network, then a perceptible delay is possible due to the nature of Bluetooth communication with the iPhone (which the watch will mostly use for network access).

The best approach is to make the user feel that things are happening even when they are not. Although you could use a classic spinner to indicate progress, this is often the kiss of death for user attention. A better approach is to present the basic user interface as soon as possible, and update it when the required information becomes available.

For the example app, you want to ensure that the table will default to displaying two inactive rows while you wait for guidance to come from the glance commander.

1. Create a method named `activateCommands(stop:continue:)` in the GlanceController. swift file that does the heavy lifting:

```swift
private func activateCommands(stop stop: Bool, kontinue: Bool) {
    var commands = [String]()
    commands.append(stop ? "GlanceCommandActive" : "GlanceCommandInactive")
    commands.append(kontinue ? "GlanceCommandActive" :
"GlanceCommandInactive")

    commandTable.setRowTypes(commands)
    let command1 = commandTable.rowControllerAtIndex(0) as! GlanceCommand
    let command2 = commandTable.rowControllerAtIndex(1) as! GlanceCommand
    stop ? command1.activateStop() : command1.deactivateStop()
    kontinue ? command2.activateContinue() : command2.deactivateContinue()
}
```

NOTE: Because `continue` is a reserved word in Swift, we've taken the traditional approach of substituting the C for a K (for example, `class` becomes `klass` and `continue` becomes `kontinue`).

2. Initialize both rows as inactive by adding the following code to the `willActivate()` method:

```swift
override func willActivate() {
    super.willActivate()
    activateCommands(stop: false, kontinue: false)
}
```

SNEAKING A GLANCE

You've spent quite a bit of time preparing the glance, but you have yet to see it in action. Running a glance in the Watch simulator is not quite as straightforward as accessing the glances directly on the hardware. Although you can swipe upward to view glances in a running simulator, you won't find your glance among them. Fortunately, it's possible to launch a Watch app directly to a specific interface mode (Main, Glance, or Notification) that can be configured through the Scheme editor. For more information, refer to the "Manufacturing a Glance" section earlier in this chapter. Let's run the GlanceCommander example.

1. Choose the Glance - GlanceCommander WatchKit App scheme from the scheme selector pop-up menu.

2. Click Run, and prepare to await your command.

   Although it's nice to finally see the glance in action, we currently find ourselves waiting for a command that never comes (**Figure 8.21**). Remember that feeling, because that is what you want the users of your glance to never experience.

   To simulate an update, you'll create an updateCommands() method that randomly chooses a command to be issued to the user. To further simulate waiting, you'll use Grand Central Dispatch (GCD) to delay the execution of this update by one second.

FIGURE 8.21 Awaiting instructions from the glance commander...

3. Add the following code to handle the updates:

```
private func updateCommands() {
    let delayTime = dispatch_time(DISPATCH_TIME_NOW,
        Int64(1 * Double(NSEC_PER_SEC)))
    dispatch_after(delayTime, dispatch_get_main_queue()) {
        if (arc4random_uniform(2) != 0) {
            self.activateCommands(stop: false, kontinue: true)
        } else {
            self.activateCommands(stop: true, kontinue: false)
        }
    }
}
```

4. Add the following highlighted code to the `willActivate()` method to cause the update to be triggered:

```
override func willActivate() {
    super.willActivate()
    activateCommands(stop: false, kontinue: false)
    updateCommands()
}
```

5. Try it for yourself. Run the app, and see if you should stop or continue (**Figure 8.22**).

FIGURE 8.22 Stop! or Continue!

This is a very simple example, but the pattern it illustrates can be extrapolated out to handle real-world data. Initiating a costly (in terms of time) task as soon as the glance is ready, and updating the UI when the required data has been received, is the ideal way to ensure that your user feels like something is happening and that the glance hasn't just silently failed.

WRAPPING UP

In this chapter, you learned how to add a glance to your WatchKit app and what you can, and can't, do within that glance. We've also discussed the techniques that you can apply to make the user experience of viewing your glance as pleasant as possible.

Next, we'll look at notifications, the push operation to a glance's pull. Whereas a glance has to request data to be displayed, a notification is fed some initial information, which adjusts the dynamic of how it's designed and implemented.

CHAPTER 9

Working with Notifications

The ability to receive notifications directly, and discreetly, to your wrist is a top selling point of the Apple Watch for many users. Although every notification that an iPhone receives can be displayed on the watch, it requires a bit more effort to make sure the notifications your app users receive are tailored to the new device and its capabilities.

WHAT ARE NOTIFICATIONS?

Although using apps, browsing the web, or scanning a Twitter timeline are actions initiated and driven by the users of mobile devices, notifications are how the devices, or the sites and services they subscribe to, can get your attention—usually when you're about to settle down to a productive writing session. The nature of the relationship between the Apple Watch and the iPhone means that notifications follow something of a two-tier existence—starting life on the phone and making their way to the watch.

iPHONE NOTIFICATIONS

Notifications on the iPhone are by no means a new experience to most users, but there's a good chance that users are not completely aware of where they come from and who, or what, creates them. They can be broken down into two general categories: remote and local.

REMOTE NOTIFICATIONS

A remote notification is one that has been created by an online system and has been pushed to a device. The concept of push notifications to mobile devices was established in the late 1990s through the use of UP.Notify and WAP Push technologies, but the modern equivalent for iOS devices is the Apple Push Notification Service (APNS).

When an iPhone has network access (via Wi-Fi or cellular) it establishes a long-lived connection to servers maintained by Apple. While connected to these servers, the APNS has a direct connection to the iPhone and can send it information such as new mail notifications and iMessages received. The APNS also has a public interface that trusted third-party developers can use; the developers can send to the APNS carefully formatted messages that have been targeted for a specific app on a specific user's device. If the message is valid, and the sender is authorized, the APNS will deliver a notification directly to the device if it is currently connected, or dispatch it later if the device is offline.

LOCAL NOTIFICATIONS

When most people think about iOS notifications, they tend to focus on remote notifications and overlook the obvious: local notifications. If you have ever created a calendar event with an alert, or a reminder with an alarm, you have received a local notification on your device. Local notifications are not limited to first-party apps created by Apple; third-party developers have access to a local notification API that they can use to trigger timed or scheduled notifications, or even to provide an alert as part of a background job.

It's therefore important to consider locally originated notifications in the same way as remote notifications. As far as the user is concerned, notifications arrive at their phone in the same way, and so local notifications are dispatched similarly to the watch regardless of origin.

WATCH NOTIFICATIONS

Apple Watch does not have the ability to receive direct notifications from third-party apps by itself; any notifications you wish your watch app to display must originate from a remote service via APNS or be triggered locally on the user's iPhone. So how does the notification get from the phone to the watch?

GETTING A NOTIFICATION TO THE WATCH

On receipt of a notification, iOS and the target phone app have a number of decisions to make. Is the app that the message is intended for still installed on the device? Does the user have Do Not Disturb enabled? Is the app currently running? Is the app in the foreground or the background? And of course, iOS now has an additional decision: Does the iPhone have an Apple Watch paired? As a developer, you have no say over the decision-making process, but it certainly helps to be aware of what is happening.

When a notification is received by the iPhone, iOS performs a number of checks:

- If the user *is* using the phone at the time and is using the target app, the app accepts and handles the notification directly.

- If the user *is* using the phone at the time and *is not* using the target app, the notification is displayed at the top of the screen in a notification banner.

- If the user *is not* using the phone at the time and *is also not wearing* the watch, then the notification is displayed on the lock screen of the phone.

- If the user *is not* using the phone at the time and *is wearing* the watch, then the wearer will feel a "tap" from the haptic feedback mechanism, though the screen will not light up.

> **TIP:** When it comes to testing both local and remote notifications using real devices, make sure to put your phone to sleep or you won't get the notifications delivered to your watch!

Although it may seem like a miracle that a notification gets to the watch at all, it really happens quite often, so it's time to think about how you want to present your notifications to your users.

WHILE THE APP IS ACTIVE

One annoyance many users had with watchOS 1 was that notifications were an interruption even while they were actively using the app that had received the notification. This was a source of frustration for developers as well; if you had an app with a stream of information (like a Twitter client, a messaging service, or a podcast feed), your users would be interrupted with a notification when what you really wanted was to simply update the UI in response.

Thankfully, Apple has remedied this in watchOS 2, and it's now possible for your app to respond directly to incoming notifications if it's already active. To achieve this, you must implement one or more optional methods on the class that implements the WKExtensionDelegate protocol—in most templates this will be the ExtensionDelegate class.

The methods you need to implement are didReceiveRemoteNotification() or didReceiveLocalNotification(). They receive a copy of the notification and can pass the information off to whichever part of the app is active at the time.

THE SHORT LOOK

If the user is not actively using the app receiving the notification, they will feel a haptic "tap" of a notification arriving, and will commonly respond by raising the watch to see what app or service the notification was for. At this point, the watch will display a simple view that Apple has named a *short look*.

The short look is an almost completely static view that is displayed for just a few seconds. It consists of three interface elements: the app icon, a title string for the notification, and the app name (**Figure 9.1**). Your only customization option here is the title string. It's defined in the notification itself, so if your app supports Apple Watch, you should endeavor to make sure there is enough information in the title—usually the first two or three words—to adequately inform the user.

FIGURE 9.1 The short-look interface

THE LONG LOOK

Should the user continue to keep their watch raised while the short look is being displayed, it will be replaced with a view named the *long look*. So far, notifications have been fairly inflexible with regard to customization, but this is where it all changes. The long look comes in two further flavors: static and dynamic.

The *static notification* is a single page of information that cannot be programmatically updated. That is not to say that the notification does not change at all—the message body and the action buttons can vary according to the payload of the notification—but the customization must all be carried out in the static interface scene in the Interface.storyboard file and is baked into your application at compile time.

If you want to customize your static interface scene based on the type of notification to be handled, you can take advantage of notification categories. Notification payloads contain a category field, and you as a developer can set this to whatever you want; for example, you might want to have a calendarInvite category for new meeting requests and a calendarAlert category to remind the user to attend an imminent meeting. Static interface scenes can specify a category to which they should respond, and you can create multiple static interface scenes for handling different notification categories.

Alternatively, a *dynamic notification* can be displayed by including a dynamic interface scene in your storyboard; this is an optional extra to the static interface scene, and it comes with a whole lot more capability. The interface scene for a dynamic notification can be customized to a much greater extent than the static notification, and more importantly it can be updated programmatically by implementing a subclass of the WKUserNotificationInterfaceController (described in more detail later).

As a developer, you have only one way that you can force which type of long-look notification to display and that is by implementing only the static interface scene. Otherwise, it is up to watchOS to determine the type of long look to display. The predetermined nature of the static interface scene means that it can be displayed in many more situations than the dynamic interface scene. When battery life is limited, or the network connection to the paired iPhone is not functioning correctly, the watch may stick with the static interface scene so that the user experience is not compromised.

Given the large amount of customization that you can perform to both static and dynamic interface scenes, how do you add this capability to Watch apps? If your development schedule is tight, you'll be pleased to know that any iOS app that runs on the iPhone is capable of delivering a plain notification style to the watch. Although this is perfectly functional, it employs a very standard template and doesn't allow your app to stand out. To really make the notification your own, you need to create a notification interface scene in your storyboard.

CREATING A NOTIFICATION SCENE

As with glances, there are two ways to create a notification scene in your own app: at target creation time and as a storyboard modification. Unlike with glances, however, it's possible to create more than one notification scene per app, so although you'll often create a notification scene up front, it's very possible that you'll want to create an additional notification scene by hand at a later stage.

CREATING A NOTIFICATION IN A NEW PROJECT

Adding a notification to a new project requires that you select the Include Notification Scene option in the options dialog for the iOS App with WatchKit App project template.

1. Create a new project by selecting File > New > Project from the Xcode main menu.

2. In the project template selection dialog, navigate to the watchOS Application category, select the iOS App with WatchKit App template, and click Next.

3. Give the project a name, and customize the template options to ensure that the Include Notification Scene option is selected (**Figure 9.2**).

    We're going to name this project **Heres Me**; it's a location- and status-sharing project for natives of Belfast, Northern Ireland.

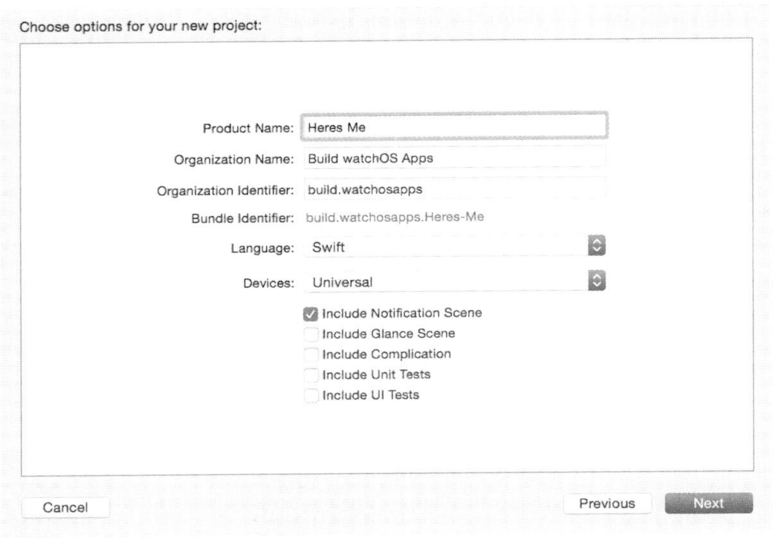

FIGURE 9.2 WatchKit App target options with the Include Notification Scene option selected

Choose options for your new project:

Product Name: Heres Me
Organization Name: Build watchOS Apps
Organization Identifier: build.watchosapps
Bundle Identifier: build.watchosapps.Heres-Me
Language: Swift
Devices: Universal

☑ Include Notification Scene
☐ Include Glance Scene
☐ Include Complication
☐ Include Unit Tests
☐ Include UI Tests

Cancel   Previous   Next

4. Click Next to proceed to the save dialog.

5. Choose a location on disk, and click Create to save it.

The result of this process will be two additional scenes in `Interface.storyboard` that provide both static and dynamic notification capabilities (**Figure 9.3**). You'll also be the proud owner of a Swift file named `NotificationController.swift` in the Heres Me WatchKit Extension group, and a file named `PushNotificationPayload.apns` under Supporting Files in the same group. We'll talk more about this file later when it comes to testing notifications.

FIGURE 9.3 Freshly minted static and dynamic notification scenes

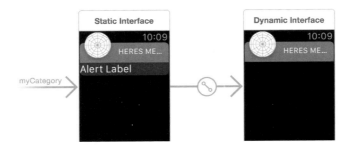

ADDING A NOTIFICATION TO AN EXISTING PROJECT

Maybe you forgot to add a notification when you first created your Watch app, or maybe you just want to add an additional notification handler. Adding notification handling is a relatively painless process, so let's add an additional notification type to the scene you created in the previous section:

1. In the Project Navigator, expand the WatchKit App group, and click the `Interface.storyboard` file to open it in Interface Builder.

2. Open the Object Library, and find the Notification Interface Controller (**Figure 9.4**).

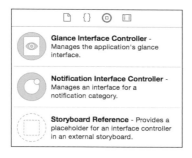

FIGURE 9.4 The Notification Interface Controller in the Object Library

3. Drag the Notification Interface Controller onto the storyboard canvas.

Be aware that the Notification Interface Controller *always* produces a static/dynamic notification pairing when added to the storyboard.

If you don't want them all and only want an additional static scene, add the pair, select the static scene, open the Attributes inspector, and deselect the Has Dynamic Interface option.

To add a dynamic scene to a static scene, select the Has Dynamic Interface option again. You can even connect two or more static scenes to a single dynamic scene (thus sharing code) by Control-clicking the unpaired static scene and dragging to the body of the dynamic scene—a popup will be displayed offering you the opportunity to create a dynamic notification relationship segue.

You now have two static notification scenes and a dynamic scene all ready to be worked with. Before you can start writing any code, you need to determine what the notification interactions will be and how they can be presented to the user.

DESIGNING YOUR NOTIFICATIONS

The Heres Me app can receive two types of notifications: location updates and status updates. The key information for each type varies—location updates need to display the location, whereas status updates need to display the status—so you need to customize the notification layout accordingly.

NOTIFICATION LAYOUT

Understanding the layout of the notification can help you make the most of the space available to you. The default static notification layout can be seen in **Figure 9.5**. The position of the sash (the area containing the app icon and the app name) is fixed, and the action buttons (not shown while in Interface Builder) will move up or down depending on the size of the content area you create. The number of buttons and their labels are controlled by registering notification actions in your iOS app.

FIGURE 9.5 The static notification interface layout

Notification actions are a means by which your iOS app can specify the action buttons to display alongside a notification. The buttons can be customized on a per-notification category basis if you wish, and the same actions will be passed down to the watch if the notification is not going to be displayed on the phone. For more information about notification actions, have a look at the Apple documentation for local and remote notification programming (bit.ly/bwa-notif-guide).

The content area is where the real customization takes place. As with glances, there are limitations to what can be included in the content area; once again, you cannot take advantage of interactive controls such as sliders, switches, and buttons, though you do of course get a set of buttons for free if you have registered notification actions in your iOS app.

If you are using a static notification scene, you must include a label that is linked to a `notificationAlertLabel` outlet by default (**Figure 9.6**). You are free to delete the existing label (or simply reconfigure it), but your project will fail to build unless a label is connected to the outlet.

NOTE: Although the dynamic notification scene also has the same `notificationAlertLabel` outlet, you won't get in trouble if it isn't hooked up.

This label is your only way to display content from the notification payload in a static notification scene, because it isn't possible to change the underlying view controller for a static scene. When the scene is displayed, the alert label is updated, as are the action buttons, and everything else remains, well, static!

FIGURE 9.6 The `notificationAlertLabel` outlet is essential.

If you want to be able to customize and programmatically update the notification scene, you instead have to rely on a dynamic notification scene, which we will examine in a later section of this chapter.

STATIC NOTIFICATIONS

The basic notification that your app needs to deal with is the status update notification. Although a status update could contain a lot of distinct information, which your main Watch app should be capable of handling at some stage, we're going to assume that the notification will send a simple string that contains both the name of the sender and its status. For example, a user named Wez could send a status notification like this: "Wez says: headin downa art callidge wimme glubeg!"

If your notification payload contains the status message as the body property, it will replace the content of the label currently displaying the text "Alert Label." If you use the default configuration for the static scene, you will quickly be disappointed because the text will be truncated. You would also like the status message to be right-aligned, which is the convention that makes it look as though it was said by someone else:

1. Select the alert label on the static notification scene that has no dynamic scene associated with it.

2. Open the Attributes inspector to show the normal attributes available for a WKInterfaceLabel.

3. Change the Width attribute to Relative to Container.

4. Change the Alignment attribute to right-aligned.

5. Change the Lines attribute to 0.

    It would be useful to have a clear indicator that this message is something that was said by someone else, so you will add a custom label to the content area.

6. Open the Object Library, and find a Label element.

7. Drag the Label element over the static scene, and make sure it is located *above* the alert label.

8. Open the Attributes inspector.

9. Change the Text attribute to **Yer mucker sez:**.

10. Click the Font attribute, and change it from Body to System Italic.

11. Change the font size to 12.

    So the user can immediately tell what type of notification has been received, you will use different sash colors to distinguish the *status* notification from a *location* notification.

12. Select the notification category for the scene (the arrow that points *into* the scene from the left side).

13. Open the Attributes inspector.

14. Change the Sash Color attribute to a hex value of #D00000—you can do this through the RGB sliders on the standard color picker.

15. Change the Name attribute to `statusNotification`. You will use this later to customize your notification payload.

You now have a distinct style and layout for your status notification (**Figure 9.7**), but the other static notification for location updates looks a bit plain in comparison.

16. Repeat steps 1 through 15 for the other static notification scene but with the following changes:

- For step 9, set the label text to **Yer muckers at:**.
- For step 14, set the Sash Color attribute to #00D000.
- For step 15, set the Name attribute to `locationNotification`.

The location update notification now has a layout that's consistent with the status notification (**Figure 9.8**).

FIGURE 9.7 The static status update notification design

FIGURE 9.8 The static location update notification design

DYNAMIC NOTIFICATIONS

At a bare minimum, the location update will display a textual representation of the user's location, but ideally it would also feature a map representation, where network access permits. You could include the map in the static notification, but we would like to reserve the static notification for quick information that doesn't require loading of extra data (for example, map tiles).

Instead, you'll take advantage of the dynamic notification, which can perform live processing of the notification information to determine exactly what to display. If the location update contains a geolocation field, you can choose to display a Map element that can be hidden otherwise.

Start by replicating the location update labels in the dynamic notification scene.

1. Select the dynamic interface scene in the `Interface.storyboard` file.
2. From the Object Library, drag two Label elements to the dynamic scene.
3. Select the first Label element, and open the Attributes inspector.
4. Change the Text attribute to **Yer muckers at:**.

5. Click the Font attribute, and change it from Body to System Italic.

6. Change the font size to 12.

7. Select the second Label element.

8. Change the Width attribute to Relative to Container.

9. Change the Alignment attribute to right-aligned.

10. Change the Lines attribute to **0**.

    Your dynamic notification now matches the static location notification, but you still need the map.

11. From the Object Library, drag a Map element onto the dynamic notification scene, ensuring it's located below the two labels (**Figure 9.9**).

FIGURE 9.9 The dynamic location update notification design

The scene has been set, but the dynamic aspect of the dynamic notification needs to be controlled by something. As you would expect, there's a controller for that.

THE WKUSERNOTIFICATIONINTERFACECONTROLLER

Because you selected the Include Notification Scene option at project creation time, Xcode created a file named NotificationController.swift in the Heres Me Watch-Kit Extension file group. It contains a class named NotificationController, which is a subclass of WKUserNotificationInterfaceController (itself a specialized subclass of WKInterfaceController).

As well as having access to the normal lifecycle methods of WKInterfaceController (covered in detail in Chapter 3), it also has two extra callback methods that you can use to customize your dynamic notification scene in response to the local or remote notification. The method didReceiveRemoteNotification(_:withCompletion:) will be called when watchOS has received a remote notification destined for your app, and the method didReceiveLocalNotification(_:withCompletion:) can be used in the same way for local notifications. In both cases, you should remember to execute the supplied completion block to ensure that watchOS knows you have finished processing the notification.

To achieve the best results, you should perform any initial setup in the init() method as usual, process the notification in the appropriate callback method, and perform any additional setup in the willActivate() method.

In addition, you have two other optional methods that can be implemented: suggestionsForResponseToActionWithIdentifier(_:forRemoteNotification: inputLanguage:) and suggestionsForResponseToActionWithIdentifier(_: forLocalNotification:inputLanguage:). These can be implemented when handling notifications that require a text response from the user. This is covered in the section "Text Responses" later in this chapter.

For our example, you need to have access to the lower Label element and the Map element to change their values in response to the notification payload. You can do this by adding some outlets to NotificationController that are connected to the UI elements.

1. Open the Interface.storyboard file, and ensure that the assistant editor is open and displaying the NotificationController.swift file.

2. Control-click the lower Label element, and drag it into the assistant editor to create an outlet named alertLabel (**Figure 9.10**).

FIGURE 9.10 Creating an outlet for the Label element

3. Control-click the Map element, and drag it into the assistant editor to create an outlet named locationMap.

   You now have the ability to change the UI, but you need to extract payload data in order to do so.

4. Replace the commented-out didReceiveRemoteNotification(:withCompletion:) method with the following code:

```
override func didReceiveRemoteNotification(remoteNotification:
→ [NSObject : AnyObject], withCompletion completionHandler:
→ ((WKUserNotificationInterfaceType) -> Void)) {
    let apsDictionary = remoteNotification["aps"] as! NSDictionary
    let alertDictionary = apsDictionary["alert"] as! NSDictionary
```

```
let bodyText = alertDictionary["body"] as! String
let locationCoord = alertDictionary["locationCoord"] as! String
let (location, region) =
  → createLocationAndRegionFromCoordinate(locationCoord)

alertLabel.setText(bodyText)
locationMap.setRegion(region)
locationMap.addAnnotation(location, withPinColor: .Red)

completionHandler(.Custom)
}
```

Most of the method involves the extraction of data from the notification, which is received as a dictionary. You already know that the dictionary contains a property named aps, which references another dictionary and which in turn contains a property, named alert, that contains yet another dictionary of properties. These properties are parsed to extract the data that is needed to populate the label and the map.

5. Add a helper method named createLocationAndRegionFromCoordinate() to the same file using the following code:

```
func createLocationAndRegionFromCoordinate(coordinate: String)
    -> (CLLocationCoordinate2D, MKCoordinateRegion) {
    let coordinateArray =
        coordinate.characters.split { $0 == "," }.map(String.init)
    let lat = (coordinateArray[0] as NSString).doubleValue
    let long = (coordinateArray[1] as NSString).doubleValue
    let location = CLLocationCoordinate2DMake(lat, long)

    let span = MKCoordinateSpanMake(0.1, 0.1)
    let region = MKCoordinateRegionMake(location, span)

    return (location, region)
}
```

Now you're ready to test the code and view the notification you've just created, but how exactly do you do that?

TESTING NOTIFICATIONS

Testing the notification-handling capabilities of your app requires that you have a notification payload to send and a means of sending it to your app. When testing with a real device, it's advantageous to have access to an APNS, but in the early stages of development you'll likely be using a simulator, which is more difficult to send pushes to. Fortunately, Xcode and the watchOS SDK provide a way to directly launch your app in notification-handling mode with a specific payload.

NOTIFICATION PAYLOADS

Xcode helpfully provided a file named PushNotificationPayload.apns when you created your project; you can find this file in the Supporting Files subgroup of the WatchKit Extension file group in the Project Navigator. This file contains an example of the data that your app can receive when it receives a push notification.

It takes the format of a JSON dictionary containing two properties that will be processed by the simulator when the payload is received: aps and WatchKit Simulator Actions. The sample contains a third property (customKey) that exists solely as a comment and is not actively processed by the simulator. We have reproduced the sample content that follows (without customKey) for ease of reference as we discuss it further.

```
{
    "aps": {
        "alert": {
            "body": "Test message",
            "title": "Optional title"
        },
        "category": "myCategory"
    },

    "WatchKit Simulator Actions": [
        {
            "title": "First Button",
            "identifier": "firstButtonAction"
        }
    ]
}
```

THE APS PROPERTY

The aps property represents the data that would be received by a real device when a push notification has been received. Associated with the property is another dictionary containing two more properties: alert and category.

- alert

  The alert property contains yet another dictionary that is home to the real substance of the notification—two properties named body and title. The use of these properties depends on the way the notification is being displayed:

  - Short look: The title property is optional, but it is worth including whenever you can do so; if watchOS finds that property in your payload, it will substitute it into a short-look notification. This makes the difference between your app displaying just the name of your app or instead displaying some useful information. **Figure 9.11** shows the difference between short-look displays for notifications that do and don't include title. It also highlights the fact that the title property has limited space to occupy (and is displayed for a short time), so keep the title short but meaningful!

FIGURE 9.11 Short-look notifications without title (left) and with title (right)

  - Static long look: If you have included a static notification scene in your storyboard, then the body property is the bare minimum that you should include in your test data. The value associated with this key is a text string that watchOS will inject into the notificationAlertLabel in the static notification scene.

  - Dynamic long look: A dynamic notification scene does not actually require either the body or title property; you write the code, so you are free to extract whatever data you wish from the notification payload. However, we still recommend including the properties because there is no guarantee that your dynamic scene will be displayed. Remember that watchOS can decide when to show the static and dynamic scenes, and the short look can be displayed as well.

- category

  When creating your static notification scenes earlier (in the section "Designing Your Notifications"), you did so with the intention of having two different notification types: status and location. You were able to do this by updating the Name attribute in the Notification Category element in the storyboard (**Figure 9.12**).

FIGURE 9.12 Configuring the status update notification category

The category property in the alert dictionary corresponds directly to the value entered in the Name attribute of the Notification Category element in the storyboard. When a notification is received by a watchOS app, it can inspect the category property value and direct the payload to the static notification scene with the same Name attribute.

WATCHKIT SIMULATOR ACTIONS

The aps property of the payload file is included to simulate the data received as part of a push notification, but the WatchKit Simulator Actions property is unique to the payload file created by Xcode, and will not be sent to a real device from the APNS. The purpose of this property is to allow you to add a collection of actions to your device based on the actions that your parent iOS app would respond to.

This may seem confusing—after all, we're talking about the watch so why are we concerned with the iOS app—but it makes more sense when you consider that notifications are part of the larger ecosystem. At the beginning of the chapter we explained that notifications are first delivered to the iPhone, which makes the decision to display or forward to the watch. iOS apps have an API that allows developers to register actions that are associated with a notification for display to the user. For example, Apple's own Mail app offers the user an opportunity to reply to or archive/delete an email from the lock screen or when a banner notification is tapped.

The sample payload in Xcode includes the WatchKit Simulator Actions so that the simulator can receive and parse a collection of actions as though they had come from the iOS device. The property value itself is composed of an array, each element of which represents an action in the form of a dictionary. Each action requires a title property—the text displayed on the button—and an identifier property—the unique identifier that is passed to watchOS so that it knows which button the user actually tapped. An additional, optional property named destructive can be supplied; it takes a 1 or a 0 to indicate whether the button should be displayed in a way that indicates a destructive action (where 1 represents the destructive action).

NOTE: watchOS automatically adds a Dismiss button for you, so there is no need to create it for yourself.

To handle notification actions, you must implement a number of optional methods on the ExtensionDelegate class—this is a class that implements the WKExtensionDelegate protocol and is found in the file named ExtensionDelegate.swift in the default Xcode project templates. The methods are named handleActionWithIdentifier(_: forRemoteNotification:) and handleActionWithIdentifier(_:forLocalNotification:), and, as the names suggest, they apply to remote and local notifications, respectively.

How you handle the actions is up to you and your application logic, but a suggested pattern would be to use a switch statement using the identifier parameter. This parameter tells you which button the user tapped, and you can call for each identifier a separate method that contains logic specific to the type. The identifier parameter can be an empty string in the circumstance where the user didn't tap an action button but instead tapped elsewhere on the notification to launch the app. You also receive a copy of the notification so that you have some context on what the user has responded to.

An additional pair of methods can be implemented if you have allowed the user to make a text response to the notification. These methods have the same format as those listed previously, but also include the text response from the user as an additional parameter. The methods are named handleActionWithIdentifier(_:forRemoteNotification: withResponseInfo:) and handleActionWithIdentifier(_:forLocalNotification: withResponseInfo:). You can learn more about text responses in the "Text Responses" section later in this chapter.

CREATING ADDITIONAL PAYLOADS

You have more than one notification category for your app, so you'll need more than one payload file to test with. Rather than just editing the existing file, you will instead create two new files and populate them with test data—you can delete the existing one if you wish. To create a new payload file:

1. Right-click the Supporting Files subgroup within the Heres Me WatchKit Extension, and select the New File command from the popup menu.

2. In the new file template chooser, choose iOS > Apple Watch, select the Notification Simulation File option, and click Next (**Figure 9.13**).

> **NOTE:** The location of the Notification Simulation File option in the iOS category may be a mistake in the current version, and it's possible that it may have been moved by the time you read this. If so, you may find it under the watchOS category instead.

FIGURE 9.13 The Notification Simulation File template in the new file template chooser

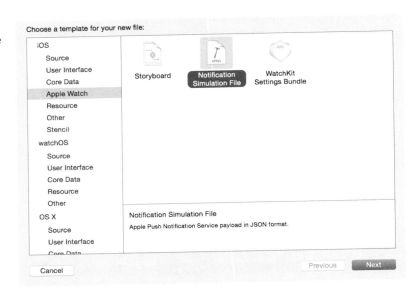

3. Choose a location to save the file, give it a name—we used `PushNotificationPayload-status.apns`—and click Next.

   You don't need to worry about including the file in a target; it isn't going to be bundled with any of the app or test targets.

4. Repeat steps 1 to 3 to create a second file; this time we named it `PushNotificationPayload-location.apns`.

5. Open the first payload (for the status category), and update it with the following test data:

```
{
    "aps": {
        "alert": {
            "body": "Headin downa snooks",
            "title": "Status Update"
        },
        "category": "statusNotification"
    },
    "WatchKit Simulator Actions": [
        {
            "title": "Reply",
            "identifier": "statusReplyAction"
        }
    ]
}
```

You've added the status message to the body property, and set the `title` property to "Status Update" so that the type of notification is clearer on a short look. The `category` property has been set to `statusNotification` so that it matches the status notification scene.

You also added a single action to the `Watch Simulator Actions` property. The Reply button is intended to trigger a `statusReplyAction` so that the user can instantly reply to their friend's status and attempt to top it.

6. Repeat step 5 for the second payload (for the location category) with the following test data:

```
{
    "aps": {
        "alert": {
            "body": "Already downa Art Callidge",
            "title": "Location Update",
            "locationCoord": "54.603264, -5.929300"
        },
        "category": "locationNotification"
    },
    "WatchKit Simulator Actions": [{
            "title": "Post Location",
            "identifier": "postLocationAction"
        }, {
            "title": "Reply",
            "identifier": "locationReplyAction"
        }
    ]
}
```

Again you've added the body and `title` properties, and set the category property to be `locationNotification` so that it matches the location scene. You have also added a custom property named `locationCoord` with a value containing a coordinate that can be extracted by the dynamic notification.

NOTIFICATION TEST SCHEMES

Now that you know how to get the data into a payload file, how do you go about sending it to the simulator for testing? Apple has solved this problem with schemes in Xcode. When you created the project, the template included a scheme named Notification - Heres Me WatchKit App. Selecting and running the scheme will cause Xcode to start the watchOS simulator, launch the Heres Me app in a notification handling mode, and inject a payload file to be handled.

To use the one of the new payload files you just created, you need to update the scheme.

1. Select Product > Scheme > Manage Schemes from the Xcode main menu.

2. Click the scheme name—Notification - Heres Me WatchKit App—and change it to **Status Notification**; a bit of brevity never hurt nobody.

3. Ensure that the Status Notification scheme is highlighted, and click the Edit button.

4. Select the Run action, click the Watch Interface popup menu, and select the Static Notification option, if it is not already selected (**Figure 9.14**).

FIGURE 9.14 The Run action for the status notification scene

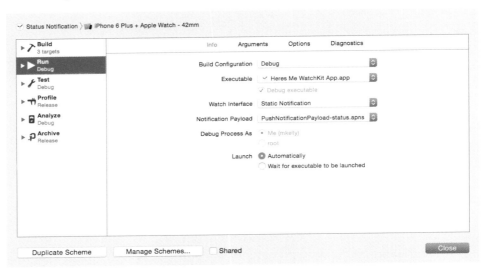

5. Click the Notification Payload popup menu, and select the PushNotificationPayload-status.apns option.

6. Click Close.

7. Click Run to test the status notification.

   The iOS and watchOS simulators should start up, and after a little initialization time, the status notification will be displayed (**Figure 9.15**). Not only is the correct status message displayed, but your Reply button shows and the correct static notification scene is selected (as evidenced by the red sash).

FIGURE 9.15 The status notification running in the watchOS simulator

It has been quite the journey, but you have finally tested your status notification. Of course there is still the location notification to test, and an easy way to do so would be to edit the Status Notification scheme, changing the Notification Payload setting to select the location payload instead. Although it would be quite quick to do this, it would become tedious, so instead you will create a new scheme for the location notification.

8. Select Product > Scheme > New Scheme from the Xcode main menu.

9. In the dialog, select the Heres Me WatchKit App target, enter the name **Location Notification**, and click OK (**Figure 9.16**).

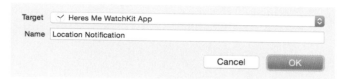

FIGURE 9.16 The scheme creation dialog

10. Select Product > Scheme > Manage Schemes from the Xcode main menu.

11. Select the Location Notification scheme, and click Edit.

12. In the Run action, click the Watch Interface popup menu, and select the Static Notification option.

13. Click the Notification Payload popup menu, and select the PushNotificationPayload-location.apns option.

14. Click Close.

15. Click Run to test the location notification.

Again, the simulators should start up and the location notification should be displayed (**Figure 9.17**). The appropriate location information should be displayed, and the green sash confirms that the location scene is correctly displayed. The Post Location and Reply action buttons also show that the WatchKit Simulator Actions data has been successfully extracted from the payload.

FIGURE 9.17 The location notification running in the watchOS simulator

There is one thing missing, however. When you created the location notification scene, you added a dynamic notification that included a map. The notification displayed in Figure 9.17 doesn't contain a map, so you are displaying only the static notification right now. That is because you set the Watch Interface setting to Static Notification; you really wanted Dynamic Notification instead.

16. Select Product > Scheme > Edit Scheme from the Xcode main menu.

17. In the Run action, click the Watch Interface popup menu, and select the Dynamic Notification option.

18. Click Close.

19. Click Run to test the dynamic notification.

This time you can see the map view appear in the notification (**Figure 9.18**), confirming that the dynamic notification scene is displayed.

FIGURE 9.18 The dynamic location notification

NOTE: Unfortunately, the watchOS simulator is unable to load the map view correctly at the time of this writing. Trust us that it will work on a physical device, and hopefully Apple will correct this soon.

ACTIONING NOTIFICATIONS

So what happens when your user actions a notification? Ultimately, actioning a notification will end up dismissing it, but what happens after the dismissal is determined by how, and where, you tap the notification.

TAPPING THE NOTIFICATION

The result of tapping a notification can be roughly divided into three categories:

- Tapping the Dismiss button.
- Tapping the action buttons.
- Tapping the main notification area; this includes the sash and any non–action-button UI components.

The easiest tap to understand is that of the Dismiss button—this will very simply dismiss the notification with no other action. Your app will not be launched at all, and you are free to go about your business. This is the notification equivalent of saying, "These aren't the droids you're looking for."

Tapping the action buttons causes your app to launch, and if you have taken the time to implement it, either the handleActionWithIdentifier(_:forRemoteNotification:) or the handleActionWithIdentifier(_:forLocalNotification:) method will be executed. Tapping an action button causes the associated action identifier name to be passed as a string through the identifier parameter. An exception to this behavior is described in the "Text Responses" section.

Tapping elsewhere in the main notification area and not on a button will also cause your app to launch, and these methods, if implemented, will be executed. This time, however, the identifier parameter will remain as an empty string.

The following code shows how you might handle actioning a notification in your Heres Me app. Add these methods to the ExtensionDelegate.swift file:

```swift
func handleActionWithIdentifier(identifier: String?,
    forRemoteNotification remoteNotification: [NSObject : AnyObject]) {
    guard let identifier = identifier else { return }
    switch (identifier) {
        case "statusReplyAction":
            handleStatusReplyForNotification(remoteNotification)
        case "locationReplyAction":
            handleLocationReplyForNotification(remoteNotification)
        case "postLocationAction":
            handlePostLocationForNotification(remoteNotification)
        default:
            handleGeneralTapForNotification(remoteNotification)
    }
}
func handleStatusReplyForNotification(notification: [NSObject:AnyObject]) { }
func handleLocationReplyForNotification(notification: [NSObject:AnyObject]) { }
func handlePostLocationForNotification(notification: [NSObject:AnyObject]) { }
func handleGeneralTapForNotification(notification: [NSObject : AnyObject]) { }
```

> **NOTE:** As of Xcode 7 beta 6, tapping the main notification area attempts to launch the app, but the handleActionWithIdentifier(_:remoteNotification:) method is not executed, and the app eventually exits. We're assuming this to be a bug in the simulator right now.

TEXT RESPONSES

With the introduction of watchOS 2, interaction with notifications took on a whole new dimension. It is now possible to mark a specific action as expecting a text response—doing so causes the normal flow to be interrupted, and watchOS will prompt the user for a personal response. The response can take the form of a dictated message, emoji, or choosing from a selection of predefined messages.

Your `statusReplyAction` and `locationReplyAction` buttons are the perfect candidates for a text response. You set this up to reply to a location notification as follows:

1. Open the file `PushNotificationPayload-location.apns`.

2. Replace the existing `WatchKit Simulator Actions` property with the following:

```
"WatchKit Simulator Actions": [
    {
        "title": "Post Location",
        "identifier": "postLocationAction"
    }, {
        "title": "Reply",
        "identifier": "locationReplyAction",
        "behavior": "textInput"
    }
]
```

3. Click the Scheme Selection popup menu, and choose the Location Notification scheme.

4. Click Run to execute the scheme.

5. Click the Reply action button.

   Instead of switching to the main app, watchOS instead displays the inline-text response screen (**Figure 9.19**).

FIGURE 9.19 The inline-text response screen

At this point the options available are a bit sparse—the dictation button is understandably disabled within the simulator, but there are also no canned responses for the user to choose from. The reason for this is simple: You haven't provided any yet!

To provide a canned response, you need to implement the suggestionsForResponseTo ActionWithIdentifier(_:forRemoteNotification:inputLanguage:) method on the NotificationController class. You can remedy that by presenting some very generic responses.

6. Open the NotificationController.swift file, and add the following method to the class:

```
override func suggestionsForResponseToActionWithIdentifier(identifier:
→ String, forRemoteNotification remoteNotification:
→ [NSObject : AnyObject], inputLanguage: String) -> [String] {
    return ["Swet", "Na mate!"]
}
```

7. Run the scheme again, and you should see a populated response like that shown in **Figure 9.20**.

FIGURE 9.20 A more useful inline-text response screen

Such generic responses are rarely going to cover everything your users might want to say, so you can use the parameters passed to the method to make better decisions. Use the identifier to know what type of action the user has taken, and the remoteNotification parameter will give you the context in which the user is replying. You could parse the notification for keywords, use time and location information for ideas, or, if you're feeling particularly adventurous, you could have your push service pass a list of potential responses down to the user through the notification payload.

When the user has picked or dictated a response, the flow of control will return to your app; this time the optional methods handleActionWithIdentifier(_: forRemoteNotification:withResponseInfo:) and handleActionWithIdentifier(_: forLocalNotification:withResponseInfo:) will be called if implemented. The responseInfo parameter will contain a dictionary; a key named UIUserNotificationActionResponseTypedTextKey can be used to access the response as a string of text.

LOCAL NOTIFICATIONS

Most of what we've discussed so far has dealt primarily with remote notifications. This is understandable given that remote notifications are the most commonly used type. Every app is different, though, and you may rely on the creation and receipt of local notifications for your core functionality, whether that be reminders, timed events, or geolocation triggers.

Handling a local notification differs only in the names of the methods you need to implement and in the format of the notification parameter. A remote notification handler will receive a dictionary, whereas a local notification receives a `UILocalNotification` object.

The local notification is dispatched to watchOS from the companion iOS app running on the user's iPhone. A notification is created and scheduled for `fireDate`—a time in the future when it should fire. When the notification fires, it will follow the aforementioned rules for determining where it should be displayed; if the user is not using his phone and is wearing his watch (and it is unlocked!), the notification will be displayed on the watch.

It isn't possible to create a local notification on the watch. Instead, you need to use the Watch Connectivity framework to send a request to the iOS app on the iPhone. Your iOS app should understand this request and use any data sent with it to construct a local notification and schedule it. The Watch Connectivity framework was covered in detail in Chapter 6.

WRAPPING UP

This has been quite the chapter—and with good reason: Although your main app and glances are important, the primary entry point to your app will likely be notifications. Apple has recognized this and has given you a tremendous level of control over your users' experience. Ensuring they get the right level of information at the right time is essential in a device that is so much about the moment.

This also ends the section on the core technologies in watchOS. In the next part, we show you how to make the most of the platform by delving deeper into some of the frameworks that let you take input from users and their environment, and we give you some guidance on working with physical devices.

PART III

Making the Most of the Platform

CHAPTER 10

Communicating with the Outside World

What is it that makes a smartwatch "smart"? When your authors were but young lads of fewer than 10 years, one had a digital watch that, as well as telling the current time in his chosen alternate time zone, had an alarm function, included a couple of very basic games, and could be used as a calculator—complete with a fiddly, rubbery keypad! Best of all—unless you were a schoolteacher, that is—it could be set to play two quick pips at the top of every hour.

At the time, that author and his peers thought that watch was pretty smart. (Let's be honest. We still do.) But it was no *smartwatch*. The defining characteristic of the modern smart-watch is its communication with the outside world, particularly via the Internet.

In this chapter, we examine how watchOS enables your watch apps to communicate with the world outside the watch itself. There are two aspects to this: making network requests via the Internet, and communicating with the host iOS app installed on the user's iPhone. By the end of this chapter, your apps will be merrily doing both.

NETWORK REQUESTS WITH NSURLSESSION

Apple introduced the NSURLSession networking API with iOS 7, updating the longstand-ing, familiar NSURLConnection—which is deprecated as of iOS 9. This being the case, NSURLSession is the API available for use by watchOS apps.

The Cocoa URL loading system is flexible and powerful, but in this chapter we cover only the basics of making network requests from Apple Watch. For more on all you can do with this family of APIs, check out Apple's documentation on the URL loading system, at http://bit.ly/bwa-url.

THE WATCH AND THE NETWORK

Apple Watch's primary connection with the outside world is via its host iPhone, connected over Bluetooth. The phone's network connection, whether Wi-Fi or cellular, is available to the watch to make requests to any server accessible over that connection. Additionally, if the watch is in range of a known Wi-Fi network, it can connect directly without communicating via its host phone. (These "known networks" are those that the watch's host phone is able to connect to automatically.)

Many use cases require an app to connect to a server for which you, as the developer of both the client and the server, control the response that is returned. Where that is the case, there are a couple of things to think about as you define the communication between your app and your server.

- Reduce the information in the response to only that needed by the watch app. Receiving and decoding data takes time and power, and the less of each you can use, the better the experience will be for your users.

- App Transport Security, introduced with iOS 9 and watchOS 2, requires that all network requests be made over HTTPS, with servers supporting TLS 1.2. Although it is possible to exclude requests from the oversight of App Transport Security—and developers using third-party APIs may need to do so—you have no excuse for not ensuring that your own servers meet the requirements of the system.

- As with any network-connected app, remember to handle the case where the server is unreachable, whether the watch and its host phone are out of range of a connection or the server itself is down.

MAKING THE REQUEST

A great number of moving parts are involved in requesting and receiving data from a remote server, but NSURLSession makes the most common cases very quick and easy for the developer.

Requests are managed by an NSURLSession and its delegate and are represented as *tasks*. A task is a subclass of NSURLSessionTask and may be of one of three types:

- NSURLSessionDataTask sends and receives arbitrary data, working with instances of NSData.
- NSURLSessionDownloadTask saves its received data to a file.
- NSURLSessionUploadTask provides the ability to use a file as the source of its request body, such as when uploading a file or storage.

Initializing an NSURLSession requires an NSURLSessionConfiguration object, which provides a great deal of control over the behavior of the session. Additionally, for even more control, it is possible to provide a custom delegate to the session. However, the simplest uses are satisfied by using the system shared session, obtained by calling NSURLSession.sharedSession(). This shared session uses the system session delegate, which is also available to your app's own NSURLSession instances. Some forms of the various NSURLSessionTasks take completion handler blocks; these are the forms that must be used if not providing a custom delegate.

To try out the basic use of NSURLSession, create a simple app with the following steps:

1. Open Xcode, and create a new WatchKit App project. Deselect the options for Notification, Glance, Complication, Unit Testing, and UI Testing. We named this project **Humoji**, for reasons that will become clear.

2. In the WatchKit App's Interface.storyboard, select the interface controller scene, and add an image and a picker as in **Figure 10.1**.

FIGURE 10.1 The image and picker in the storyboard scene

Here, the image is configured to Center-Top and the picker to Center-Bottom. The image has a fixed width and height of 64pt in each dimension.

3. In the WatchKit Extension group, open InterfaceController.swift and replace its contents with the following empty implementation:

```
import WatchKit
import Foundation

class InterfaceController: WKInterfaceController {
}

// MARK: Emoji list loading
extension InterfaceController {
}

// MARK: Emoji image loading
extension InterfaceController {to
}
```

Note that this project won't be an example of perfectly architected software. We're keeping everything together in one class for ease of demonstration and using Swift extensions to break it up into logical parts.

4. Add the following two @IBOutlets to the main class block, and connect them to the interface objects in the storyboard scene:

```
@IBOutlet var image: WKInterfaceImage!
@IBOutlet var picker: WKInterfacePicker!
```

Now you need to add a few more properties and a couple of methods to coordinate the behavior of the interface and the loading content.

5. Add the following properties to the main class block of InterfaceController:

```
private var pickerIndex = 0
private var imageLoadTimer: NSTimer?
private var emojiList: [(String, String)] = []

private var pickerItems: [WKPickerItem] = [] {
    didSet {
        picker.setItems(pickerItems)
        picker.focus()
    }
}
```

You're using Swift's didSet feature on the pickerItems property so that when it is set it will automatically update the items on the picker itself.

6. Add the following @IBAction method to the class block, and connect it to the picker in the storyboard scene:

```
@IBAction func emojiSelected(value: Int) {
    pickerIndex = value

    imageLoadTimer?.invalidate()
    imageLoadTimer = NSTimer(
        timeInterval: 0.3,
        target: self,
        selector: "imageTimerFired:",
        userInfo: nil,
        repeats: false
    )
    NSRunLoop.mainRunLoop().addTimer(imageLoadTimer!, forMode:
    → NSDefaultRunLoopMode)
}
```

7. Add the method that the timer calls:

```
func imageTimerFired(timer: NSTimer) {
    timer.invalidate()
    loadImageFromAddress(emojiList[pickerIndex].1)
}
```

To keep this example simple, you'll be triggering the download of an image depending on the value of the picker. This timer makes sure that the download isn't triggered for each value as the user scrolls the picker; instead, it inhibits the action by putting a 0.3-second delay on the start of the download.

8. Complete the implementation of the main class by adding the following three methods:

```
override func awakeWithContext(context: AnyObject?) {
    super.awakeWithContext(context)

    if pickerItems.isEmpty {
        pickerItems = [loadingPickerItem()]
        requestData()
    }
}

private func loadingPickerItem() -> WKPickerItem {
    let item = WKPickerItem()
    item.title = "Loading..."
```

```
        return item
    }

    private func pickerItems(emoji: [(String, String)]) -> [WKPickerItem] {
        return emoji.map { (name, _) in
            let item = WKPickerItem()
            item.title = name
            return item
        }
    }
}
```

At this point, Xcode will be complaining about some unknown methods. To fill out the functionality here, you need to complete the two extensions in InterfaceController.swift.

The first extension handles making a request to the GitHub API. The endpoint you're using is unauthenticated and returns a JSON dictionary of the names and URLs of all the emoji supported in GitHub's issues and comments.

9. Add the following method to the Emoji list loading extension.

It handles the data received from the API request and uses it to populate the picker with the names of the emoji.

```
    private func processData(data: NSData?, error: NSError?) {
        guard let data = data else {
            if let error = error {
                print(error.description)
            }
            return
        }

        do {
            if let receivedEmojiList = try NSJSONSerialization.
            → JSONObjectWithData(data, options:.AllowFragments) as?
            → [String:String] {
                emojiList = receivedEmojiList.map { name, address in (name,
                → address) }
                picker.setItems(pickerItems(emojiList))
            }
        }
        catch {
            print("Error decoding emoji list")
        }
    }
```

The JSON is an array of dictionaries of the form {"emoji_name": "emoji_image_url"}, which this method maps to an array of tuples containing the names and URLs.

The other method to add to this extension is the one that makes the actual API request.

10. Add the following method to make the API request:

```
private func requestData() {
    let url = NSURL.init(string: "https://api.github.com/emojis")!
    let urlSession = NSURLSession.sharedSession()
    let task = urlSession.dataTaskWithURL(url) { data, response, error in
        self.processData(data, error: error)
    }

    task.resume()
}
```

This method gets the shared NSURLSession and then uses it to create an NSURLSessionDataTask. This is the simplest use of NSURLSession: The data task asynchronously performs an HTTP GET to the URL provided, then passes the response to the completion handler provided. Note that all NSURLSessionTasks are created in a suspended state and must be started with a call to their resume() method.

The second extension to the InterfaceController class handles the loading and display of the emoji images in the WKInterfaceImage added earlier to the storyboard scene.

11. Add the following method to the Emoji image loading extension:

```
private func loadImageFromAddress(address: String?) {
    guard let address = address else {
        image.setImage(nil)
        return
    }

    let url = NSURL.init(string: address)!
    let urlSession = NSURLSession.sharedSession()
    let task = urlSession.downloadTaskWithURL(url) { tempFileUrl, response,
        error in
        if let tempFileUrl = tempFileUrl,
                imageData = NSData.init(contentsOfURL:tempFileUrl),
                downloadedImage = UIImage.init(data:imageData) {
            self.image.setImage(downloadedImage)
        } else {
            self.image.setImage(nil)
        }
    }
}
```

```
        task.resume()
}
```

This method creates an NSURLSessionDownloadTask used to download the image for the currently chosen emoji. Although the data task in the code passes an instance of NSData to its completion handler, a download task provides the URL of a temporary file in which the download is stored. The file is not guaranteed to be available at the temporary URL when the completion handler has finished executing, so you need to make sure that you have processed the downloaded file before the handler returns. This will often mean copying the file to a more permanent location (your app's Documents, or Caches, directory). For simplicity in demonstration, this implementation simply loads the downloaded image into memory and sets it to the WKInterfaceImage.

You can run the app is it now stands, but when the emoji list loads, no image displays until you have scrolled the picker.

12. To load the first image in the list when it becomes available, add the following in the body of the processData(_:error:) method:

```
do {
    if let receivedEmojiList = try NSJSONSerialization.
    → JSONObjectWithData(data, options:.AllowFragments) as?
    → [String:String] {
        emojiList = receivedEmojiList.map { name, address in (name, address)
    }

        picker.setItems(pickerItems(emojiList))
        loadImageFromAddress(emojiList[0].1)
    }
}
catch {
    print("Error decoding emoji list")
}
```

Now you can run the app and explore all the emoji options available to GitHub users (**Figure 10.2**). We, being cheerful authors, are particularly fond of expressionless.

FIGURE 10.2 Humoji in action

Although any production app would give more attention to a number of obvious areas than we have in this example (caching of the downloaded data and images, for one), we really should go into one detail specifically.

HANDLING PREMATURE DEACTIVATION

Because of the nature of Apple Watch and watchOS, it is possible—even likely—that your app will be deactivated at some time. With the basic use of the default NSURLSession shown here, this would mean that the completion handler isn't called and the received data is never processed.

One option to handle this situation is to use a custom background NSURLSession and treat the request as a download, but there is another approach whereby your app can request a little extra time to complete the task before it exits. NSProcessInfo provides the method performExpiringActivityWithReason(_:usingBlock:), which asks the system to allow the provided block to complete execution before suspending the process. This block, as with the completion handlers of the NSURLSessionTasks earlier, is executed asynchronously on a concurrent queue. Consequently, a little bit of work is required to coordinate the execution of the different blocks.

Return to the example project, and make the following updates:

1. Add the following property to the main class block of InterfaceController:

```
private var emojiListDataTask: NSURLSessionDataTask?
```

This property will be used to store the task that is in progress. Checking the state of this task makes it possible to avoid creating a repeat task for one that is already in progress.

> **NOTE:** For the purposes of this demonstration, we will be updating only the behavior of the initial request for the emoji list. The image downloads would be better handled by a background NSURLSession working together with a sensible approach to caching the downloaded images.

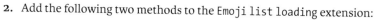

2. Add the following two methods to the Emoji list loading extension:

```
private func beginBackgroundTask(semaphore: dispatch_semaphore_t) {
    NSProcessInfo.processInfo().performExpiringActivityWithReason
    ("emojiListRequest") { expired in
        if !expired {
            let fifteenSecondsFromNow = dispatch_time(DISPATCH_TIME_NOW,
            Int64(15 * NSEC_PER_SEC))
            dispatch_semaphore_wait(semaphore, fifteenSecondsFromNow)
        } else {
            print("No more background activity permitted")
            self.endBackgroundTask(semaphore)
```

```
                }
            }
        }

    private func endBackgroundTask(semaphore: dispatch_semaphore_t) {
        dispatch_semaphore_signal(semaphore)
    }
```

The closure provided for execution simply blocks until a provided semaphore is signaled. If the signal is sent when the data task and its completion handler have finished, this closure waits to return until that task's asynchronous work is done. The 15-second delta provided to dispatch_semaphore_wait is an effective timeout for the request. If that period passes and the process is suspended, then it will be as if the request never happened.

The closure passed to performExpiringActivityWithReason(_:usingBlock:) takes a Boolean parameter named expired. This parameter is used to indicate to the closure whether its work can be extended into the background. The same closure may be called a second time if the process is to be suspended, so you should handle that case. In this example, this situation is handled by signaling the semaphore.

Now, you need to make use of this mechanism.

3. Make the following updates to the requestData() method:

```
    private func requestData() {
        guard emojiListDataTask?.state != .Running else {return}

        let semaphore = dispatch_semaphore_create(0)
        beginBackgroundTask(semaphore)

        let url = NSURL.init(string: "https://api.github.com/emojis")!
        let urlSession = NSURLSession.sharedSession()
        emojiListDataTask = urlSession.dataTaskWithURL(url) { data, response,
        ⟶ error in
            self.processData(data, error: error)
            self.endBackgroundTask(semaphore)
        }

        emojiListDataTask?.resume()
    }
```

The initial guard clause in this implementation makes sure that a request in progress is allowed to carry on rather than being duplicated.

Running the app now will demonstrate apparently unchanged behavior. However, the request to the GitHub API is now much more robust in the face of process suspension.

The most complicated aspect of this approach to sustaining an NSURLSessionTask is the coordination of the two asynchronously executed blocks of code. However, in this case where there are only two blocks to be coordinated, semaphores provide a straightforward and simple way to manage the problem.

NSURLSession has many capabilities beyond those demonstrated in this simple app, ranging from highly configurable handling of authentication challenges and encrypted connections to making download requests in the background and pausing and resuming downloads. It's an API that is definitely worth getting to know well.

TALKING TO THE PHONE WITH WATCHCONNECTIVITY

With watchOS 2 and iOS 9, Apple introduced a new way for the WatchKit extension running on an Apple Watch to communicate with its companion app on the watch's host iPhone: the WatchConnectivity framework. (Although the communication is with the WatchKit extension running on the Apple Watch, for brevity we will mostly refer to it as the app.)

> **NOTE:** In order to use WatchConnectivity, the framework must be available to both the WatchKit extension and the iOS app. This means that it is only possible if the watch is running at least watchOS version 2 and the host iPhone is running at least iOS version 9.

It is pleasingly straightforward to use WatchConnectivity for inter-device communication. The process relies on both the WatchKit extension and the iOS app each maintaining a WCSession and providing it with a delegate (conforming to the WCSessionDelegate protocol). Because each app sends data via the WCSession, its counterpart receives that data and acts on it via calls to its session delegate.

> **NOTE:** All calls to methods specified in the WCSessionDelegate protocol are guaranteed to be made on a background queue. Remember to make sure that any code called in response to a received transfer is executed on the correct queue (for example, if UI updates are necessary or if a Core Data model will be involved).

Communication using WatchConnectivity can take place when one or both apps are in the background on their respective devices, or can also be run in real time using the message-sending methods. The key characteristics of the two types are as follows:

- Background transfer is for cases where the information isn't needed immediately by the counterpart app. With a little care, this can cover most cases for data transfer between devices.
- Background transfers are handled by the OS, which means that once the call to the WCSession has been made, the sending app can be safely backgrounded or terminated and the transfer will still take place.
- Background transfers are handled by the OS, so the system optimizes the sending of data by considering device battery levels, current device load and user activity, and the use pattern of the app.
- When background transfers are made to a receiving app that is inactive, they are queued and the receiving delegate methods are called when the app is launched and its WCSession is activated. (On the host iPhone side, this doesn't necessarily mean the app is in the foreground.)
- Live message sending can take place when the app on the watch is running in the foreground. If a message is sent to the iPhone app and it is not running, it will be launched in the background to receive the message.
- Both types of communication allow for the transmission of dictionaries, which makes it trivial to send any property list–compatible type. Because this includes NSData, it is possible to send anything you can encode as such. Additionally, the background transfer type has methods that allow for the convenient sending of files referenced by local file URLs, and the live messaging methods can take NSData instances without wrapping them in dictionaries.

BACKGROUND TRANSFER

Three types of background transfer are available: Application context updates are useful for synchronizing application state; user info transfer permits the transmission of dictionaries of arbitrary data; and file transfer simplifies sending files.

APPLICATION CONTEXT UPDATES

An application context update is sent with updateApplicationContext(_:) method of WCSession and triggers a call to the receiving WCSessionDelegate's session(_:didReceiveApplicationContext:) method. The context to send is a dictionary of the form [String : AnyObject].

The WCSession has two properties related to the application context: applicationContext is the last context dictionary sent to the app's counterpart, and receivedApplicationContext is the last context dictionary received from the app's counterpart. If a context update is called while a previous update is queued to send, then the most recent call *replaces* the previous one. In this way, the application context is best used as some state that can be updated.

USER INFO TRANSFER

Similarly to the application context, user info transfer allows your apps to send dictionaries of arbitrary data to their counterparts. Unlike with the application context method, successive transfers are queued for delivery in order when the receiving app is launched.

User info dictionaries are sent via the WCSession using its transferUserInfo(_:) method. On delivery, the WCSessionDelegate method session(_:didReceiveUserInfo:) is called.

A call to transferUserInfo(_:) returns an instance of WCSessionUserInfoTransfer that can be used to monitor the status of the transfer and cancel it if necessary. Additionally, when a transfer finishes (either successfully or in failure), the *sending app's* session delegate will receive a call to session(_:didFinishUserInfoTransfer:error:).

FILE TRANSFER

Although it would be perfectly possible to transfer files between devices by reading them into memory and storing them as NSData in a transmitted user info dictionary, WCSession provides a method to directly send a file referenced by URL: transferFile(_:metadata:).

File transfers are queued in a manner similar to user info transfers, with the difference that in the case of files, the order of delivery is not guaranteed.

When creating a file transfer, the metadata parameter accepts an optional dictionary to deliver alongside the file, and the method returns a WCSessionFileTransfer object that can be used to monitor and, if necessary, cancel the transfer. When the file has been transferred, the sending app's session delegate will receive a call to its session(_:didFinishFileTransfer:error) method and the receiving app's delegate will be informed with a call to session(_:didReceiveFile:).

When the receiving delegate method is called, the URL it receives (contained, along with any metadata dictionary, in a WCSessionFile instance) refers to a temporary copy of the received file, which *will* be deleted when the delegate method returns. As a consequence, the file must be read or moved to more permanent storage before the method exits and the URL becomes invalid. (This behavior is very similar to that of the completion handler on an NSURLSessionDownloadTask, as discussed earlier in this chapter.)

As with the other background transfer methods, queued file transfers are handled by the system with sympathy to current system state and activity. Larger files will, of course, take longer to transfer and expend more energy doing so.

LIVE MESSAGE TRANSMISSION

Although background transfers are queued and delivered at the system's discretion, it is also possible to use the WatchConnectivity session to send messages for immediate delivery. In order to do so, the recipient device must be available to receive the message. This is determined with WCSession's reachable property, which will be true if the paired device is able to receive a message, and false otherwise.

Reachability depends on two factors:

- For the app on the phone to be reachable from the watch, the phone and the watch need to be connected. If the companion app on the phone is not running, it will be launched in the background to receive the incoming message.

- For the watch app to receive a message from the app running on the iPhone, not only must the devices currently be connected and in range, but the watch app must be running in the foreground. (Unlike iOS apps, WatchKit extensions do not have a background execution state.)

Attempting to send a message for delivery to a companion app that is not reachable will result in an error, with a call to any error handler provided to the message-sending method. It is, of course, also possible for a counterpart that was reachable to become unreachable while a message is being sent, which will result in the same call to the error handler.

When multiple messages are sent in sequence, they are delivered in the order that they are sent.

Two methods on WCSession may be used to send messages. The first method, sendMessage(_:replyHandler:errorHandler:), takes a dictionary to send, and the other, sendMessageData(_:replyHandler:errorHandler:), takes an instance of NSData to send to the counterpart app. The replyHandler and errorHandler parameters are optional, and if handlers are provided, they are used as follows:

- The reply handler is a block with a signature of either ([String : AnyObject]) -> Void or (NSData) -> Void that is called if the receiving app's WatchConnectivity session delegate sends a reply—in the form of the dictionary passed to this handler.

- The error handler is a block of the form (NSError) -> Void, called if an error occurs when sending the message.

Receipt of a message will result in a call to one of four methods on the WCSessionDelegate:

- If the message was in the form of a dictionary, the possible methods are session(_:didReceiveMessage:) and session(_:didReceiveMessage:replyHandler:).

- If the message was an NSData object, then the methods are session(_:didReceiveMessageData:) and session(_:didReceiveMessageData:replyHandler:).

In each case, the shorter form is used when the sender did not provide a reply handler, and the longer form is called when a reply handler was provided. The reply handler will accept either a dictionary or an instance of NSData according to the form of the message that was received, and the delegate method *must* call the reply handler if one is provided.

PREPARING THE iPHONE APP

In order to try out WatchConnectivity-based messaging between devices, you will return to the Humoji project from earlier in this chapter and build a basic companion iPhone app.

1. From the iPhone app's group in the Project Navigator, open `Main.storyboard` (**Figure 10.3**).

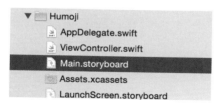

FIGURE 10.3 The storyboard file

The storyboard will contain one blank scene, corresponding to the `ViewController` class created from the project template.

2. Add an image view to this blank scene by dragging an image view from the Object Library.

3. Select the image view and apply layout constraints to center it in its containing view. Do this by clicking the Align button at the bottom of the canvas pane and selecting both Horizontally in Container and Vertically in Container. Then click the Add 2 Constraints button (**Figure 10.4**).

FIGURE 10.4 Setting alignment constraints

4. Again, select the image view. To apply constraints to give it a fixed width and height, click the Pin button (next to the Align button). Select the options for Width and Height and set the value for each to 64. Click the Add 2 Constraints button (**Figure 10.5**).

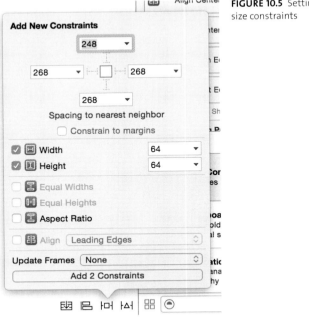

FIGURE 10.5 Setting size constraints

Selecting the image view will cause its constraints to show, and the scene should appear as in **Figure 10.6**.

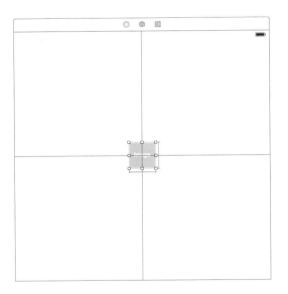

FIGURE 10.6 The completed scene

5. Open `ViewController.swift`, and replace the contents with the following:

```
import UIKit

class ViewController: UIViewController {
    @IBOutlet weak var imageView: UIImageView!
}
```

6. Connect the image view in the storyboard scene to the `@IBOutlet` in `ViewController`.

RECEIVING WATCHCONNECTIVITY MESSAGES

We now have a very simple iPhone app that displays an image. The phone app will receive the image in a WatchConnectivity message from the watch.

> **NOTE:** Although the two apps will be using different methods of the WatchConnectivity delegate, in this simple example we'll keep them together in one class that is present in both apps.

1. Create a new group at the top level of the project, and name it `Inter-Device Communication`. Create a new Swift file in this group, and name it `CommunicationManager.swift`.

2. Replace the contents of `CommunicationManager.swift` with the following:

```
import Foundation
import WatchConnectivity

class CommunicationManager : NSObject {
    static let sharedInstance = CommunicationManager()
    private override init() {
        super.init()
    }
}
```

This class will act as the delegate to the app's `WCSession`—and because there can be only one instance of `WCSession`, this implementation ensures that you will always know where to find its delegate.

3. Add the following property to `CommunicationManager`:

```
var session: WCSession?
```

4. Add the following extension to the file:

```
extension CommunicationManager : WCSessionDelegate {
    private func setupSession() {
        if (WCSession.isSupported()) {
            session = WCSession.defaultSession()
            if let session = session {
                session.delegate = self
                session.activateSession()
            }
        } else {
            print("WCSession unsupported")
        }
    }
}
```

5. Add the following to the class's initializer:

```
private override init() {
    super.init()
    setupSession()
}
```

6. Make sure that `CommunicationManager.swift` belongs to both the iPhone app's target and to the WatchKit Extension target by selecting the file in the Project Navigator and ensuring that the File inspector matches **Figure 10.7**.

FIGURE 10.7 Target membership for `CommunicationManager.swift`

7. Return to `ViewController.swift`, and add the following property to the `ViewController` class:

```
internal var communicationManager: CommunicationManager?
```

8. In `AppDelegate.swift`, add the following to the implementation of `application(_:didFinishLaunchingWithOptions:)`:

```
if let rootViewController = window?.rootViewController as? ViewController {
    rootViewController.communicationManager = CommunicationManager.
    → sharedInstance
}
```

9. Returning to CommunicationManager.swift, add the following property to the class block:

```
var onReceivedMessageData: (NSData -> Void)?
```

10. Add the following method to the extension:

```
func session(session: WCSession, didReceiveMessageData messageData: NSData)
{
    onReceivedMessageData?(messageData)
}
```

11. In ViewController.swift, add the following didSet block to the communicationManager property:

```
internal var communicationManager: CommunicationManager? {
    didSet {
        communicationManager?.onReceivedMessageData = { data in
            self.dataReceived(data)
        }
    }
}
```

12. To complete the work in the phone app, add the following method to ViewController.swift:

```
private func dataReceived(data: NSData) {
    dispatch_async(dispatch_get_main_queue()) {
        if let image = UIImage(data: data) {
            self.imageView.image = image
        }
    }
}
```

SENDING WATCHCONNECTIVITY MESSAGES

With the phone app complete (we did say it was basic), you need to make a few changes to the watch app to send the image data when an emoji is selected.

1. In the WatchKit Extension group in the Project Navigator, open ExtensionDelegate.swift and add the following property:

```
var communicationManager: CommunicationManager?
```

2. Instantiate the `CommunicationManager` by adding the following line to the extension delegate's `applicationDidFinishLaunching()` method:

```
func applicationDidFinishLaunching() {
    communicationManager = CommunicationManager.sharedInstance
}
```

3. Once again, open `CommunicationManager.swift` and add the following method to the class block:

```
func sendMessageData(data: NSData) {
    if let session = session where session.reachable {
        session.sendMessageData(data, replyHandler: nil, errorHandler: nil)
    }
}
```

4. Add the following property to `InterfaceController.swift`:

```
private var communicationManager: CommunicationManager?
```

5. Still in `InterfaceController.swift`, add the following to `awakeWithContext(_:)`:

```
if let extensionDelegate = WKExtension.sharedExtension().delegate as?
→ ExtensionDelegate {
    communicationManager = extensionDelegate.communicationManager
}
```

6. Finally, in `InterfaceController`'s Emoji image loading extension, update `loadImageFromAddress(_:)` as follows:

```
private func loadImageFromAddress(address: String?) {
    guard let address = address else {
        image.setImage(nil)
        return
    }

    let url = NSURL.init(string: address)!
    let urlSession = NSURLSession.sharedSession()
    let task = urlSession.downloadTaskWithURL(url) { tempFileUrl, response,
    → error in
        if let tempFileUrl = tempFileUrl,
            imageData = NSData.init(contentsOfURL:tempFileUrl),
            downloadedImage = UIImage.init(data:imageData) {
            self.image.setImage(downloadedImage)
            self.communicationManager?.sendMessageData(imageData)
```

```
        } else {
            self.image.setImage(nil)
        }
    }

    task.resume()
}
```

Run the apps, making sure that both the phone app and the watch app are active. When an emoji image is loaded in the watch app, you will see the same image appear in the phone app. Feels good, doesn't it?

This is the simplest demonstration of WatchConnectivity's power. When the watch app's interface controller downloads and displays an image, it then uses the `CommunicationManager` to access the app's `WCSession` and send a message with the `NSData`-encoded image as the payload. On receipt in the counterpart app, the `CommunicationManager`, acting as the `WCSession`'s delegate, calls its `onReceivedMessageData` block. The called code displays the image on the phone.

MAKING THE MOST OF INTER-DEVICE COMMUNICATION

If you have an app in which data received from a server needs to be shared between the Watch app and its iPhone companion app, there are a couple of possible approaches to making sure both devices have all the data they need.

Often the simplest way is for both devices to download their own copy of the information from the server and use WatchConnectivity to synchronize their state. When user-generated data is not available from the server, then it will, of course, need to be transferred directly between the devices. Another case may be that there is substantial expensive (in time or power) processing that needs to be performed on received data; in this circumstance, the most effective technique might be to download the data to the phone, process it, and then transfer it to the watch.

Perhaps most likely, a combination of these techniques could work best for your app—it all depends on what you need to achieve.

CONTINUING USER ACTIVITY WITH HANDOFF

An Apple Watch app can communicate with its counterpart on the iPhone using Handoff, but it is quite different from WatchConnectivity in intent and in how it is put to use. Handoff is a part of the Continuity feature set introduced in iOS 8.0 and OS X 10.10 and has been available in watchOS since the Apple Watch was introduced.

Handoff allows the user to begin a task in a watch app and then seamlessly continue that task from an iPhone, as long as the devices are connected. For example, if you were to launch the Maps app on your Apple Watch and browse to find a location, then look to

FIGURE 10.8 The Maps Handoff icon

the lock screen on your iPhone, you would see a Handoff icon in the lower-left corner (**Figure 10.8**). Swiping up from that icon will launch the phone's Maps app and open it to the location being viewed on the watch.

The key to making the most of Handoff is remembering that it is not an active communication on the part of your app. Rather, it provides the opportunity to maintain a lightweight snapshot of the user's current activity and use it to respond appropriately if the user decides to continue that activity on another device.

In a watch app, it is very simple to make a task available to be handed off to its companion app—or even to a webpage, if that makes sense for your app. `WKInterfaceController` provides the method `updateUserActivity(_:userInfo:webpageURL:)`, which your subclasses call to register the current user activity for handoff. The parameters are:

- A string indicating the type of activity, which will be received and used by the counterpart app to take over the activity. This string is defined by the developer and should not be blank, and Apple's documentation recommends it be in the normal reverse-DNS style for app-specific identifiers—for example, `"build.watchosapps.humoji.view-emoji"`.

- A `userInfo` dictionary providing any information needed by the receiving app to correctly resume the activity. Being a dictionary, this can contain any property list–compatible type. However, the usual admonition applies: Keep this as lightweight as possible to help with transfer and decoding time.

- A web URL (with a scheme of either `http` or `https`) can be provided as well as or in place of the `userInfo`, which will allow the handoff to take place to the browser rather than to the counterpart app.

Your app's controller classes should call this `updateUserActivity(_:userInfo:webpageURL:)` method as often as necessary to keep the current registered user activity up to date and ready to be handed off to the user's phone. Whenever the current activity state should no longer be available to hand off, the `WKInterfaceController` method `invalidateUserActivity()` should be called to cancel the activity.

TIP: The Handoff APIs are also useful to pass information to your app when it is launched from its glance. The glance controller may also call `updateUserActivity(_:userInfo:webpageURL:)`, and when the user taps the glance to launch the app, then the `WKExtensionDelegate` will receive a call to `handleUserActivity(_:)` with the `userInfo` dictionary. If the extension delegate doesn't implement that method, then the app's initial interface controller may do so instead.

When your watch app's user opts to continue activity with the iPhone companion app, the phone app is notified via its `UIApplicationDelegate`. A number of application delegate methods may be involved:

- If the app is launching, it is not already in memory, and its `application(_:willFinishLaunchingWithOptions:)` and `application(_:didFinishLaunchingWithOptions:)` methods are called, the

launchOptions dictionary will contain the UIApplicationLaunchOptionsUser
ActivityTypeKey and UIApplicationLaunchOptionsUserActivityDictionaryKey keys.
These methods may return false to indicate that they will not be continuing the user
activity. In that case, neither of the following methods will be called.

- application(_:willContinueUserActivityWithType:) is called to warn your app that
the user has opted to continue an activity. Note the absence of any information beyond
the activity type; the data associated with the activity may not yet be available when this
method is called.

- application(_:continueUserActivity:restorationHandler:) is the main method
for picking up an activity from Handoff. The userActivity parameter is of type
NSUserActivity. This class provides a great deal of functionality useful for managing Handoff between iOS and OS X. For the purposes of a watch app, it contains the
activity's type identifier, its userInfo dictionary, and any web URL that was provided.
The restorationHandler is a block that your app can call with an array of instances
of UIResponder subclasses that need to be informed of the user activity (for example,
UIViewControllers). Each will receive a call to restoreUserActivityState(:_). Note
that it is your code's responsibility to call the restorationHandler if needed—but it
is not compulsory to do so. Indeed, if appropriate, your application code may copy the
block and call it at a later date.

Beyond its use in watch apps, Handoff is a powerful and detailed feature to enable silky
smooth transition between activity on iOS and OS X. If this is relevant to your apps, and
even if it *may* be relevant in the future, we suggest digging into the documentation to learn
more about how your apps can use it to delight your users.

WRAPPING UP

This chapter has been a quick demonstration of the options available for getting data in and
out of an Apple Watch app—at least in those cases where the data is sent and received by
other devices.

There is more to the story of getting information into your app, though. Until the day
when we are all assimilated into the Digital Robotic Overmind, users will also want to provide their own input directly to the apps that they use. Read on to get to know the possibilities for user input on watchOS.

CHAPTER 11

Accepting User Input

Taps of the finger and clicks of the digital crown can go a long way to getting all the input needed from your app's users, but sometimes it's necessary to capture a word, a sentence, or more of textual input. With larger devices, this is trivial; whether a keyboard has physical keys or is presented onscreen, we're used to tapping away quickly to "say" what we need. Apple Watch is different. It simply does not have enough room for a keyboard, but through some clever ideas and technology we can receive our users' words all the same.

SPEECH TO TEXT

In the absence of a keyboard, there are three ways to provide text input to a watch app:

- The app can provide prepared strings that are presented to the user as options. The user can select one by tapping it.
- The user can select an emoji from a range of options that include the standard Apple set and the animated emoji introduced in watchOS 1.
- The user can speak into the watch's microphone and have their speech transcribed to text.

The third option is by far the most versatile and is the one that has the benefit of letting your app's users feel a bit like secret agents sending the message that will save the world. Or perhaps just self-consciously adding chocolate-hazelnut spread to their shopping list. But then, even secret agents need to take a chocolaty meal break every now and then.

The dictation capability of watchOS is powerful and easy to use—both for users and for developers. From the users' point of view, all they have to do is tap the dictation button when it's presented, speak, and confirm that the dictation has been correctly captured. For the developer, very little needs to be done to enable dictation input. The system handles the capture of audio, its transcription, and the user's confirmation, passing the resulting string to your app to deal with as you wish. All the hard work is done for you.

The dictation input on watchOS has one limitation: The transcription takes place on Apple's servers, with the captured audio uploaded for processing. This means that dictation input is not available when the watch has no network connection.

The reliance on remote processing raises two other considerations that may be relevant to your app:

- There is a slight delay while the audio is uploaded and the transcription received, although in our experience the process is impressively quick.
- The transmission of your users' input to a third party for processing might be a privacy or security concern. We expect that this isn't an issue for most apps, but it's something you should consider during development.

All this possibility for input is provided through one simple interface supplied by the system: the text input controller.

THE TEXT INPUT CONTROLLER

Text input on watchOS is handled via a modal text input controller (**Figure 11.1**). This modal controller is created and managed by the system and invoked with a call to one of these WKInterfaceController's methods:

- `presentTextInputControllerWithSuggestions(_:allowedInputMode:completion:)`
- `presentTextInputControllerWithSuggestionsForLanguage(_:allowedInputMode:completion:)`

FIGURE 11.1 A text input controller

The first method accepts an optional array of strings as suggestions, whereas the second takes a `suggestionHandler` block that receives a string representing the user's currently selected language and should return an array of suggestions for that language.

These two `WKInterfaceController` methods are executed asynchronously, and their completion blocks are called when the user either confirms their input or cancels the task, dismissing the text input controller. The completion block will receive an optional array that may contain a string containing the user's input or—in the case of an animated emoji input—an image packaged as `NSData`.

Because the calls to present text input controller are made asynchronously, it is also possible to force the input controller to dismiss without input from the user, via `WKInterfaceController`'s `dismissTextInputController()` method. Be aware, though, that if you dismiss the input controller programmatically, then its completion block will not be called, in contrast to the behavior when the controller is dismissed by the user.

INPUT TYPES

As mentioned earlier in this chapter, the text input controller allows users to provide their input in three ways. Your app can define which of these input types are available using the constant provided to the `allowedInputMode` parameter of the invoking method. This parameter is an enumeration of type `WKTextInputMode`, with the following possibilities available:

- `Plain` specifies text from the provided suggestions or from dictation.
- `AllowEmoji` includes text suggestions and dictation, plus selection from the standard set of non-animated emoji.
- `AllowAnimatedEmoji` augments the possible inputs with a selection from Apple's animated emoji.

Availability of suggestions is controlled by the optional array or the `suggestionHandler` provided when the text input controller is invoked. Passing `nil` presents no suggestions to the user.

The combination of the `allowedInputMode` and the provided suggestions modifies the behavior of the input controller. Ordinarily, the input controller is presented and the user can, for example, tap the dictation button (**Figure 11.2**) to trigger dictation. However, if the input mode is specified as `Plain` and no suggestions are provided, then the controller will present directly in dictation mode (**Figure 11.3**), with only a haptic tap to notify the user. In this case you may want to present an initial alert to prepare the user.

FIGURE 11.2 The dictation button

FIGURE 11.3 Text entered in dictation mode

TRYING OUT THE INTERFACE

The best way to get to know the different parts of the text input controller interface is to try it out.

1. In Xcode, create a new project with the iOS App with WatchKit App template. For this example, leave the Complication, Glance, and Notification options deselected.

2. Open the WatchKit App's `Interface.storyboard` and add an image, a label, and a button to the interface controller scene. Align the image and label to Center-Top and the button to Center-Bottom. Set the label's text alignment to Center and its number of lines to 0. The scene should resemble that shown in **Figure 11.4**.

FIGURE 11.4 The interface controller storyboard scene

3. Open `InterfaceController.swift` and replace its contents with the following:

```
import WatchKit
import Foundation
```

```
class InterfaceController: WKInterfaceController {
    @IBOutlet var image: WKInterfaceImage!
    @IBOutlet var label: WKInterfaceLabel!

    @IBAction func buttonTapped() {
    }
}
```

4. Connect the image, label, and button in the storyboard scene to the `@IBOutlet`s and the `@IBAction` in `InterfaceController.swift`.

5. Add the following property and method to the interface controller:

```
private var text = "Tap the button to say something"

override func willActivate() {
    super.willActivate()

    label.setText(text)
}
```

6. Update the `buttonTapped()` method to have the following implementation:

```
@IBAction func buttonTapped() {
    let suggestions = [
        "Game over, man! Game over!",
        "Hello. My name is Inigo Montoya.",
        "That's a big Twinkie.",
        "Let's see what happens when we take away the puppy.",
        "In the end there can be only one."
    ]

    presentTextInputControllerWithSuggestions(suggestions,
      → allowedInputMode: .Plain) { responses in
        if let responses = responses where responses.count > 0 {
            if let response = responses.first as? String {
                self.text = response
                self.label.setText(self.text)
            }
        }
    }
}
```

Running this app and tapping the button will display the text input controller shown in **Figure 11.5**. Selecting a suggested response or dictating your own will update the label once the input controller has dismissed. The dictation option will be disabled when running the app in the simulator. To try out the dictation, you'll need to run the app on a physical device. See Chapter 13 for a guide to getting up and running with the hardware.

FIGURE 11.5 The plain input controller

7. To handle emoji input, add the following property to `InterfaceController`:

   ```
   private var imageData: NSData?
   ```

8. Make the following changes to `buttonTapped()`:

   ```
   @IBAction func buttonTapped() {
       let suggestions = [
           "Game over, man! Game over!",
           "Hello. My name is Inigo Montoya.",
           "That's a big Twinkie.",
           "Let's see what happens when we take away the puppy.",
           "In the end there can be only one."
       ]

       presentTextInputControllerWithSuggestions(suggestions,
       → allowedInputMode: .AllowAnimatedEmoji) { responses in
           if let responses = responses where responses.count > 0 {
               if let response = responses.first as? String {
                   self.text = response
                   self.label.setText(self.text)
               } else if let response = responses.first as? NSData {
                   self.imageData = response
                   self.image.setImageData(self.imageData)
               }
           }
       }
   }
   ```

Run the app and try selecting an emoji as your response. Note that "normal," non-animated emoji are handled as a text response, whereas it is the animated emoji that are handled as image data. At the time of this writing, it appears that the received data is not sufficient to animate the emoji. Instead, its first frame is displayed (**Figure 11.6**).

FIGURE 11.6 Displaying the chosen emoji

PREPARING SUGGESTIONS

Dictation is useful for free text input, but it is limited by its reliance on network connectivity and the need for the user to be in a relatively quiet environment where background noise won't overshadow their voice. There's also the social factor: Although such practice may soon become commonplace and unremarkable, for the moment not everyone is comfortable talking into their wrist in public. And although the dictation is surprisingly accurate and effective, some regional accents can present it with quite a challenge. Your authors hail from a small country with a range of accents that are sometimes difficult for human ears to understand, never mind digital ones!

The ability of the text input controller to present suggested responses for the user to choose from is a way to work around these limitations. In their most simple use, as in the previous example, suggested responses can be hardcoded in the app, but it is perfectly possible to generate them at runtime. How you do so, and the question of whether it is even necessary, will depend on the app.

For example, a messaging app could suggest certain phrases based on the content of previous messages. A social media update app could learn what you regularly have for lunch and have those phrases ready to post. An app that lets you record what you watch at the cinema might cross-reference your location with a list of showtimes and have current films ready to be entered. You can do a lot with a network-connected, location-aware wrist computer.

You could even consider allowing the user to define their own suggested responses for different uses, be it in the companion iPhone app or via settings exposed in the iOS Watch app (see Chapter 6 for more on that functionality).

INPUT FROM NOTIFICATIONS

One more indirect way to trigger the text input controller is available. Notifications, local or remote, forwarded to a watchOS app can be configured so that they can accept a text response. This is analogous to how iOS 9 can present interactive notifications that accept text input.

We spent some time in Chapter 9 discussing how to make a text-based response to a notification, so if you skipped ahead to here, you may want to go back for a quick read of the section "Text Responses."

WRAPPING UP

Although it is true that text input is more restricted on Apple Watch than it is on an iOS device, it is still very capable—albeit with a little creativity, both from the watchOS development team and from third-party developers working with the platform. As has been a theme in previous chapters, careful planning to match the use of your app to the strengths of the platform is the key to a quality user experience.

It is unlikely anyone will want to compose their next best-selling novel by speaking at their wrist, but for a great many shorter pieces of text input, watchOS apps are ready and waiting.

CHAPTER 12

Playing and Recording Media

"Media player" may not be the first phrase that comes to mind to describe Apple Watch, but with its high-quality screen and native support for Bluetooth audio, it is surprisingly capable of useful audio and video playback. You may not be settling down to watch eleven and a half hours of fantasy epic on your wrist, but the watch is very well suited to quick bites of video and audio from messages or social media. These same media-handling capabilities are available to third-party apps.

WORKING WITH MEDIA

watchOS provides the ability to play audio and video content while your app is running in the foreground, to play audio in the background while your app isn't in active use, and to record audio.

Audio is played over the watch's built-in speaker or is automatically routed to Bluetooth headphones if any are connected.

MEDIA TYPES AND ENCODINGS

If you will be controlling the media that your watch app will be playing (whether by providing the media yourself or by processing user-supplied content on a server), it's worth making sure that the media files match Apple's recommendations. The recommendations are in the WatchKit documentation for `WKInterfaceMovie`, and the highlights are as follows:

- Video should be encoded as H.264 at a bit rate of 160 kbps and 30 frames per second. Video that has larger dimensions than the screen of the watch hardware will result in unnecessarily large files, so limit the files to a width of 320 pixels and a height of 260 pixels.
- Audio should be in stereo, at 32 kbps.

Of course, the watch can handle files at greater resolution than these, but without benefiting from the extra resolution.

STORING MEDIA

Where and how video and audio files are stored for access by your app depends primarily on whether the files are bundled with the app or are provided later. For example, your app may download content from the network or work with user-supplied content. In either case, remember the storage limitations of Apple Watch—media files tend to be large, and there isn't much space to store them locally on the watch. You may be able to cache files locally for only a short time, or you may be able to use WatchConnectivity to transfer files to and from the host iPhone (see Chapter 10 for an introduction to the WatchConnectivity framework).

When files are provided with the app, they should be added to the WatchKit extension's bundle. In this way they can be easily accessed by your extension code. When a file is downloaded from the network or is otherwise received at runtime, it should be saved into a shared App Group container accessible to both the WatchKit extension and the WatchKit app.

If necessary, `WKInterfaceMovie` also has the ability to load a file from a remote URL. Note, though, that the entire file will have to be downloaded before playback can begin.

FOREGROUND PLAYBACK

The simplest use of media in a watch app is playing it while the app is in the foreground. Most of the hard work for this is done for us, with easy access to a player interface via the WatchKit APIs. You can trigger the player programmatically or, even more simply, with a WKInterfaceMovie control.

USING WKINTERFACEMOVIE

The WKInterfaceMovie control displays a simple interface to the user, showing a poster image with a Play button superimposed (**Figure 12.1**). When the user taps the Play button, a modal player displays (**Figure 12.2**).

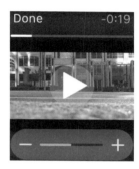

FIGURE 12.1 A WKInterfaceMovie control

FIGURE 12.2 The video player interface

WKInterfaceMovie can play audio content as well as video.
You manage the control with the following methods:

- setMovieURL(_:) takes the URL of the media file to be played by the control.
- setVideoGravity(_:) decides how the video should be sized to fit the screen on playback. Possible values are the cases of the WKVideoGravity enumeration type. These are .ResizeAspect, .ResizeAspectFill, and .Resize. The video gravity property can also be set in the storyboard editor.
- setPosterImage(_:) takes an optional WKImage to be used as the poster image for the control. A nil value clears the image. This can also be set in the storyboard editor.
- setLoops(_:) takes a Bool to control whether the media file will be played in a continuous loop or played once and stopped.

To demonstrate the use of WKInterfaceMovie, the following example uses media files available for download at bit.ly/bwa-media-assets.

1. In Xcode, create a new project from the watchOS > iOS App with WatchKit App template. When creating the project, leave the options for complications, glances, notifications, and tests unselected.

2. In the WatchKit Extension project group, add the file `poster.png` (downloaded from bit.ly/bwa-media-assets) to the `Assets.xcassets` asset catalog.

3. Add the file `FirstSnow.m4v` to the WatchKit Extension group, selecting "Copy items if needed" and ensuring that the file is added to the WatchKit Extension target (**Figure 12.3**).

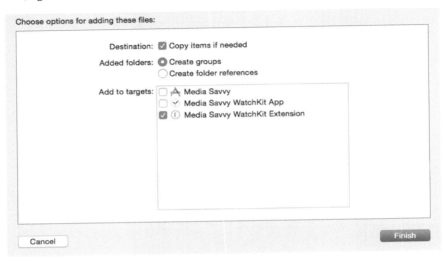

4. In the WatchKit App project group, open `Interface.storyboard`, and add a `WKInterfaceMovie` control to the interface controller scene (**Figure 12.4**).

FIGURE 12.4 The storyboard scene

5. Use the Attributes inspector to set the `WKInterfaceMovie`'s Video Gravity setting to Resize Aspect.

6. Open the WatchKit Extension's `InterfaceController.swift`, replace it with the following, and then connect the movie control to the `@IBOutlet`:

```
import WatchKit
import Foundation
```

```
class InterfaceController: WKInterfaceController {
    @IBOutlet var player: WKInterfaceMovie!
}
```

7. Add the following method to `InterfaceController`:

```
override func awakeWithContext(context: AnyObject?) {
    super.awakeWithContext(context)

    var posterImage: WKImage?
    if let image = UIImage(named: "poster") {
        posterImage = WKImage(image: image)
    }
    player.setPosterImage(posterImage)

    let bundle = NSBundle(forClass: InterfaceController.self)
    if let movieUrl = bundle.URLForResource("FirstSnow", withExtension:
    → "m4v") {
        player.setMovieURL(movieUrl)
    }
}
```

8. Run the app, and you will be able to play the movie via the `WKInterfaceMovie` in the interface.

Exactly the same approach can be used to play audio files.

PRESENTING A PLAYER PROGRAMMATICALLY

`WKInterfaceMovie` is very easy to use, but it also takes up a lot of screen space, even in its initial state. It is also possible to trigger the player UI programmatically, perhaps in response to a button press.

1. Return to `Interface.storyboard`, and delete the `WKInterfaceMovie` from the interface controller scene.

2. Add a button to the storyboard scene, and give it the title **Play** (**Figure 12.5**).

FIGURE 12.5 The button in the storyboard scene

3. In InterfaceController.swift, replace the existing @IBOutlet with the following, and connect it to the button in the storyboard scene:

```
@IBOutlet var button: WKInterfaceButton!
```

   Because you removed the movie control from the interface, the code to configure it is no longer needed.

4. Delete the awakeWithContext(_:) method from InterfaceController.

5. Add the following method to InterfaceController:

```
@IBAction func play() {
    let bundle = NSBundle(forClass: InterfaceController.self)
    if let movieUrl = bundle.URLForResource("FirstSnow", withExtension:
    → "m4v") {
        presentMediaPlayerControllerWithURL(movieUrl, options: nil)
        → {finished, endTime, error in
        }
    }
}
```

6. Connect the button in the storyboard scene to the @IBAction.

7. Run the app, and tap the button.

   You will see the same player interface displayed for the video.

   The method presentMediaPlayerControllerWithURL(_:options:completion:) of WKInterfaceController allows you to refine the user experience using its options and completion parameters. The options parameter is an optional dictionary that can have any or all of the following keys:

- WKMediaPlayerControllerOptionsAutoplayKey takes a Boolean value indicating whether the media should be automatically played on presentation rather than requiring the user to tap to play.

- WKMediaPlayerControllerOptionsStartTimeKey takes an NSTimeInterval value, indicating the point in the file from which playback should begin.

- WKMediaPlayerControllerOptionsVideoGravityKey corresponds to the Video Gravity setting on WKInterfaceMovie and takes the same enumeration values.

- WKMediaPlayerControllerOptionsLoopsKey takes a Boolean value to control whether the media will play once through or continuously on a loop until dismissed—either programmatically or by the user.

   The completion handler will receive three arguments: a Bool indicating whether or not the media file played to its end, an NSTimeInterval with the time index of playback when the player was dismissed, and an optional NSError that will be populated if an error occurs.

The completion handler is called when the user dismisses the player interface. It is also called if the player interface is dismissed programmatically. This is done with a call to the WKInterfaceController method dismissMediaPlayerController().

You need to make some changes to InterfaceController.swift.

1. Add the following property to InterfaceController:

    ```
    private var playbackPosition: NSTimeInterval = 0
    ```

2. Update the play method:

    ```
    @IBAction func play() {
        let bundle = NSBundle(forClass: InterfaceController.self)
        if let movieUrl = bundle.URLForResource("FirstSnow", withExtension:
        → "m4v") {
            let playerOptions = [
                WKMediaPlayerControllerOptionsStartTimeKey: playbackPosition
            ]
            presentMediaPlayerControllerWithURL(movieUrl, options:
            → playerOptions) {finished, endTime, error in
                self.playbackPosition = finished ? 0 : endTime
            }
        }
    }
    ```

The completion handler on presentMediaPlayerControllerWithURL(_:options: completion:) makes sure that when the player is dismissed and then presented again, playback will resume where it left off.

BACKGROUND AUDIO PLAYBACK

Any media playing in the foreground by a WatchKit app is paused when the app is no longer running—and remember that the system will stop the app after a period of user inactivity. In keeping with the nature of the watch, foreground playback is best suited to short pieces of content.

If your app needs to play a longer piece of audio, it can handle this limitation by handing the file off to the system to be played in the background. It will even appear in the Now Playing glance (**Figure 12.6**). However, background audio playback is available only when a Bluetooth audio device is connected to the watch.

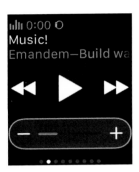

FIGURE 12.6 The Now Playing glance

To play background audio, the app needs to register for the audio background mode. Let's return to the media playback app from earlier in this chapter.

1. Open `Info.plist` from the WatchKit App project group (*not* the WatchKit Extension project group).

2. Add the key `UIBackgroundModes` with a value of `audio`.

   These values, when entered, will be translated by Xcode and displayed as shown in **Figure 12.7**.

▼ Information Property List		Dictionary	(14 items)
▼ Required background modes	⬍	Array	(1 item)
Item 0		String	App plays audio or streams audio/video using AirPlay

FIGURE 12.7 The audio background mode setting

3. Add an audio file to the WatchKit Extension group by dragging and dropping it from the Finder. Make sure that "Copy items if needed" is selected and that the file is assigned to the extension's target (as in Figure 12.3).

   If you need to find a suitable audio file for this exercise, we suggest browsing http://freemusicarchive.org. (In this example, we will proceed on the assumption that the file you have just added is named `music.mp3`. You should substitute the actual name of your file.)

4. Open `Interface.storyboard`, and add a second button to the interface controller scene, as in **Figure 12.8**. Give it a title of **Play Music**.

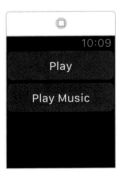

FIGURE 12.8 Adding the second button

5. Add the following @IBOutlet and @IBAction to InterfaceController.swift, connecting them both to the button that you just added.

```swift
@IBOutlet var backgroundButton: WKInterfaceButton!
@IBAction func toggleBackgroundPlayback() {
}
```

6. Add the following property and method to InterfaceController.swift.

```swift
private var isPlaying = false
private func updatebackgroundButton() {
    if (isPlaying) {
        backgroundButton.setTitle("Stop Music")
    } else {
        backgroundButton.setTitle("Play Music")
    }
}
```

7. Add an implementation of awakeWithContext(_:) as follows:

```swift
override func awakeWithContext(context: AnyObject?) {
    super.awakeWithContext(context)
    updatebackgroundButton()
}
```

8. Add the following to the implementation of InterfaceController:

```swift
// MARK: Background audio
private var musicItem: WKAudioFilePlayerItem?
private var backgroundPlayer: WKAudioFilePlayer?

private func startBackgroundPlayback() {
}

private func stopBackgroundPlayback() {
}

private func prepareAudioItemAndPlayer() {
}
```

9. Update toggleBackgroundPlayback() with the following:

```swift
@IBAction func toggleBackgroundPlayback() {
    isPlaying = !isPlaying
```

```
        if (isPlaying) {
            startBackgroundPlayback()
        } else {
            stopBackgroundPlayback()
        }

        updatebackgroundButton()
    }
```

10. Update the background audio methods to read as follows:

```
    private func startBackgroundPlayback() {
        prepareAudioItemAndPlayer()
        guard let _ = musicItem, backgroundPlayer = backgroundPlayer else
        → {return}

        backgroundPlayer.play()
    }

    private func stopBackgroundPlayback() {
        guard let backgroundPlayer = backgroundPlayer else {return}

        backgroundPlayer.pause()
    }

    private func prepareAudioItemAndPlayer() {
        guard musicItem == nil else {return}

        let bundle = NSBundle(forClass: InterfaceController.self)
        if let audioUrl = bundle.URLForResource("music", withExtension: "mp3") {
            let asset = WKAudioFileAsset(
                URL: audioUrl,
                title: "Music!",
                albumTitle: "Build watchOS Apps",
                artist: "Emandem"
            )

            musicItem = WKAudioFilePlayerItem(asset: asset)
            if let musicItem = musicItem {
```

```
            backgroundPlayer = WKAudioFilePlayer(playerItem: musicItem)
        }
    }
}
```

11. Run the app.

You'll be able to start and stop the background audio playback using the button in the app or via the Now Playing glance.

Note the use in the example of the `WKAudioFileAsset` initializer `init(URL:title:albumTitle:artist:)`. This is a simpler intializer that requires only the URL of the file, `init(URL:)`. If the audio asset is initialized with only the URL, the other properties can be set after initialization. Any properties that do not have values will be set from the metadata of the audio file, if available.

> **TIP:** The media files used as examples in this chapter are much larger than we recommend shipping in the bundle of a production watch app. If you need to bundle such large files, we recommend including them in the companion iPhone app and transferring them to the watch on demand using the WatchConnectivity framework (see Chapter 10).

AUDIO RECORDING

Any subclass of `WKInterfaceController` may use that class's method `presentAudioRecorderControllerWithOutputURL(_:preset:options:completion:)` to present a simple interface for recording short clips of audio via Apple Watch's microphone (**Figure 12.9**).

FIGURE 12.9 The audio recording interface

That method's URL parameter specifies the file to which the audio recording will be saved. The URL has two restrictions:

- The provided URL must be a file URL in a shared app group's container, to which both the WatchKit app and extension have access.
- The final segment of the URL is the name of the file, and the extension of the file is used to determine its format. Valid extensions are `.wav`, `.mp4`, and `.m4a`. Using any other file extension will result in an error.

The preset parameter takes one of three cases of the `WKAudioRecorderPreset` enumeration:

- `.NarrowBandSpeech` is for standard-quality speech recording.
- `.WideBandSpeech` is suitable for high-quality recordings of speech.
- `.HighQualityAudio`, as its name suggests, is the highest-quality recording available.

The options dictionary may be set to `nil`, which accepts the default recording setup, but it can accept any of the following keys:

- `WKAudioRecorderControllerOptionsActionTitleKey` is used to set an alternative label to the Save button of the recording modal.
- `WKAudioRecorderControllerOptionsAlwaysShowActionTitleKey` is a `Bool` that controls whether the Save button is shown even before the user has made a recording. The default value is `true`.
- `WKAudioRecorderControllerOptionsAutorecordKey` is a `Bool` specifying whether or not recording will begin automatically once the recording interface is presented. This defaults to `true`, and the user is prompted with a tap from the watch's haptic motor.
- `WKAudioRecorderControllerOptionsMaximumDurationKey` takes an `NSTimeInterval` specifying the maximum length of the recording. If this is unspecified, then it has no maximum length.

The default values of the various options are practical for many recording scenarios.

Finally, `presentAudioRecorderControllerWithOutputURL(_:preset:options:completion:)`'s completion handler receives two arguments. The first is a `Bool` indicating whether or not an audio recording was saved (perhaps the user canceled without saving), and the second is an optional `NSError` containing details of any error encountered.

The first time a watch app presents the recording interface, an alert will be displayed on the host iPhone, requesting access to the microphone. This is easy to miss, so it may be appropriate to present an alert in the watch app prompting the user to look to their phone.

MAKING A RECORDING

Using watchOS's recording interface requires only a little effort from you as the developer.

1. In Xcode, create a new project using the watchOS > iOS App with WatchKit App template. This example will use none of complications, glances, notifications, or tests, so leave the options for those unselected.

In preparation for saving a recording, you need to create an App Group identifier. This is done in the App Groups section of the Certificates, Identifiers & Profiles screen in the Developer Center.

2. In a browser, go to http://bit.ly/bwa-adc-groups. Create a new group by clicking the + button shown in **Figure 12.10**.

FIGURE 12.10 Adding an app group

3. Specify a description and identifier for the group. Note that the form will enforce that the group identifier be prefixed with group. (**Figure 12.11**).

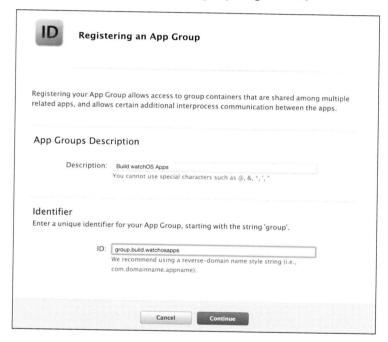

FIGURE 12.11 Setting up the app group

4. Click Continue, then click Register, then click Done to move through the screens.

5. Back in Xcode, select the top-level project from the Project Navigator, then select the WatchKit App target. Navigate to the Capabilities tab, and switch the App Groups setting to On (**Figure 12.12**).

Xcode will access your developer account and retrieve the available app groups.

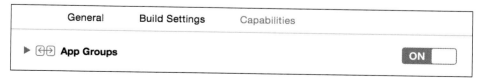

FIGURE 12.12 Enabling app groups

6. Select the checkbox beside the identifier you created in steps 2–4.

   Xcode will make sure that the app has a specific bundle identifier and will register it in the developer portal for you. When the process is complete, you should see three checkmarks, as in **Figure 12.13**.

Steps: ✔ Add the "App Groups" entitlement to your entitlements file
✔ Add the "App Groups" entitlement to your App ID
✔ Add the "App Groups containers" entitlement to your App ID

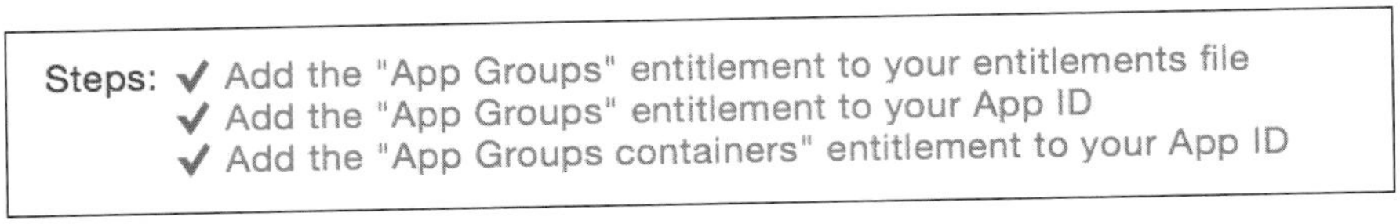

FIGURE 12.13 A correctly set up app group

7. Repeat steps 5 and 6 for the WatchKit Extension target.
8. Open the WatchKit App's `Interface.storyboard`, and populate the default scene with two button like the ones in **Figure 12.14**.

Interface Controller
10:09
Record
Play

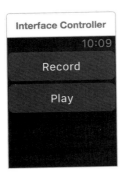

FIGURE 12.14 The buttons in the storyboard scene

9. Open `InterfaceController.swift`, and replace its contents with the following, connecting the buttons in the storyboard to the two `@IBOutlets`:

```
import WatchKit
import Foundation

class InterfaceController: WKInterfaceController {
    @IBOutlet var recordButton: WKInterfaceButton!
    @IBOutlet var playButton: WKInterfaceButton!
}
```

10. Add the following property and method to `InterfaceController`:

```
private var audioUrl: NSURL?
private func updatePlayButtonState() {
    playButton.setEnabled(audioUrl != nil)
}
```

11. Add an implementation of willActivate() as follows:

```swift
override func willActivate() {
    super.willActivate()

    updatePlayButtonState()
}
```

In order to save an audio file, you need to find the App Group container and specify the URL to a target file there.

12. Add the following method to specify the URL:

```swift
private func generateAudioUrl() {
    let containerUrl = NSFileManager.defaultManager().containerURLFor
    ⤳ SecurityApplicationGroupIdentifier("group.build.watchosapps")!
    let filename = String(NSDate().timeIntervalSince1970)

    audioUrl = containerUrl.URLByAppendingPathComponent("\(filename).m4a")
}
```

13. Add two @IBAction methods as follows, and connect them to the appropriate buttons in the storyboard scene:

```swift
@IBAction func record() {
    generateAudioUrl()

    if let url = audioUrl {
        presentAudioRecorderControllerWithOutputURL(
            url,
            preset: .NarrowBandSpeech,
            options: nil) { didSave, error -> Void in
                if !didSave {
                    self.audioUrl = nil
                }

                self.updatePlayButtonState()
        }
    }
}

@IBAction func play() {
    guard let url = audioUrl else {return}
```

```
presentMediaPlayerControllerWithURL(url, options: nil) { finished,
→ endTime, error -> Void in
    if finished {
        do {
            try NSFileManager.defaultManager().removeItemAtURL(url)
            self.audioUrl = nil
            self.updatePlayButtonState()
        } catch {}
    }
}
}
```

In the completion handler of the media player, this example checks whether the file was played to its end. If it was, the file is deleted to save on storage.

14. Run the example.

   You will be able to record audio and play it back. Note that if you are running the example in a simulator, everything will work as it should, except that the recorded audio track will consist only of silence. This is a limitation of the simulator. Deploying to a physical device, as described in Chapter 13, will allow you to experience this app in all its glory.

HANDLING RECORDED AUDIO

As noted, audio recordings should be saved to a shared container to which both the Watch-Kit app and the WatchKit extension have access. This provides flexibility in accessing the saved file, but you should consider what your app should do with the audio.

Depending on the duration and quality of the recording, files can get quite large. Apple Watch's storage space is constrained, so these files should be dealt with and deleted as soon as possible. Your app might need to upload the file to a server, which can be done directly from the watch, but if it is to be stored for later access, consider transferring it to the host iPhone using the WatchConnectivity framework (see Chapter 10). Any intensive processing can be carried out on the more powerful phone, or it can be used as a place to keep the file and retrieve it later. Remember, though, that the larger the file, the longer it will take to transfer between devices. And since the transfer takes place over a Bluetooth connection, the larger the file the more power will be consumed.

Ultimately, of course, how an app handles the recorded audio will be decided by the reason it was recorded in the first place—be that for sharing online or storing for later use.

WRAPPING UP

The media handling facilities offered by Apple Watch may be limited, but there is great strength in their ubiquity. A screen, a speaker, and a microphone are right there on the user's wrist, ready to be called into action at the shortest of notice and with a minimum of hassle.

These media capabilities are much less impressive in the simulator than they are when displayed by an actual watch on your wrist. In Chapter 13, we will walk through how to deploy your watchOS apps to a physical device. Then you can see just how impressive these media capabilities can be in reality.

Deploying to Physical Devices

We have spent most of the book running the example code in the Watch simulator supplied with Xcode. Although this is invaluable in terms of time and cost efficiency, nothing beats the feeling of deploying your app to a physical device. And no matter how good a simulator is, there's always the chance that what works in the simulator may not work on a real device.

MANAGING DEVICES

Apple Watch devices cannot be directly connected to your Mac in order to be deployed onto, so instead you must connect the iPhone that the watch has been paired with. Once it's connected, you can open the Device Manager by selecting Window > Device Manager from the Xcode main menu.

When you do so, you may be surprised to see that your iPhone has appeared in the device list but the watch has not. Strangely, there are also no watch devices configured in the list of simulators. This is to be expected—given the close bond between iPhone and Watch, you can only see watch devices in the Device Manager by viewing the details for the iPhone that it has been paired with. Select your iPhone in the device list to see the information for the watch (**Figure 13.1**).

FIGURE 13.1 Viewing your iPhone and paired watch in the Device Manager

Most of the information shown in the Device Manager is of little use to you during the development process, but it is worth recording the Identifier property in case you need to add it manually through the online Developer Center at some stage.

NOTE: The watch details will only be shown if your watch is currently paired with the iPhone. If the watch is moved out of range of the iPhone, the details will disappear from the Device Manager, and you may need to deselect and reselect the iPhone to refresh them.

Simulator devices that are configured with a paired watch simulator are not easily identifiable in the list, but you can find them by clicking a simulator in the list and navigating using the Up and Down Arrow keys. When you encounter a phone and watch combination, the device information will show the paired watch information as well. If you want to configure more combinations, click the plus (+) button to start creating a new simulator and choose an iPhone 5 or higher as the Device Type. You will then get the option to assign a paired Apple Watch.

CONFIGURING PROVISIONING PROFILES

If you want to run your watchOS app on a physical device, you need to make sure your project is configured with a development team. We'll assume that you already have a development team set up in the Developer Center as part of your iOS development workflow, but you should ensure that your copy of Xcode is configured with an Apple ID to make the team available to your projects. You can do this by adding your Apple ID as an account in the Accounts tab in the Xcode settings.

As of version 6.0, Xcode learned a few tricks that involved the magic Fix Issue(s) buttons that would often appear in response to device provisioning issues. Although clicking the button often results in success, it can regularly result in a partially configured nightmare that no amount of "fixing issues" can resolve. To account for this, we will take a trip through the manual process in a later section.

TIP: If your Apple ID belongs to multiple development teams, you can explicitly choose which one to use for a target by opening the project settings and changing the Team pop-up menu setting to the correct one.

AUTOMAGIC SETUP

Let Xcode do a lot of the work for you.

1. Select Xcode > Preferences from the Xcode main menu, then select the Accounts tab.

   If you already have an account set up, then you can jump ahead to step 3.

2. Click the plus (+) button to create an account, and select Add Apple ID from the pop-up menu to enter your Apple ID and password.

After you sign in, Xcode will contact the Developer Center and retrieve the list of teams to which you belong and display them in the right pane of the Accounts tab.

3. Close the Preferences window, pick a WatchKit App scheme from the scheme selector pop-up menu, and then select a physical phone and watch combination as the destination (**Figure 13.2**).

FIGURE 13.2 Selecting the scheme and devices

4. Press Command-B to start a build of the WatchKit App scheme.

The build process will quickly stop and present you with a warning that it was unable to code sign the WatchKit extension (**Figure 13.3**). To code sign an executable, Xcode needs two things: a valid development certificate and a provisioning profile that can include the bundle identifier of the WatchKit extension.

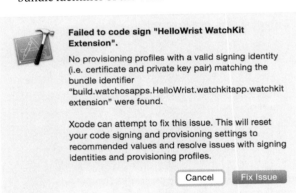

FIGURE 13.3 The warning message displayed when a valid provisioning profile cannot be found

5. Click the Fix Issue button to let Xcode attempt to fix the issue for you.

It is hard to specify exactly what Xcode will do in response to clicking the Fix Issue button. Some things it might do include:

■ Prompt you to choose a development team. If you are a member of multiple teams, you will need to choose one to continue the process with.

■ Prompt you to import a developer profile from another computer. If you have a valid development certificate in the Developer Center but do not have the necessary keys in your local keychain, you can import a developer profile from the machine you created the profile on.

- Prompt you to reset the development certificate. If you have a valid development certificate in the Developer Center but do not have the necessary keys in your local keychain, you can instead revoke the existing certificate and create a new one.

- Prompt you to create a new provisioning profile. If there is a valid provisioning profile but it does not contain the correct device identifiers or development certificate, Xcode can delete the existing profile and create a new one for you.

MANUAL SETUP

Unfortunately, sometimes Xcode will not quite manage to complete the process, so it helps to be aware of what actually needs to happen at the Developer Center in order to repair a partially completed provisioning attempt. In the following steps, we illustrate the entire process from scratch. Where Xcode has performed some of the actions, you may need to check the validity of the output.

1. In a web browser, navigate to the Certificates, Identifiers & Profiles section of the Apple Developer Center (bit.ly/bwa-adc-certs).

   Unless you have visited the Developer Center very recently, you will be prompted to sign in using your Apple ID. If you are a member of multiple teams, you will be prompted to select a team to use as well.

2. Under the iOS Apps column, click the link to Certificates.

3. In the Certificates section, check to see if you have a valid (non-expired) iOS Development certificate for which you have the original signing keys.

   If you have a valid certificate with the signing keys, you can jump ahead to step 8.

   If your certificate is invalid or you no longer have access to the keys used to sign the certificate in the past, you may need to create a new certificate instead.

4. Click the plus (+) button near the upper right of the screen to start the process of creating a certificate.

5. In response to the question "What type of certificate do you need?" you should choose iOS App Development (**Figure 13.4**) and click Continue at the bottom of the screen.

FIGURE 13.4 Creating an iOS App Development certificate

6. Create a Certificate Signing Request (CSR) by following the instructions provided onscreen (they're good instructions so why try to better them?) and then click Continue.

7. Upload the CSR to the Developer Center, and click Generate.

The result of this process is a new valid certificate. You can download this certificate and directly install it by double-clicking it in the Finder, or you can let Xcode retrieve it later. With the certificate resolved, you can now move on to registering your development devices in the Devices section.

TIP: If you intend to use the certificate on more than one Mac, you will need to export the signing keys created when you generated the CSR. The Keychain Access application can be used to export these from one Mac and import them to another. Refer to the in-app documentation for more guidance.

8. Click the All link under the Devices section of the page.

9. Check whether your iPhone and your Apple Watch need to be registered by looking for their name and device identifier in the list of devices.

The device identifier for your phone and watch can be found in the Device Manager when they are connected (Figure 13.1). If they already exist, you can jump ahead to step 13. If they don't exist in the list of registered devices, you will need to register them.

10. Click the plus (+) button near the upper right of the page, and enter the name of your watch—make it meaningful so that you understand what it is when you see it again (**Figure 13.5**).

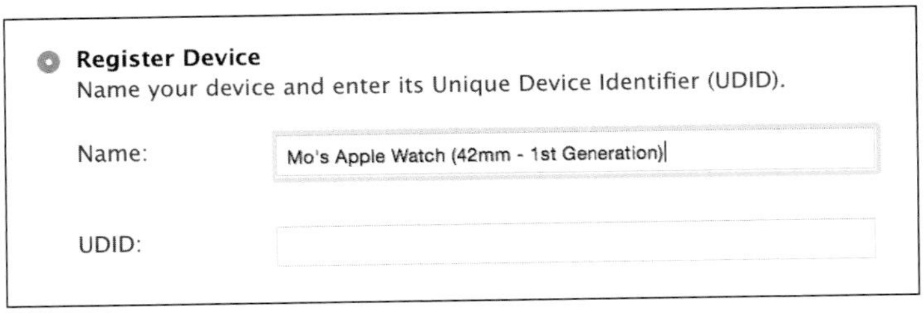

FIGURE 13.5 Registering a new device

Register Device
Name your device and enter its Unique Device Identifier (UDID).

Name: Mo's Apple Watch (42mm - 1st Generation)

UDID:

11. Enter the device identifier (found in the Device Manager in Xcode) in the UDID field, click Continue to submit the details, and then click Register to confirm your decision.

Apple recently increased the limit for the number of devices you can register; you can now have up to 100 devices for each of the following categories: iPhone, iPad, iPod touch, Apple Watch, and Apple TV. Yes, Apple TV. Now there's another book.

12. Repeat steps 10 and 11 for your iPhone.

By this stage, you should have both your watch and phone registered as devices. This means that you will be able to include them both in a provisioning profile (along with the development certificate).

13. Click the Development link under the Provisioning Profiles section to view the list of existing profiles.

If you already have a profile that you wish to amend with extra devices, you can choose to edit and regenerate it instead of creating a new one from scratch. You cannot, however, change the development certificate associated with a provisioning profile.

14. Click the plus (+) button to add a new provisioning profile, and select the iOS App Development profile type (**Figure 13.6**).

FIGURE 13.6 Creating a new provisioning profile

15. Click Continue to confirm your choice.

16. Unless you need something more specific, choose the Xcode iOS Wildcard App ID, and click Continue.

At this stage, we don't need to be more specific, and so we're creating a provisioning profile that will match the bundle identifier in any app. If you want to be more specific, you should create an App ID in the Identifiers section for your specific app and select it instead. You will have to do this later in Chapter 15 in order to produce provisioning profiles for app distribution.

17. Select the certificates you wish to include in the profile.

This example includes the certificate you created in steps 2 through 7, but you can opt for any that may already exist (**Figure 13.7**).

FIGURE 13.7 Selecting a development certificate for inclusion with a provisioning profile

18. Click Continue.

19. Select the registered devices that you wish to include in the provisioning profile.

   The provisioning profile will be usable only with the devices that you specify at this stage. Note that you can edit the devices at a later stage (causing the profile to be regenerated), but it usually makes sense to just click the Select All checkbox. Having too many devices included in a profile doesn't do any harm. At the bare minimum, make sure your iPhone and Apple Watch devices are selected.

20. Click Continue.

21. Give your profile a meaningful name, and click Generate to complete the process (**Figure 13.8**).

   You can download the profile and double-click it in the Finder to install it to Xcode directly, or you can follow along and get Xcode to refresh the certificates and profiles from the Developer Center.

FIGURE 13.8 The final steps in creating your provisioning profile

22. Return to Xcode, and select Xcode > Preferences from the Xcode main menu.

23. In the Accounts tab, select your Apple ID, and then select the appropriate team name.

24. Click View Details.

   Xcode will connect to the Developer Center and show the list of Signing Identities (certificates) and Provisioning Profiles belonging to you for that team (**Figure 13.9**).

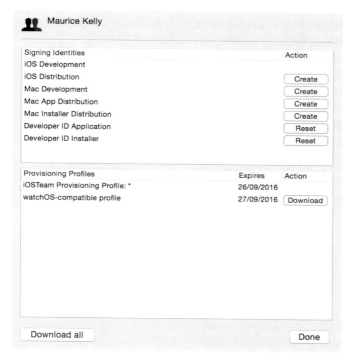

FIGURE 13.9 Xcode's view of your certificates and profiles

FIGURE 13.9 Xcode's view of your certificates and profiles

25. If the Signing Identity or Provisioning Profile has a Download button beside it, click it to download it from the Developer Center.

Now that you've got everything you need to deploy onto a physical device, it's time to start testing your apps for real.

DEPLOYING TO A DEVICE

The line that determines when you should switch between using a simulator and a real device for watchOS app development is not a clear one. In fact, there is another point to consider: distribution of beta test versions of your app to a wider audience. The decision to use a simulator or a real device is analogous to the decision to use CPU cache, main memory, or a solid state drive (SSD) in computing.

Working with the simulator is very much like relying on CPU cache: It is fast and convenient because it lives right on the machine you are developing on. But it isn't as practical for demonstrations because it is tied to your Mac, and simulators never impress as much as running on a physical device. Working with a real watch (paired with a phone connected to your Mac) is the equivalent of working with main memory: The testing cycle is somewhat extended, but it is more convenient for getting "fingertips-on" experience with the real device. Finally, wider distribution is much like using a bigger but much slower SSD: Although it is better for getting test versions of your app out to many beta testers, it really suffers from latency between build and deploy to devices (especially if you use Apple's TestFlight system).

Although it does not have the same kind of instant feedback as working with a simulator, running your app on a physical device isn't so challenging once you have the necessary provisioning steps set up.

1. Pair your Apple Watch with your development iPhone, if it has not already been paired.

2. Connect the iPhone to your Mac by plugging it into a USB port.

   All being well, the scheme selection pop-up menu updates to indicate that the device pairing has been correctly picked up.

3. Click the scheme selection menu, and select the pairing as the destination for running any of the watchOS specific schemes (Figure 13.2).

4. Click the Run button to start the build and deploy to the device.

   This process can take some time because it has a number of things to do. The first task is to rebuild the iOS app and the watchOS app for physical devices instead of simulators (building for the ARM architecture instead of Intel).

   Once it's built, Xcode begins the process of copying the app bundles to the devices. The iOS app will first be copied to the iPhone; this is relatively quick because it is being copied over the USB connection. The slower phase is extracting the watchOS app and copying it over the Bluetooth connection between the phone and watch. This can take some time, and you may soon get used to seeing messages such as those in **Figure 13.10**.

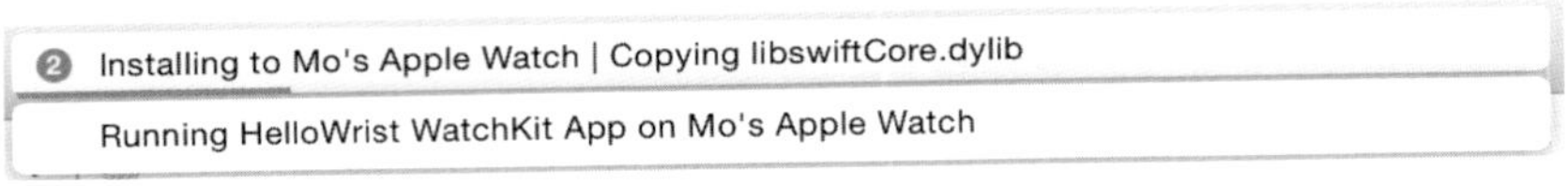

FIGURE 13.10 Copying the watchOS app to the device

> ❷ Installing to Mo's Apple Watch | Copying libswiftCore.dylib
>
> Running HelloWrist WatchKit App on Mo's Apple Watch

NOTE: The process of deploying to the watch may be interrupted by Xcode prompting you to unlock your phone; if your phone is locked the deployment cannot be completed. If you're going to be settling down for a long session of device testing, it may be wise to disable the automatic locking of the phone for the duration of the session. We've also experienced fewer failures to launch the app on the watch when its PIN has also been disabled.

The wait is worth it—running your own app on a physical device is exciting, and it seems even more magical when it is running on a mini computer mounted on your wrist.

WRAPPING UP

Testing your app on a physical device is always an exciting experience, and running watchOS apps on an Apple Watch is particularly exciting. It is also a vital part of the testing process and can make the difference between the first view of a prototype app being of merely passing interest to a customer and thrilling them.

In the next chapter, we take advantage of our newfound ability to run the app on a physical device and examine the Apple Watch hardware capabilities that are available to you as a developer.

CHAPTER 14

Using Hardware APIs

Since iPhone SDK was first made available to developers, in 2008, one of the most exciting aspects of developing for Apple platforms has been access to the varied capabilities of the hardware itself. Apple Watch and watchOS are no different, allowing developers access to the potential of the heart rate sensor, the accelerometer, and the much-vaunted haptic feedback system dubbed the Taptic Engine.

USING SENSOR DATA

WatchKit apps can access data from two of the watch's sensors: the heart rate sensor on the underside of the watch and the internal accelerometer. The data from these sensors is available via the HealthKit and CoreMotion frameworks.

ACCESSING HEART RATE DATA VIA HEALTHKIT

In iOS 8, Apple introduced the Health app, backed by the HealthKit framework. The intention is to provide a central repository of health-related data, populated by any app (and informed by any device) to which the user grants access.

The core design principle for HealthKit is to keep the user in control of their data at all times. This is enforced at the API and interface level by requiring an app to request access to each type of data (weight, heart rate, or step count, for example), with the user being able to authorize or deny each app's ability to read or write each type of data. As a matter of policy, Apple insists that only apps with a clear health and fitness purpose may access health data.

Another example of how seriously Apple takes user privacy in the implementation of HealthKit and the Health app is that the database is stored and encrypted on the user's iPhone rather than in a cloud-based repository. Of course, there are by now plenty of apps and services that can synchronize HealthKit data to their own database, and this is a valid and permitted use of the data, but again, this is only possible after the user has explicitly granted those apps access to the data.

When an app has received the necessary permission from the user, it can query the HealthKit database for a wide variety of types of data (and, with the right permissions, write data to the database). The query engine is detailed and powerful, providing a mechanism for very fine-grained queries according to timeframe and data type, but a proper exploration of its facilities is outside the scope of this book.

Instead, we will look at how to access streaming heart rate data during a *workout*. In the context of HealthKit and watchOS, a workout is a period of focused activity that contributes to the user's daily Exercise total (the green ring in the Activity app). It is possible to access recorded heart rate data without initiating a workout, but for our purposes here, a workout provides two benefits: It allows the app to stay in the foreground rather than being deactivated after a short time without user interaction, and it provides frequent, streamed updates of the user's activity.

In the following example, we will work through the various points of contact with the HealthKit APIs. There are quite a few, so prepare yourself for a workout indeed!

PREPARING THE USER INTERFACE

This app will have a very simple interface. It will use a HealthKit workout to access heart rate data, so it will need a button to start and stop the workout. You will also include a label for your output.

1. In Xcode, create a new app using the watchOS > Application > iOS App with WatchKit App template. Do not select the options for notification, glance, complication, or tests, since you won't be using them here.

2. Open the WatchKit app's `Interface.storyboard`, and add a button and a label as shown in **Figure 14.1**.

FIGURE 14.1 The button and label in the storyboard scene

3. Open the WatchKit extension's `InterfaceController.swift`, and replace its contents with the following; then connect the button and the label in the storyboard scene to the relevant `@IBOutlets` and `@IBAction`:

```swift
import WatchKit
import Foundation

class InterfaceController: WKInterfaceController {
    @IBOutlet var button: WKInterfaceButton!
    @IBOutlet var label: WKInterfaceLabel!

    @IBAction func buttonTapped() {
    }
}
```

4. Add the following property and method to `InterfaceController`:

```swift
private var readingHeartRate = false {
    didSet {
        updateButton()
    }
}

private func updateButton() {
    if readingHeartRate {
```

```
            button.setTitle("Stop")
        } else {
            button.setTitle("Start")
        }
    }
```

5. Add the following implementation of awakeWithContext(_:) to initialize the user interface when the app launches:

```
override func awakeWithContext(context: AnyObject?) {
    super.awakeWithContext(context)

    label.setText("-")
    updateButton()
}
```

6. Add the following two methods. For now they will simply trigger the UI updates by changing the value of readingHeartRate:

```
private func beginReadingHeartRate() {
    readingHeartRate = true
}

private func endReadingHeartRate() {
    readingHeartRate = false
}
```

7. Update the implementation of buttonTapped to read as follows:

```
@IBAction func buttonTapped() {
        if readingHeartRate {
            endReadingHeartRate()
        } else {
            beginReadingHeartRate()
        }
    }
```

Now that you have the user interface in place and the necessary @IBOutlets and @IBAction connected, the next task is to request access to heart rate data from HealthKit.

SETTING UP HEALTHKIT ACCESS

In order to access heart rate data through a HealthKit workout, some preparation is required. First, the app must check that HealthKit data is available and request access to heart rate data. If the access request is successful, then the workout can be created and started.

In order to access HealthKit data, the WatchKit Extension must have the necessary entitlement.

1. In Xcode's Project Navigator, select the top-level project. Then select the WatchKit Extension target, and navigate to the Capabilities tab. Switch on the HealthKit capability (**Figure 14.2**). Do the same for the iPhone app target.

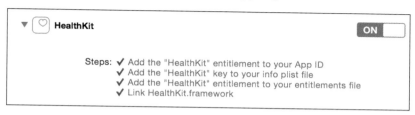

FIGURE 14.2 Selecting the HealthKit entitlement

2. In InterfaceController.swift, add the following line at the top of the file:

```
import HealthKit
```

3. Still in InterfaceController.swift, add the following extension at the end of the file:

```
// MARK: HealthKit access
extension InterfaceController: HKWorkoutSessionDelegate {
    // MARK: HKWorkoutSessionDelegate

    func workoutSession(
        workoutSession: HKWorkoutSession,
        didChangeToState toState: HKWorkoutSessionState,
        fromState: HKWorkoutSessionState,
        date: NSDate
    ) {
    }

    func workoutSession(
        workoutSession: HKWorkoutSession,
        didFailWithError error: NSError
    ) {
    }
}
```

4. In the main body of the InterfaceController class, add the following properties:

```
let healthStore = HKHealthStore()
var quantityType: HKQuantityType?
var workoutSession: HKWorkoutSession? {
```

```
        didSet {
            workoutSession?.delegate = self
        }
    }
```

5. Add the following method to the main body of the class (it will be used to signal the various error conditions):

TIP: Using emoji in source code is one of the more whimsical things enabled by the Swift programming language's Unicode support. You can insert them using the OS X symbol picker, triggered by pressing Ctrl+Cmd+Space.

```
private func updateWithNoAccess() {
    label.setText("⚠️")
    endReadingHeartRate()
}
```

6. To request HealthKit access, add the following method to the HealthKit access extension in InterfaceController.swift:

```
private func beginWorkout() {
    guard HKHealthStore.isHealthDataAvailable() else {
        updateWithNoAccess()
        print("HealthKit unavailable")
        return
    }

    quantityType = HKQuantityType.quantityTypeForIdentifier(HKQuantity
    → TypeIdentifierHeartRate)
    if let quantityType = quantityType {
        healthStore.requestAuthorizationToShareTypes(
            nil,
            readTypes: Set([quantityType]),
            completion: accessRequestReturned
        )
    } else {
        updateWithNoAccess()
        print("No quantity type")
    }
}
```

HealthKit supports a number of different sample and query types. Heart rate is an HKQuantityType, and you will be using an HKAnchoredObjectQuery to access it. See Apple's HealthKit documentation for information on the other possibilities.

7. Add the following method to the HealthKit access extension to handle the authorization request:

```
private func accessRequestReturned(allowed: Bool, error: NSError?) {
    guard allowed else {
        updateWithNoAccess()
        print(error?.description)
        return
    }

    workoutSession = HKWorkoutSession(activityType: .Other, locationType:
    →.Indoor)

    if let workoutSession = workoutSession {
        healthStore.startWorkoutSession(workoutSession)
    }
}
```

8. Add one more method to the extension:

```
private func endWorkout() {
    if let workoutSession = workoutSession {
        healthStore.endWorkoutSession(workoutSession)
    }
}
```

9. Update beginReadingHeartRate() and endReadingHeartRate() to call the beginWorkout() and endWorkout() methods you just added:

```
private func beginReadingHeartRate() {
    readingHeartRate = true
    beginWorkout()
}

private func endReadingHeartRate() {
    readingHeartRate = false
    endWorkout()
}
```

When the user is prompted to allow access to HealthKit data, the interface is presented by the iPhone app. This requires the addition of one method to the iPhone app's application delegate.

10. Open `AppDelegate.swift`, and add the import for HealthKit:

```
import HealthKit
```

11. Add the following method to AppDelegate:

```
func applicationShouldRequestHealthAuthorization(application:
→ UIApplication) {
    HKHealthStore().handleAuthorizationForExtensionWithCompletion
    → { (success, error) -> Void in
    }
}
```

RESPONDING TO HEART RATE UPDATES

As mentioned in the previous section, this example queries for heart rate data using an `HKAnchoredObjectQuery`. This type of query is so named because it has an *anchor*—a point in time that acts as a boundary on the results. Only data from after the anchor will be returned.

Once the query is created, it is possible to add an update handler that is called when new data that match the query is added to the HealthKit store. You will use this technique to receive heart rate data as it becomes available.

1. Returning to `InterfaceController.swift`, add three new properties to `InterfaceController`:

```
var unit: HKUnit?
var queryAnchor: HKQueryAnchor?
var query: HKAnchoredObjectQuery?
```

2. Update the two `HKWorkoutSessionDelegate` methods as follows:

```
func workoutSession(
    workoutSession: HKWorkoutSession,
    didChangeToState toState: HKWorkoutSessionState,
    fromState: HKWorkoutSessionState,
    date: NSDate
) {
    if toState == .Running {
        workoutStarted()
    } else if toState == .Ended {
        workoutEnded()
    }
}
```

```
func workoutSession(
    workoutSession: HKWorkoutSession,
    didFailWithError error: NSError
) {
    print(error.description)
    endReadingHeartRate()
    label.setText("Error!")
}
```

3. Add the following method to stop the query (which you will be creating shortly) when the user ends the workout:

```
private func workoutEnded() {
    if let query = query {
        healthStore.stopQuery(query)
    }
}
```

4. Add the workoutStarted(_:) method, which is where you will create and execute the query, as follows:

```
private func workoutStarted() {
    unit = HKUnit(fromString: "count/min")

    if queryAnchor == nil {
        queryAnchor = HKQueryAnchor(fromValue: Int(HKAnchoredObject
        ⇢ QueryNoAnchor))
    }

    query = HKAnchoredObjectQuery(
        type: quantityType!,
        predicate: nil,
        anchor: queryAnchor,
        limit: Int(HKObjectQueryNoLimit),
        resultsHandler: queryUpdateReceived
    )

    if let query = query {
        query.updateHandler = queryUpdateReceived
        healthStore.executeQuery(query)
    }
}
```

Two more methods are required. The first is the callback for the query.

5. Add the following callback method:

```
private func queryUpdateReceived(
    query: HKAnchoredObjectQuery,
    samples: [HKSample]?,
    deletedSamples: [HKDeletedObject]?,
    updatedAnchor: HKQueryAnchor?,
    error: NSError?
) -> Void {
    if let updatedAnchor = updatedAnchor {
        self.queryAnchor = updatedAnchor
        self.heartRateSamplesReceived(samples)
    }
}
```

Finally, add the method to update the user interface as heart rate data is received. Callbacks from HealthKit are executed on a background queue, so you need to make sure that UI updates are properly dispatched to the main queue.

6. Add the following to update the user interface:

```
private func heartRateSamplesReceived(samples: [HKSample]?) {
    guard let quantitySamples = samples as? [HKQuantitySample] else
    → { return }

    dispatch_async(dispatch_get_main_queue()) {
        guard let sample = quantitySamples.first, unit = self.unit else
        → { return }
        self.label.setText("\(sample.quantity.doubleValueForUnit(unit))")
    }
}
```

7. Run the app on your watch, and tap the Start button.

An alert on the paired iPhone will prompt you to allow the app to access your heart rate data (**Figure 14.3**). Once you allow access, the interface will start to update as the app receives heart rate data from HealthKit. If you stop and start the workout session, the queryAnchor property will make sure that only new, up-to-date data is received in each session.

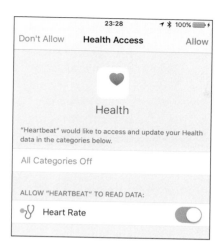

FIGURE 14.3 Authorizing access to HealthKit data

READING ACCELEROMETER DATA WITH COREMOTION

HealthKit is only one of the new (to the watch) frameworks that were made available in watchOS 2. CoreMotion has been giving developers bright ideas since the first iPhone SDK release (iPhoneOS 2), and watchOS 2 has brought it to the watch. Although CoreMotion on the iPhone has access to an exciting variety of sensors, apps running on Apple Watch have only the accelerometer. It is possible to access both the raw accelerometer data and to read step counts calculated by the system.

READING RAW ACCELEROMETER DATA

You'll be glad to hear that accessing accelerometer data requires much less work than using HealthKit.

1. Open Xcode and create a new app using the watchOS > Application > iOS App with WatchKit App template. Don't select the options for notification, glance, complication, or tests.

2. Open the WatchKit app's `Interface.storyboard`, and add three labels to the interface controller scene, as in **Figure 14.4**.

FIGURE 14.4 Labels for the accelerometer data

3. Open the WatchKit Extension's InterfaceController.swift, and replace its contents with the following:

```swift
import WatchKit
import Foundation
import CoreMotion

class InterfaceController: WKInterfaceController {
    @IBOutlet var xLabel: WKInterfaceLabel!
    @IBOutlet var yLabel: WKInterfaceLabel!
    @IBOutlet var zLabel: WKInterfaceLabel!
}
```

4. Connect the labels in the storyboard scene to the matching @IBOutlets in InterfaceController.swift.

This app will take the simple approach of starting to read accelerometer data when the interface controller becomes active, and stopping when it becomes inactive. To do so, it needs an instance of CMMotionManager.

5. Add one more property to InterfaceController:

```swift
let manager = CMMotionManager()
```

6. Add the following implementation of willActivate() to the interface controller:

```swift
override func willActivate() {
    super.willActivate()

    guard manager.accelerometerAvailable else {
        xLabel.setText("⚠")
        yLabel.setText("⚠")
        zLabel.setText("⚠")
        return
    }

    manager.accelerometerUpdateInterval = 0.2
    manager.startAccelerometerUpdatesToQueue(NSOperationQueue.
    → currentQueue()!) { data, error in
        if let data = data {
            self.xLabel.setText("X: \(data.acceleration.x)")
            self.yLabel.setText("Y: \(data.acceleration.y)")
            self.zLabel.setText("Z: \(data.acceleration.z)")
        } else {
```

```
            print(error?.description)
        }
    }
}
```

7. Add the `didDeactivate()` method:

```
override func didDeactivate() {
    super.didDeactivate()

    manager.stopAccelerometerUpdates()
}
```

When you run the app on your watch, you will be able to see the accelerometer data update rapidly as you swing your arm around. Go on—try it!

READING PEDOMETER DATA

The raw data produced by the accelerometer is precise and updates quickly, but such unprocessed data needs interpretation. CoreMotion provides one such interpretation of the data, provided via the `CMPedometer` class.

You can use `CMPedometer` to query historical data or to receive live streaming updates. It provides instances of `CMPedometerData`, which can include a variety of information, each relative to the object's `startDate` and `endDate` properties:

- `numberOfSteps`
- `distance`, estimated in meters
- `currentPace`, estimated as seconds per meter (available only in live updates)
- `currentCadence`, in steps per second (available only in live updates)
- `floorsAscended` while walking or running
- `floorsDescended` while walking or running

Much like the previous example, accessing pedometer data requires only a little code. The following example measures the user's maximum number of steps per second while the app is running.

1. Open Xcode, and create a new app, selecting the watchOS > Application > iOS App with WatchKit App template. Don't select the options for notification, glance, complication, or tests.

2. Open the WatchKit app's `Interface.storyboard`, and add a label to the interface controller scene (**Figure 14.5**).

FIGURE 14.5 The label in the storyboard scene

3. Replace the contents of the WatchKit extension's `InterfaceController.swift` with the following, then connect the label in the storyboard scene to the `@IBOutlet`:

```
import WatchKit
import Foundation
import CoreMotion

class InterfaceController: WKInterfaceController {
    @IBOutlet var label: WKInterfaceLabel!
}
```

4. Add the following properties and method to `InterfaceController`:

```
let pedometer = CMPedometer()
var maxCadence: Double = 0

private func updateLabel() {
    label.setText(String(maxCadence))
}
```

5. Add the following implementation of `willActivate()` to `InterfaceController`:

```
override func willActivate() {
    super.willActivate()

    guard CMPedometer.isCadenceAvailable() else {
        label.setText("⚠")
        return
    }

    updateLabel()
```

```
pedometer.startPedometerUpdatesFromDate(NSDate()) { data, error in
    guard let data = data else {
        print(error?.description)
        self.label.setText(" ⚠ ")
        return
    }

    if let cadence = data.currentCadence?.doubleValue
        where cadence > self.maxCadence {
        self.maxCadence = cadence
        self.updateLabel()
    }
  }
}
```

6. Add the following didDeactivate() method to the interface controller:

```
override func didDeactivate() {
    super.didDeactivate()
    pedometer.stopPedometerUpdates()
}
```

When you first install and run this app, keep an eye on the screen of your iPhone; you will be prompted to allow the app access to your motion activity. Upon authorization, the app will display your maximum cadence in steps per second as you move around.

Cadence is only one of the pieces of information available via CMPedometer, and—as with the raw accelerometer data—it is possible to query for historical data as well as receive updates with live data. Although Apple Watch has fewer sensors available than the iPhone, hopefully this small taste of what is there will start you thinking of what you can achieve with this data.

PROVIDING HAPTIC FEEDBACK

One of the most intriguing hardware features of the Apple Watch is undoubtedly the haptic feedback engine. Although the screen and audio capabilities of the device are the principal forms of interactive output, it is the haptic feedback engine that will provide much of the asynchronous communication between the watch and its wearer. In watchOS 2, Apple has given developers the ability to trigger the haptic engine directly; this provides us with a wonderful opportunity to give feedback straight to the user's wrist.

PLAYING WITH HAPTICS

Experimenting with the haptic engine is trivial from an API perspective. A single method, named `playHaptic(_:)`, is available for you to call against the `WKInterfaceDevice` class. The `playHaptic(_:)` method takes a single parameter of the enum type `WKHapticType`. The enum defines the complete range of feedback styles available for you to use. Each has a different character, and they (almost) all have corresponding audio tones.

- `Notification` is the default tap that you feel when your watch has a notification to display to you. If you supply an enum value that is outside the currently defined range, this will also be "played."
- `DirectionUp` consists of two discrete taps. The name `DirectionUp` comes from the audio tone that accompanies the taps; the watch plays two ascending tones.
- `DirectionDown` also consists of two discrete taps. This time the tone that accompanies the taps consists of two descending tones.
- `Success` consists of three quick taps of equal duration. The accompanying audio consists of three ascending notes.
- `Failure` also has three quick taps, but the audio consists of two equal tones following by a tone at a lower pitch.
- `Retry` features three quick taps accompanied by three tones at the same pitch.
- `Start` is a single strong tap accompanied by a single tone.
- `Stop` has two strong taps accompanied by two tones; these tones are further apart that those for the preceding styles.
- `Click` is a very short tap and is unique in that it has no accompanying tone.

It's not that easy to mentally imagine the differences between the haptic styles, so it is worth creating a small example project; the sample app will include a Picker control to allow you to select between the different styles. On selection, the style will play for you.

1. From the Xcode main menu, select File > New > Project.

2. In the new project template chooser dialog, navigate to our old favorite watchOS > Application > iOS App with WatchKit App, and click Next.

3. Enter the Product Name as **PlayHaptic**, set the Language as Swift, and click Next.

   Feel free to choose whichever Devices setting you wish. We won't be worrying about notifications, glances, or complications, so you can deselect those as well.

4. Choose a location to save the project, and click Create.

   Now you have your familiar project template, so let's update the user interface to contain a Picker control.

5. In the Project Navigator, open the file group named PlayHaptic WatchKit App, and click the file named `Interface.storyboard` to open it in Interface Builder.

6. In the Object Library, search for the Picker control, and drag it onto the interface controller scene.

    You need to hook the Picker control up to a controller class so that you can supply it with data and monitor its changes.

7. Open the assistant editor, ensuring that it displays the file named InterfaceController.swift.

8. Control-click and drag from the Picker control onto the InterfaceController class, and create an outlet named hapticPicker.

9. Repeat step 8, but instead create an action named stylePicked.

    You now need to create the data for the Picker control.

10. In the InterfaceController class, add a read-only property that points to an array of tuples containing pairs of String and WKHapticType values:

```
let styles:[(String, WKHapticType)] = [
    ("Notification", .Notification),
    ("DirectionUp", .DirectionUp),
    ("DirectionDown", .DirectionDown),
    ("Success", .Success),
    ("Failure", .Failure),
    ("Retry", .Retry),
    ("Start", .Start),
    ("Stop", .Stop),
    ("Click", .Click)
]
```

    With the data created, you can populate it into the Picker control.

11. Update the awakeWithContext(_:) method with the following:

```
override func awakeWithContext(context: AnyObject?) {
    let pickerItems: [WKPickerItem] = styles.map { style -> WKPickerItem in
        let pickerItem = WKPickerItem()
        pickerItem.title = style.0
        return pickerItem
    }
    hapticPicker.setItems(pickerItems)
    super.awakeWithContext(context)
}
```

    You now need to be able to play the selected haptic when the Picker control has been changed.

12. Edit the `stylePicked(_:)` method with the following code:

```
@IBAction func stylePicked(value: Int) {
    let hapticStyle = styles[value].1
    WKInterfaceDevice.currentDevice().playHaptic(hapticStyle)
}
```

Everything is ready to go, although you need to test this on a device because the Watch simulator cannot do justice to haptic feedback.

13. Plug your iPhone into your Mac, choose PlayHaptic WatchKit App as the scheme, and choose your iOS device and watch combination in the scheme selector pop-up menu.

The project will build and the app will eventually be transferred to the watch, presenting the Picker control with a list of haptic styles when it has loaded (**Figure 14.6**). Scrolling with the digital crown will cause the different haptics to play—make sure to enable sound on the watch to hear them as well as feel them!

FIGURE 14.6 Playing with haptics

TAP CAREFULLY

Unlike the vibration motors within many phones, the haptic feedback engine in the Apple Watch—or the Taptic Engine, as it is known from a marketing perspective—is inside a device that is in permanent physical contact with the user. Instead of providing jarring actions designed to be felt through clothing or to vibrate through desks, the Taptic Engine can instead provide extremely discreet taps directly to the wrist.

The beauty of such a system is that because it can be felt directly rather than being heard or transferred through layers of clothing, the patterns of feedback can be distinguished and these patterns can be ascribed meanings. This is what allows wearers to know whether the watch is telling you to stand up or turn right or that an urgent notification has been received.

This gives you a great opportunity for your app to establish a truly intimate relationship with your users. It is also something that you should be wary of; just having the ability to trigger a vibration on your user's wrist does not mean that you have to take advantage of it.

In those circumstances in which haptic feedback is appropriate, always strive to make those haptics meaningful. The value of such feedback can be severely diminished through overuse and can lead to notification fatigue in your users. You should also be aware that although you may have sounds turned off on your watch, your users may not have made the same decision. Excessive haptics can result in a barrage of noise coming from your app, and could result in it being deleted from the watch by a frustrated user. Too many haptics will also have a detrimental effect on battery life; every vibration requires power, and it may not take long for users to connect your trigger-happy tendency toward haptic feedback with the quick depletion of their precious battery.

WRAPPING UP

Apple Watch is a very capable piece of hardware, and some of its best bits are hidden from view as sensors and haptic motors. By now you have covered almost all the capabilities of the device and its SDK, and in the next chapter you will venture into what might be the most exciting—and daunting—territory yet: shipping an app to the App Store.

CHAPTER 15

Shipping Your WatchKit App

At the end of the app development journey comes arguably the most satisfying stage: shipping your app. Distribution of your app to paying customers takes place through the iOS App Store, but you have a surprising number of potential obstacles to consider along the way before you get to spend your App Store millions.

PREPARING YOUR APP FOR DISTRIBUTION

Before you can take the plunge and release your app to the public, ask yourself the following questions: Have I tried it on device? Have I done enough testing? Have I done external testing? Does it run efficiently? Have I done all the due diligence to make sure I really want to release it?

Because the pre-release checklist will vary from developer to developer and even from app to app, you should not see the following guidance as exhaustive, and it may not even be applicable in all situations. However, we still think it is worth reading if only to check that you've covered all bases and maybe to prompt yourself to think more about your specific scenarios.

DEVICE SUPPORT

In recent years, Apple has made huge strides in extending the life of older hardware by ensuring that the latest versions of iOS work on relatively ancient devices. Your opinion on that may be positive or negative, depending on whether you own, or are forced to support, an iPhone 4S or an iPad 2!

To use an Apple Watch with your app, your customers need to have at least an iPhone 5 or 5C. Even though the 4S is supported by iOS 9 in software, it does not have the hardware support that would allow it to pair with an Apple Watch. It is also worth reiterating that no currently available iPads have the ability to work with an Apple Watch.

For this reason, you should ensure that you carefully consider the types of devices used by your customers if you have access to such data. The Apple Watch is an amazingly useful device, but be careful when making the assumption that everyone who downloads your iOS app is intending to run your watch app. The key is to remember that, in the overwhelming majority of cases, a watch app is a *companion* to the iOS app.

A further point to bear in mind is that many of the frameworks and APIs used in this book are applicable to watchOS 2 only. Although watchOS 2 is a free upgrade, it is not mandatory, and some of your potential customers may still be running the original watchOS release. watchOS 2 is compatible only with iOS 9 and higher, so if large numbers of your customers are holding out on iOS 8.4, you may need to consider supporting watchOS 1 as well.

ICONS AND IMAGE RESOURCES

Although it is not a critical task, making sure that your use of icons and other image resources is appropriate can be of great benefit to your users. Fortunately, all Apple Watch devices are Retina quality, which means you don't need to worry about including anything but @2x-quality images. This is a benefit to customers because you don't have to include unnecessary extra images in the app bundle.

ICONS

When creating an icon for your iOS app, you now need to produce even more variations, to satisfy the new requirements for app icons under watchOS. You might want to start saving up to pay that designer for some extra work, because there are now eight additional icons to be produced for all the extra new places they can be displayed. You can take a look at the placeholders for the icons by navigating to the Assets.xcassets file within a WatchKit App file group in the Project Navigator (**Figure 15.1**).

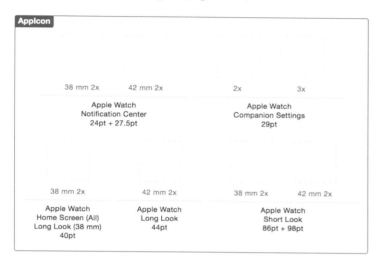

FIGURE 15.1 The range of required watchOS app icons

App icons are displayed without a name on the watch home screen, so you are relying on a familiarity with your iOS icon to help your users recognize and launch your app. Although it may be tempting to compensate by adding some text to your icon, or even just by shrinking your iOS icons to the watchOS sizes, it is a temptation worth resisting.

The Apple Watch has a small and dense display. These factors conspire to make the icon size much smaller than the iOS equivalent. Adding text to your icon will rarely result in easily readable results, and scaling down your existing icon could cause it to look like a cluttered mess. To make matters worse, watchOS icons have a circular theme—as opposed to the "squircles" employed on iOS—and the average iOS icon could be subjected to some unflattering cropping.

Redesigning your existing icon to fit the new dimensions would be a lot more sensible. Take, for example, the icons for PCalc, a successful calculator app for Mac, iOS, and now watchOS. When developer James Thomson was putting together the icons for the watchOS version, he took the time to redesign the iOS icon to fit the new circular aesthetic and to promote the most distinctive part of his icon: the number 42 (**Figure 15.2**). You can find more information about PCalc at the developer's website: www.pcalc.com/iphone.

FIGURE 15.2 The distinctive square icon of PCalc on iOS was translated to a circle for watchOS.

IMAGE ASSETS

watchOS comes prepared with the ability to support multiple devices with different screen sizes and resolutions. To make this possible, watchOS gives you the ability to configure individual user interface elements to have different property values depending on the size of the screen that the app runs on. For example, this allows you to configure your user interface elements to have different sizes, or even text contents, according to the available screen space.

Although the best user interfaces do not heavily rely on pixel-perfect images for their design, it is still possible that you will want to customize your image assets to have different sizes depending on the display size. You can of course customize the actual dimensions of the image so that it uses the available space most appropriately. **Figure 15.3** shows the image size properties customized to allow the 42mm devices to use more of the space.

FIGURE 15.3 Customizing the image properties to override size dimensions on 42mm devices

This is a very useful capability, but it does pose a problem for the app user. Using a single image for multiple sizes can lead to scaling artifacts as the image is stretched to fit a dimension it was not optimized for. Using asset catalogs to manage multiple images for the different screen sizes is the best solution to this problem.

1. In the Project Navigator, open the asset catalog named `Assets.xcassets` in the WatchKit App file group.

   Take care to open the asset catalog in the file group named WatchKit *App*, not WatchKit *Extension*.

2. In the Xcode main menu, select Editor > Add Assets > New Image Set.

   This creates a new image set named Image with a default set of image placeholders (**Figure 15.4**). Unfortunately, the default placeholders (for 1x, 2x, and 3x images) do not suit our watchOS app, so we need to change them.

FIGURE 15.4 A default image set

3. Open the Attributes inspector, deselect the Universal checkbox, and select the Apple Watch checkbox (**Figure 15.5**).

FIGURE 15.5 The Attributes inspector properties for the image set

This causes the previous placeholders to be replaced with placeholders marked 2x, 38 mm 2x, and 42 mm 2x (**Figure 15.6**).

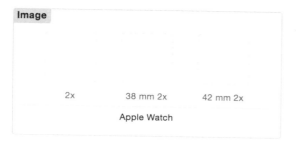

FIGURE 15.6 Placeholders for a watchOS-specific image

The next step is to place images in the appropriate placeholders. If you have only one image for all device sizes, then you can use the 2x placeholder. For our example, we want to use two images. We have created these so you don't have to, and you can obtain them from our assets repository (bit.ly/bwa-image-assets).

4. Download the sample assets, and expand the file named `image-assets.zip` to create a folder containing two image files.

5. Drag the file named app-image-38.png over the placeholder named 38 mm 2x (**Figure 15.7**).

FIGURE 15.7 Dragging the 38mm image over the placeholder

6. Drag the file named app-image-42.png to the placeholder named 42 mm 2x.

You should now have two similar but differently sized images in the image set. We've created the images with different numbers on them so that they can be more readily distinguished (**Figure 15.8**).

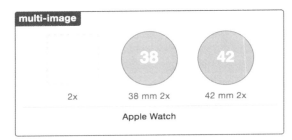

FIGURE 15.8 A fully configured image set

7. Using the Attributes inspector, change the name of the image set to **multi-image**; you don't have to, but it makes the whole process feel slightly less generic.

You should now have a nicely configured image set, ready to use in the app.

8. Open the file named Interface.storyboard, and select the interface controller scene.

9. In the Object Library, find the Image object, and drag it onto the interface controller scene.

10. In the Attributes inspector, set the Image property to **multi-image**, and the Horizontal and Vertical Alignment properties to **Center**.

Strangely, when you specify the multi-image image set, the image placeholder is replaced with a question mark. Although this may suggest that Xcode cannot find the image set, it actually indicates that it can't decide which image to display right now because Interface Builder is currently using the Any Screen Size option. If you switch to a specific size class, the correct image will be shown for that size class.

Now we are ready to check the results.

11. In the scheme selector pop-up menu, choose the HelloWrist WatchKit App as the scheme and iPhone 6 + Apple Watch – 38mm as the destination, and then build and run the app.

Once built, the app should run and display the correct image for the 38mm size class (**Figure 15.9**).

12. Repeat step 11 for the destination iPhone 6 Plus + Apple Watch – 42mm.

Again, the app should run, and this time it will display the correct image for the 42mm size class (Figure 15.9).

FIGURE 15.9 The app running in 38mm (left) and 42mm modes

This technique may seem over the top, and we readily concede that it will not be necessary for every image in your app. But it is good to be aware of its availability, especially as you move into beta testing and distribution—a phase of app development that often highlights problems on a wider range of devices than you may have access to, and a phase when you've got more eyes on your software than ever before.

BACK TO THE DEVELOPER CENTER

Despite the hassles you put up with in Chapter 13 to enable on-device testing of your app, we have some bad news for you: You need to go back to the Developer Center to do some more work if you want to be able to release your app.

APP IDENTIFIERS

If you have ever released an iOS app before, you are aware of the need to create an app identifier in the Developer Center. The app identifier is a unique string that Apple requires for every app that is to be released, and it is specified as part of the provisioning profile that you create to sign your app for installation onto physical devices.

During the development process, you can specify a wildcard app identifier for your development provisioning profile. This allows you to include your provisioning profile in any app whose bundle identifier matches the wildcard. For release, you must use a distribution provisioning profile—we'll cover that in the next section—one of the requirements for which is that a wildcard app identifier cannot be used.

For your HelloWrist app, you need to create an app identifier that matches the bundle identifier that was generated when you created the project way back in Chapter 1 (Figure 1.2). The bundle identifier—build.watchosapps.HelloWrist—was generated from the organization identifier (build.watchosapps) and product name (HelloWrist) that you supplied. Knowing this, you can log in to the Developer Center and create the corresponding app identifier.

NOTE: Unfortunately, app identifiers must be unique across all developers, so you won't be able to follow along with these exact instructions. You can instead change the bundle identifier in the target settings so that it maps onto an identifier of your own.

1. In a web browser, navigate to the App IDs subsection of the Identifiers section of the Developer Center (bit.ly/bwa-adc-appids).

   If you are a member of multiple development teams, be sure to sign in to the correct team if prompted.

2. Click the plus (+) button near the upper right of the page.

3. Enter an App ID Description for the App Identifier; for ours, we will use **HelloWrist App**.

4. In the App ID Suffix field, choose Explicit App ID, and enter your bundle ID; for ours we will enter **build.watchosapps.HelloWrist**.

   If you have any specific app services that you need to include, you can do so now. Your selection will be specific to your app, and they can be edited later anyway, so we'll skip this section.

5. Click Continue.

   The Developer Center will validate your proposed settings, and if everything is acceptable it will display a summary of your request.

6. Click Submit to register your app identifier.

   You now have an identifier that you can use when you want to create a distribution provisioning profile for your app.

   Unfortunately, the identifier we just created applies only to the iOS app. We also need identifiers for the WatchKit App and WatchKit Extension targets as well, and they should match the bundle identifiers that the project templates set up.

7. Repeat steps 2 through 6 for the WatchKit App target. We will use an App ID Description of **HelloWrist Watch App** and an Explicit App ID of **build.watchosapps.HelloWrist .watchkitapp**.

8. Repeat steps 2 through 6 for the WatchKit Extension target. We will use an App ID Description of **HelloWrist Watch Extension** and an Explicit App ID of **build.watchosapps.HelloWrist.watchkitapp.watchkitextension**.

PRODUCTION CERTIFICATES

We went through the process of creating a development certificate in Chapter 13. This was enough to code sign your app for installation on a local device, but to distribute through TestFlight or the App Store, you must use a production certificate.

1. In your web browser, navigate to the Certificates section of the Developer Center (bit.ly/bwa-adc-cert).

2. Click the plus (+) button near the upper right of the page.

3. Scroll down the page to the Production section, and select App Store and Ad Hoc as the certificate type.

4. Click Continue.

5. Create a certificate signing request by following the instructions provided, and click Continue.

   If you did this in Chapter 13 and kept the CSR file, you can use the same file instead of creating a new one.

6. Choose the CSR file, and click Generate.

7. Download the generated certificate or refresh the developer team in the Accounts section of the Xcode preferences.

DISTRIBUTION PROVISIONING PROFILE

Although we mentioned it in previous sections, it bears repeating that if you wish to distribute your app to the wider world, you need to bundle it with a distribution provisioning profile. The development profile you created in Chapter 13 is for use only with devices to which you have direct physical access, so if you want to get your app onto devices via TestFlight or the App Store, you need to move up to a distribution profile instead.

1. In your web browser, navigate to the Distribution subsection of the Provisioning Profiles section of the Developer Center (bit.ly/bwa-adc-profs).

2. Click the plus (+) button near the upper right of the page.

3. Scroll down the page to the Distribution section, and choose App Store as the profile type.

4. Click Continue.

   To create the distribution profile, you need to include an app identifier.

5. Choose the app identifier you created in the section "App identifiers," and click Continue.

6. Choose a production certification to include in the provisioning profile; the certificate created in the previous section will be sufficient.

7. Click Continue.

8. Give the profile a meaningful name so that you can identify its purpose when you stumble across it again in the future; we will call ours **HelloWrist Distribution Profile**.

9. Click Generate.

   The result is a profile that can be downloaded and installed directly to Xcode, or it can be pulled down by refreshing the developer team in the Accounts section of the Xcode preferences.

   However, we're not finished yet; we need to create similar distribution profiles for the WatchKit App and WatchKit Extension targets.

10. Repeat steps 2 through 9 for the App target. We will use the app identifier **build.watchosapps.HelloWrist.watchkitapp** that we created earlier and give the profile a name of **HelloWrist Watch App Distribution Profile**.

11. Repeat steps 2 through 9 for the Extension target. We will use the app identifier **build.watchosapps.HelloWrist.watchkitapp.watchkitextension** that we created earlier and a profile name of **HelloWrist Watch Extension Distribution Profile**.

   You now have all the pieces you need to build your app for distribution.

12. From the scheme selector pop-up menu, choose iOS Device + watchOS Device as the destination.

13. Choose Product > Archive from the Xcode main menu.

   Xcode will start the process of building for release. This differs from a normal build and run action because the release configuration settings are used. This allows the compiler to do its optimization magic to get your apps running faster than normal debug builds.

   At the end of the Archive action, Xcode will display its Organizer window, opened to the Archives tab (**Figure 15.10**). This will show you the local builds that you have available and give you the option to upload them to the App Store. Before you can do that, though, you need to make sure the App Store is ready to receive them.

FIGURE 15.10 The Xcode Organizer window

TIP: When archiving, Xcode should use the Automatic setting to choose the correct provisioning profile for each target. If the Automatic setting does not pick the correct profiles, you can set them manually in the target settings.

iTUNES CONNECT

Whether you are aiming straight for release or are going to embark on beta distribution first, you need to sign in to iTunes Connect to prepare your app before it can be uploaded from Xcode. We mentioned way back in the mists of Chapter 1 that watchOS apps are distributed along with their companion iOS apps—like a welcome Trojan Horse. This means that a lot of what needs to be done in iTunes Connect is actually for the benefit of your iOS app, so we will skate over some of the sections quite quickly in an effort to focus on what you need to do for your watch app.

CREATING AN APP RECORD

The first stage is to create an iTunes Connect entry for your app.

1. Sign in to iTunes Connect through your web browser (bit.ly/bwa-itc).
2. Click My Apps.
3. Click the plus (+) button to display the add menu, and select New App when it appears.
4. Fill in the app details, ensuring that you include the bundle identifier you created earlier.
5. Click Create.

    A new app record will be created, ready to be fleshed out with some extra information. First, though, you need to send a build to iTunes Connect from Xcode.

UPLOADING YOUR APP

To upload your build to iTunes Connect:

1. Open the Xcode Organizer by selecting Window > Organizer from the Xcode main menu.
2. In the left panel, select the app (HelloWrist for us), and then select the specific build you wish to upload (Figure 15.10).
3. Click the Upload to App Store button.

    If you are a member of more than one development team, Xcode presents a list of teams (**Figure 15.11**).

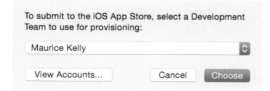

FIGURE 15.11 The development team selection dialog

4. Choose the development team that corresponds to the app identifier, and click Choose.

   Xcode will now attempt to sign the build for App Store distribution. If the provisioning profile for the app is incorrect, Xcode will display an error and some information to guide you to resolution. Once it's resolved, you will need to repeat the archiving process and then go back to step 1.

   If the provisioning profile is correct, Xcode will display a confirmation screen to indicate that it is ready to upload the build (**Figure 15.12**).

FIGURE 15.12 The upload confirmation screen

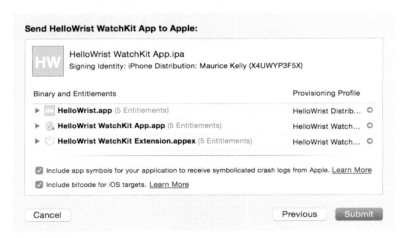

5. Click Submit to send the build to the App Store.

   Xcode will perform some additional processing and then start transmitting the archive to the App Store. When the upload is completed, you should see a confirmation message, and you're now ready to prepare for distribution to TestFlight beta testers or to put it up for sale on the App Store.

DISTRIBUTING THE APP

The best way to be ready to ship is to ensure that you've done enough on-device testing. A good QA team can go a long way toward ensuring that your app is ready, but if you want to be really sure that your code covers all the edge cases that your customers can throw at it, then beta testing with a wider audience is a must.

If you're not interested in doing so, or you simply want to get your app out there more quickly, you can jump straight into preparing your app for sale (see the "App Store Distribution" section). However, we recommend you give the following sections a read at some stage, if only to know what the rest of the Apple developer community is talking about.

TESTFLIGHT DISTRIBUTION

One of the biggest barriers to beta testing iOS (and now watchOS) apps with a wider range of customers has always been the restrictions placed on deploying builds to physical devices. Until fairly recently, Apple restricted you to being able to install onto just 100 *devices*; when taking into account the fact that testers, who are often developers as well, can have iPhones and iPads, and over the course of a year will often have multiple phones, those 100 devices are eaten up pretty quickly.

Fortunately, Apple recently bought a beta testing service named TestFlight and brought the process in-house; it is now offered for free as part of your developer program membership. TestFlight is still a little rough around the edges (and lacking some of the more advanced crash reporting features of paid competitors like HockeyApp), but for the starting developer it is a good value for the money, and so we will focus on it here.

ACCESSING TESTFLIGHT

TestFlight builds can be created through the iTunes Connect interface. When you're viewing the information page for a specific app, TestFlight will be presented as an option along the top of the page.

TestFlight builds can be one of two flavors:

- **Internal** TestFlight builds are intended for you to distribute to testers within your own organization. You are limited to 25 individual testers, although they have the ability to test the app on multiple devices. Internal builds are not subject to any form of app review, and so they are a good way to get your app out to a small group of trusted testers for immediate feedback. Internal testers can be added only if they have iTunes Connect accounts.

- **External** TestFlight builds are intended for distribution to a wider audience outside your own organization. The tester limit is significantly higher, at 1000 individuals, and again they are free to test the app on multiple devices. Due to the wider distribution, external builds are subject to beta app review. Although this is not quite as stringent as the full App Store review process, it does mean that your test builds will be placed in a queue to await review and can be delayed and even rejected if they fail the review process. This can be useful, though; beta reviews can highlight potential failures before you submit for full App Store review. External testers can be added simply by adding their email address to a tester management form, but you should make sure you have their permission first.

It is possible to maintain different internal and external builds at the same time; this gives you a way to provide a stable beta to your external testers while the internal testers could have access to daily test builds that have varying quality levels.

GUIDANCE FOR YOUR TESTERS

So what happens when you release a build of your app to your testers? If they've not received a build before, they will be sent an email to invite them to join your test program. To complete the signup they will need to install the TestFlight app from the App Store; this is not your app but an app produced by Apple to help TestFlight users maintain their test builds on their devices.

Following the link in the email will open the TestFlight app on their device and present some information about the app. When an app comes with a bundled Apple Watch app, the information page will display a banner that reads "Offers Apple Watch App" (**Figure 15.13**).

FIGURE 15.13 TestFlight information for HelloWrist

Once the tester taps the Install button, the test build will be downloaded and installed on the device. When installation has completed, the user can return to the TestFlight app to view the information for the app; this time the "Offers Apple Watch App" banner will be updated to say "Install on Apple Watch" and will feature a switch control (**Figure 15.14**). If the user taps the switch, the process of installing the app to the Apple Watch will begin. Once that's completed, the user can start experimenting with your creation.

FIGURE 15.14 The test build installation switch

It is important that your testers (especially external testers) are aware of the implications of running beta versions of your software. Although many beta testers may simply want access to an early preview of your app, they may be disappointed to find that it isn't as stable as they would like. It is in your best interests to find testers who are enthusiastic about the testing process and not just wanting access to previews. Enthusiastic testers are more forgiving of bugs and more likely to give you useful feedback.

Builds are time-limited to 30 days and will need to be replaced by App Store releases or by further test builds. If your users can create their own data within your apps, you should strive to keep providing them with a usable build before the current build has expired. You should also do your best to protect the data they create; although they know they are taking a risk using beta software, it still reflects badly upon you if every beta version destroys their data.

If the testers want to stop using the test builds, they can either remove the build from their device completely or replace it with an App Store release build. If they want to stop receiving notifications of new builds, the TestFlight app has a Stop Testing button at the bottom of the page that provides more detail about your app. Tapping the button will start the process of leaving your test program.

APP STORE DISTRIBUTION

The endgame of this whole process is to release your app to the world via the App Store. As we've said before, your watch app is delivered to users inside the iOS app bundle, so the process of releasing your watch app is almost identical to that which you will be used to for iOS app release.

The only addition to the process is the additional screenshots and icons. The app information page in iTunes Connect has an expandable section named Apple Watch. When you expand the section, it reveals two new fields. The first field is for the watchOS app icon; it should be a PNG file of 1024 by 1024 pixels. The second field can be used to add up to five screenshots from the 42mm version of your watch app (312 by 390 pixels). More guidelines are available at the app submission guide for Apple Watch: bit.ly/bwa-store-guide. With this additional data in place, users browsing iTunes or the App Store will see more about the watchOS app that you are offering.

> **TIP:** The standard product page on the iOS App Store will show the first two screenshots without scrolling, so Apple recommends that you provide at least two screenshots to take advantage of this.

WRAPPING UP

We have reached the end of our watchOS journey together, but we hope that your journey is only just beginning. The Apple Watch is an exciting new platform, and although there are numerous restrictions right now—some artificial, some natural—it has always been within the confines of restriction that iOS and Mac developers have created magical and innovative apps that continue to push the boundaries of their platforms. We look forward to seeing what you can do with watchOS.

INDEX

X

REGISTER THIS PRODUCT
SAVE 35%
ON YOUR NEXT PURCHASE

HOW TO REGISTER YOUR PRODUCT

- Go to peachpit.com/register.
- Sign in or create an account. (*If you are creating a new account, be sure to check the box to hear from us about upcoming special offers.*)
- Enter the 10- or 13-digit ISBN of your product.

BENEFITS OF REGISTERING

- A 35% off coupon to be used on your next purchase—valid for 30 days (*Your code will be available in your Peachpit cart for you to apply during checkout. You will also find it in the Manage Codes section of your Account page.*)
- Access to bonus chapters, product updates, and/or workshop files when available
- Special offers on new editions and related Peachpit products (*Be sure to check the box to hear from us when setting up your account or visit peachpit.com/newsletters.*)

Benefits for registering vary by product. Benefits will be listed on your Account page under Registered Products.

Discount may not be combined with any other offer and is not redeemable for cash. Discount code expires after 30 days from the time of product registration. Offer subject to change.

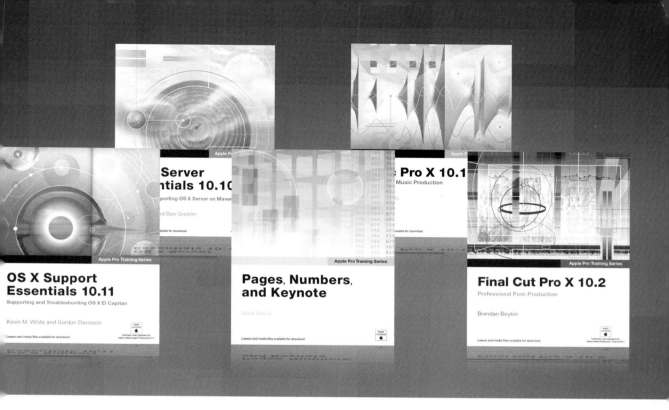

Apple Pro Training Series

Apple offers comprehensive certification programs for creative and IT professionals. The Apple Pro Training Series is both a self-paced learning tool and the official curriculum of the Apple Training and Certification program, used by Apple Authorized Training Centers around the world.

To see a complete range of Apple Pro Training Series books, videos and apps visit: **www.peachpit.com/appleprotraining**